Michael Bywater, whose 'Lost World' column appears in the *Independent on Sunday*, is a writer and broadcaster. He has written for an unfeasibly long list of publications (including *The Times*, the *Observer* and, astonishingly, the *Daily Mail*), as well as films and computer games, and teaches structured thinking without a trace of irony. He is also a pilot, cook, harpsichordist and photographer. He divides his time.

Praise for *Lost Worlds*

'Funny, erudite and fascinating, Bywater's *Lost Worlds* is a treasure trove of spectacularly miscellaneous knowledge, all of it worth knowing, about things lost and gone, many of them worth regretting. Bywater writes with a razor-sharp wit and flashes of real profundity; his magpie genius has found a dazzling outlet here' A. C. Grayling

'Bywater decodes, derides and deconstructs the major and minor arcana of world civilizations, hilariously zooming in and out from chocolate bars to cosmology: anatomizing moustaches and melancholy, dogs and democracy. This marvellous and valuable book transforms itself as you read from a quirky miscellany into something wiser, nobler, deeper, sadder and more remarkable' Stephen Fry

'Bywater has one of the most interesting and encompassing minds of the age – no one else could have written this book, particularly with such verve' Kathy Burk

'Clever, eclectic, eccentric and funny: perfect brainfood' Nigella Lawson

'Dizzyingly learned and dazzlingly inventive' Tom Holland

'The last remaindered copy should be buried in a time-capsule so that archaeologists of the distant future, rummaging through the

radioactive landscape, can dip into the learning that its author wears so lightly and wittily' Jonathan Sale, *Independent*

'*Lost Worlds* is the best thing about – better than iPods, the first rime of winter, salty porridge, Paula Rego, chocolate bars dusted with cinnamon and the Dandy annual' Andrew Marr, *Daily Telegraph*

'The fantastic, absurd exaggeration is as enjoyable as the *Hitchhiker's Guide to the Galaxy* . . . Michael Bywater can leap from kings to cabbages without drawing breath, and find amusement, if not eternity, in a grain of sand' Emily Wilson, *Times Literary Supplement*

'A lovely little book of yearning' *Herald*

'In a history of audacious indexes, the list that completes Michael Bywater's delightful volume would be up there with the greats' Brian Dillon, *Scotland on Sunday*

'What makes Bywater so good . . . is the exactitude with which he remembers . . . A seductive whirlpool of evanescence' Howard Jacobson, *Independent*

'Chastened, erudite, amused and endlessly digressive' Jonathan Derbyshire, *Time Out*

'Full of razor-sharp wit and nostalgia, there is ultimately a deep wisdom in his perspective on life' *Good Book Guide*

'Nostalgia is seldom this funny, or expressed with such tenderness' *Metro London*

LOST
WORLDS

What Have We Lost,
& Where Did It Go?

MICHAEL BYWATER

Granta Books
London

Granta Publications, 2/3 Hanover Yard,
Noel Road, London N1 8BE

First published in Great Britain by Granta Books 2004
This edition published by Granta Books 2005

A CIP catalogue record for this book is available from
the British Library.

5 7 9 10 8 6 4

ISBN-10: 1 86207 798 3
ISBN-13: 978 1 86207 798 0

Typeset by M Rules
Printed and bound in Great Britain by
Mackays of Chatham plc

To Keith Haward Bywater,
Father
&
Proper Doctor
(*see below*)

The gifts he has ... turn to dust in his hands as he realises that everything he has is merely the shadow cast by what he has lost.

DOUGLAS ADAMS & MARK CARWARDINE,
Last Chance to See

epameroi: ti de tis; ti de ou tis; skias onar anthropos?
('Gone in a day: who is someone? What is no-one? Everyone's the shadow of a dream.')

PINDAR, *Pythian Odes*

Prolegomenon[1]

From one loser to another: goodbye.

Brace ourselves against it as we will (with manners, customs, beliefs, riches, vocations, pastimes, love and learning), we will all lose in the end. What will we lose to?

We will lose to the law. And if you don't believe me, to hell with you.

And to hell with me, too. For if hell is – as it is in at least one cosmology – a region of ice and silence, we are all going there and there's nothing we can do about it.

Caprice? No, it's as far from caprice as one can get. It's physics. And physics says we've had it. You, me, the dog, the careful home, the plans, the savings, the posterity, the great globe itself, Yea, and all which it inherit: the Second Law of Thermodynamics.

That's the one which governs us. Simply but clumsily put, the Second Law of Thermodynamics says 'heat doesn't go uphill'. More clearly expressed, it says: things are getting more chaotic. Order is moving ineluctably towards disorder. The cosmos began in chaos (says Genesis) and (says physics) in chaos it will end. All

---

1 Itself a lost wor(l)d. Prologues, Forewords, Introductions by the score. But the Prolegomenon? Gone. Except, now . . .

the energy in everything that is – the energy which keeps us going, keeps our cells together, keeps the circling planets spinning on their way, *all* of it – will end up as a sort of formless heat, without order or purpose. The Heat Death of the Universe.

Entropy, the physicists call it. The amount of disorder in a system. And it goes up. Entropy keeps rising. We may cheat it for a few decades (eating and eating and eating[2] to get new energy in, to fuel the struggle against our own bodily chaos) but in the long run, like the Universal casino, entropy will triumph. The House will always win.

We've had it.

So what do we do while we're waiting? Perhaps it's a miracle that we do anything at all; the psychoanalyst Gyllian Moore once said that ninety per cent of her work was helping people come to terms with the inevitability of their own death. Most of us, though, manage to rub along, after a fashion; but much of what we do is building defences against loss. Businessmen cope with it by constantly wanting more; the great middle class copes by worrying about how to hang on to what it already has; engineers build things to outlast them; historians stare the thing in the face; artists (of whatever sort) try to stop time and freeze it in its tracks[3]. Religion tells us that loss is transient (death being but a recession) or illusory (what we lose is not worth having anyway) or the price of admission to

---

2 No matter what the politicians may say about our health. Do you think they really care?

3 A universal instinct, as shown by the huge popularity of photography and video, though the instinct can sometimes take a strange form. I remember the mother of a friend who believed she was dying took her daughter to Paris, where she took hundreds of photographs of her. We could not understand the thinking behind it, until suddenly we realized: she was taking the photographs so that, when she was no longer alive to remember her daughter, the photographs would remember her by proxy.

eternal happiness. Most explicitly of all, doctors are engaged in nothing more than keeping loss (of capability, of the faculties, of life itself) at bay.

Yet we understand little about the quiet storm of loss which blows about our lives and histories. Despite the obsession of our species with organizing, categorizing and making lists (we categorize *everything*, from Linnaean taxonomy to the 'rules' of harmony and counterpoint, from the codifying of human weakness in the form of the law to codifying ourselves both from the top down, in theology, and the bottom up, in the Human Genome Project) we have not managed to organize our thinking about loss. It still just . . . happens. It still surrounds us, dogs our footsteps, clings to our coat-tails and (as P. G. Wodehouse said of Fate) waits around every corner with a sock full of wet sand.

It's everywhere we look. Hydraulic power beneath the streets of London, the graveyard of lost books in the Geniza of Cairo, the lost world of Xanadu, the lost delights of impotency[4], lost causes of death[5]. Loss dominates our histories, and we tell stories of empires' fall more than their rise; we remember lost books more than safely delivered ones: Carlyle's first draft of *The French Revolution* burned by a servant[6] and Newton's of the *Principia* eaten by his dog Diamond[7].

---

4 Itself now becoming lost, thanks to Viagra, for those who can afford it, of course, like so many other lost losses.

5 Who now dies, as they did in 1647, of *bloudy flux* or *suffocation of the Mother?* Who of *tympany*, or of being *blasted*, of *impostume* or *King's Evil*, of *Livergrown* or *Rising of the Lights* or *Grief* or *Jaw-faln?*

6 We no longer have servants to blame; instead we have computers, and indeed the computer this book was composed on was stolen from a locked hotel room not eight hours after the manuscript was handed in.

7 Provoking Newton merely to murmur sadly 'Diamond, Diamond, thou little realiseth what thou hast done' and giving rise to an excuse gleefully rediscovered by every new generation of schoolboys.

The list could go on and on, and, very shortly, will. And the fact that the most difficult thing about writing on loss is knowing when to stop might also be the reason we have never managed to come up with a taxonomy of loss.

It's not for want of trying. We could construct endless taxonomies of loss, and indeed I did so at one stage, thinking there might be a key to it all.

'A Taxonomy of Loss,' I wrote, then put my foot down and let it rip.

Abandoned
Blown up
Bowdlerized
Burned
Cast in Resin & Sold in Museum Shops
Damnatio Memoriae, Subjected to
Decay, Natural
See also:
    Universe, The, Heat Death of
    Entropy
Destroyed by Mistake
Destroyed by Time
Destroyed by the Author
Destroyed by the *Daily Mail*
Destroyed by the Forces of Morality
Destroyed in Time of War
Destroyed in Time of Conquest
Destroyed in Time of Defeat
Died
Killed
Murdered
Disintegrated
Drowned
Eaten
Evaporated

4

Forbidden
  – By Doctors
  – By Doctors, but Rehabilitated
By God
By God, but Largely Ignored
Ignorance, Overtaken by the Advancement of
Inadequately Reassembled
Intervention, Divine, Rendered Inaccessible by
Intervention, Diabolical, Rendered Inaccessible by
Intervention, Divine, Inexplicably Withheld
Spirited away (*see* Jesus)
Should Have Been Lost but Weren't
Magicked away
Left
  – By Mistake
  – On Purpose
Lost through Catastrophe
Lost but Found Again
Lost by the Betterment of Public Taste
Lost in the March of Progress
See the Curse of Xanadu
Lost through Passing of Time
Lost through Thermodynamics
Lost to Religion
Mislaid
Never Existed
Obliterated
Place, Safe, Put in a
Recycled
Restored
Rotted
Saatchi, Charles, Bought by
Servants, Lost, Destroyed or Stolen by
Sold to the USA
Stolen

Thrown away
  - Accidentally
  - Deliberately
Lost to the Depredations of Time
Transfigured
Tidied up

And then I realized it was rubbish. I had not scratched the surface. It was just words. There was no system, because loss is not systematic, but universal. There is a fundamental law of computing which says: *you will never succeed in building a foolproof system because the fools are always one step ahead.* Loss is Nature's fool, and will always get the better of us, in the end, and on the way to the end.

When we are young, we cannot stand it. It's one of the things the young rail about: old fools banging on about the old foolish days, when Things were Different. The young are, of course, immortal. Of course they can't stand it. They don't even *believe* it. To hell with them.

Once we stop being immortal, though, the stress is off[8]. No worries. We've sung our own funeral chant often enough by then, even though we may not recognize it for what it is: a strange, valedictory litany of things which were, of things which are no longer, of the vanished, the withdrawn, the dead, the broken, the irreparable.

A song of what's gone, and the fragility of human wishes.

Of lost worlds.

And yet . . . so the dog's dead, we can't find our Meccano set, they don't make Fry's Five Boys chocolate any more, the

---

8 It happens twice: once in the late twenties, then again, beyond a shadow of doubt, when you turn forty and realize it really *will* happen, that this . . . *distinguished thing* is going to come, and something will be required of you (a cock to Aesculapius?) and will you know what to do, *how to die?*

cathedral of Ys and the town of Dunwich have vanished beneath the waves, an ounce of Baby's Bottom is beyond the reach of any mortal tobacconist, you can't get the old strawberry bonbons, hot water bottles are plastic[9], raincoats don't perish, friends have died, the beer doesn't taste the same somehow . . . is this, any of it, all of it, really Death's harbinger and a warm-up routine for the triumph of entropy? Really? Or, as the versatile Yiddish word has it: *Nu?*

Oh yes they do.

Let us take you, gentle reader[10], as our experimental subject. You may deny that your life has been, as much as anything, a process of loss; but it has. From the moment you were born, a Universal process of attrition has been waged against you, internally and externally. If Jesus wants you for a sunbeam, that far older deity, Nature, wants you for a dunghill.

And so, every day, things vanish. As you move through life, plans will fail, muscle tone deteriorate, brain cells die, vision dim, hearing muffle, taste decline. The flowers that don't smell these days: that's not the wicked Dutch flower-growers; that's your nose. Kunzle cakes, dignified officials, Remington typewriters, the smell of Paris, proper policemen, Worcester Pearmains, respect, Spangles, personal service, Bayko, efficiency, floppy floppies, family businesses, LPs, the neighbourhood, Crêpe de Chine, affordable housing, Sturmey-Archer gears, National Service, Boyards cigarettes, unspoiled beaches, built-cane fishing rods, personal security, fully fashioned stockings, God, Noddy . . . where are they?

---

9 Odd how they don't keep you warm now that they don't smell right any more; who would have thought that synaesthesia – the confusion and mingling of the senses – could have had such a long reach?

10 I told you I would.

Entropy got them. Time got them. They've gone, and every newspaper you read is a narrative of things gone: lives and aspirations, chances and hopes, possessions and opportunities. When did you last see the headline *Everything Goes Just Fine For Man, 43*? Never.

Because that's not the story we want to hear, or to tell ourselves. In the light of our own lives – no matter how 'successful' – Man, 43, can go climb up his thumb. We don't want to hear it. Tales of the rich only hook us if they themselves are barbed; who would want to hear about property millionaire Nicholas van Hoogstraten were it not that he was as he is, were it not that he has a most egregious face (think of a backstage accident in a drag club), were it not that he has been imprisoned, were it not that he is spending his money on his mausoleum: a man seemingly terrified of death, a man trying to buy immortality and, in the process of publicizing this aim, giving the rest of us the chance to lay plans for his forgetting?

The Romans had a good trick for that one: *damnatio memoriae* – the cursing of memory, the erasure of monuments, of sculptures and inscriptions. A foot wrong, the wrong man insulted, the wrong horse backed in the greasy-pole contest of imperial politics, and out came the functionaries, the little men with chisels. Off with his face! The grunt-work of despotism (whatever flag it marches under) has always been done by little men with chisels; they, at least, will never be lost from the world.

But the damning chisel was as double-edged as it was blunt. 'Who was the man with the hacked-away face, Mater?' 'That's Cestius Horribilis, darling[11]. We don't talk about him any more.' 'Why? What did he do?' . . . And so they would talk about him;

---

11 Corcula, actually: little heart. Some things don't change.

the damnation of his memory the source of his perpetual resur-rection[12].

The stories of those particular damned suit us rather well. Why? Well: here's a secret: *I can't tell you.* When I closed this file yesterday (a yesterday that's gone: a whole lost world in itself[13]) I knew *for certain* how I was going to continue when I took it up again. So certain that I didn't even make a note of it. Today: nothing. Meaningless. That terrible moment when you look inside your mind and there is absolutely nothing going on, not even a decent perplexity. Nowt. Like peering into an abandoned house. Who knows; perhaps that sentence – *The stories of those particular damned suit us rather well* – was going to lead on to something stunning. We will never know. Not me; not you. Gone.

Which is pleasingly appropriate.

If this is – as indeed it is – a *salmagundi* of transience, a *pot-pourri* of the Vanished, a taxonomy of loss and the vanity of human wishes, does that therefore mean that it is sad, gloomy, a lowering of the spirits? No. We can leave that task to government and international politics. For ourselves, as individual human beings, we are certainly all in the same boat.

And that boat is sinking. But it is sinking into the warm, comfortable waters of time and entropy, and on our gentle way down to whatever marvels may lie upon the sea-bed of

---

12   And what, one might wonder, if the Sanhedrin had said 'Jesus – Issa bar-Yussuf – thinks he's the Meshiach? Ach, never mind; he's harmless enough, and a decent fellow of good family; why, we knew his daddy well . . .'?

13   If it helps, and for the record, it was Thursday, 19 February 2004, on the 16.22 train from Bath Spa to London Paddington, about five miles east of Slough. Now you know. And what good has it done you to know? What good does it do anyone to know anything? Follow that line of thinking and you could become the Secretary of State for Education faster than you could say 'Oh Mr Blair, you are *so* right.'

14   As the poet Virgil – arguably the greatest of all poets, at whatever time and in whatever language – demonstrably knew, once you hit upon a metaphor, flog it to death.

eternity[14] we can be as diverted by what has gone as by the wonders coming our way, and the way of our descendants whom we shall never meet. Just as they, in their turn, will look back at what *they* have lost, and find comfort in their own transience.

Mundus senescit: the world grows old. But it grows old slowly, and has been growing old far longer than the nanosecond flash of our clever little species. The turpitude of the world has been a figure which authors (and preachers, and moralists, and snake-oil salesmen) have turned in neat phrases since the first scribe scratched out the first cuneiform[15]. And that in itself is a comfort: everything going down the tubes, and always has been, *and yet we are still here.* We can content ourselves, perhaps, by travelling back a mere couple of millennia, to the frantic, portly, wheezing, affable Uncle Pliny, the besotted encyclopaediacerast of first-century Rome, who first of all got it wrong –

> Thus these things every one doe enwrap and entangle
> silly mortall men, void of all forecast and true under-
> standing: so as this only point among the rest remains
> sure and certain, namely, That nothing is certaine . . .

– by missing out (a) death and (b) taxes; but who then redeemed himself by taking a pop at the nearest thing the Ancients had to entropy: God Himself:

---

15 A lie, actually. Early writings, once deciphered, are almost invariably disappointing, tending to be bald accounts, tallying goats. But where are those goats? Gone. QED.

Moreover, the chiefe comfort the man hath, for his imperfections in Nature, is this, That even God him-selfe is not omnipotent, and cannot do all things: for neither he is able to worke his owne death, would he never so faine, as man can do when he is wearie of his life [. . .] ne yet recall, raise and revive those that once are departed and dead: nor bring to passe that one who lived, did not live; or he that bare honorable offices, was not in place of rule and dignity. Nay, he hath no power over things done and past, save only oblivion . . .[16]

And yet the paradox of oblivion is this: by remarking it, we hold it at bay. Damned or not, memory is stronger than oblivion. Let us leave it at that, and move on; I had something else to say, but I have forgotten what it was. Onward. Onward, before entropy gets us all.

---

16 See Philemon Holland's *Pliny*. Holland and Pliny are long gone, yet his wonderful translation – 'done into English', as they more precisely said in those times – captures and conjoins Pliny's own enchanting 'catalogue of unreliable wonders' and his own, marvelling age. I once was invited to lunch with Dr Peter Fox, the Librarian at the Cambridge University Library. It was a bit like being asked to lunch with God, the Library being an earthly paradise; all the more so at the end of lunch. 'I've something to show you,' he said, removing the baize cover from a folio volume on a book-stand. It was the first edition of Holland's *Pliny*, open at the beginning of Book II: *The World, and this, which by another name men have thought good to call heaven (under the pourprise and bending cope whereof, all things are emmanteled and covered) beleeve we ought in all reason to be a God, eternall, unmeasurable, without beginning, and likewise endlesse* . . . You, too, would have been shaken; you, too, would have had to reach for your handkerchief and pretend there was dust in your eye; or there is no health in you.

Lost Worlds

So let us begin; and let's start (because this is the computer age, the data age, an age where everything important to our masters must be quantified with a number) with a number.

404

That's our number.

And if any number can be said to encapsulate our times, 404 is it. There are other contenders. 999 might sum up the edgy jitteriness, the nobody-is-safe neurosis of the early twenty-first century; but it is halted at the boundaries of Great Britain. In Europe, 999 becomes 112; in America, 911. 999 (unlike the violence, the intrusion, the burglaries, lurking shadows, closing footsteps, crackling flames, smoke, crunching metal, broken glass and shrieks in the night which invoke it) does not travel. And, in a world given to globalization[17], not travelling will simply not do.

101? That, too, has a case to be argued. We may (particularly politicians, who have a vested interest) declare that we now inhabit a giant, pan-national version of Orwell's Room 101 from

---

17 Foolish phrase. The world has always been global. It's merely that we are only just noticing, and not necessarily in a helpful way either.

Nineteen Eighty-Four, in which that which we most fear will surely come to pass. But 101's case must fail. For most of us, the world has never been safer, our lives never fuller, our span of years never longer. If we inhabit World 101, it's 101 with chintz, a sofa, and soap, sanitation and antibiotics; and nor need we live in fear of World 102, the terrible, minatory Life to Come, when debts will be paid with a finality and ineluctability that taxmen can only dream of. That many of us do live in that fear (or its whorish sister, hope) is a matter of faith or choice; science, and physics in particular, has given us an alternative: that this great globe itself (yea, you will recall, all which it inherit) is simply a glorious mistake, the product of cosmic happenstance, the biggest winning payout in the history of . . . history.

No. 404 it is. Globalizers and one-worlders: both are mistaken. We inhabit not one world (whether to exploit or guard it[18]) but – at least – three. The philosopher Karl Popper classified those three worlds as:

World 1: The physical world, the world of continents and oceans, of rocks and shrubs and rainfall and volcanoes.

World 2: The psychological world: the world inside our heads, of love and hope, of anger and desire, faith and dreams, judgements, fantasies and delusions.

World 3: The – in its broadest sense – philosophical world: the world of art and books, statues and music, maps and algorithms; the world of theories and proofs, of postulates and refutations.

World 3, by its very nature, requires some sort of transcription, some kind of permanence. The writer Jorge Luis Borges isolated the problem neatly in his references to non-existent works. Why bother (he asked) writing an entire book when one might more easily imagine the book and write a review of it?

---

18 Beware, though, of those who would save the planet. The planet doesn't need to be saved. The planet is doing fine, and, if it comes to it, would shrug us off with a whisk of its climatological tail. What they mean is: us. Humankind. Not 'Save the Earth' but 'Sauve qui peut'.

So where *is* that imagined book? Is it in World 2, with the dream I had last night when the dead came back from World 102? Or is it in World 3, along with all the books ever really written, the music really composed, the sculptures really chiselled out of real stone?

The question is important for our times. Ask yourself: where is cyberspace? The computer guru (and sometime lyricist for The Grateful Dead) John Perry Barlow famously answered:

'Cyberspace is where you are when you're on the phone.'

You might prefer – or not prefer – to think of it as where your MONEY is[19].

But the key thing about cyberspace is . . . 404.

404. On the Web, it means: *Page not found.*

'Not found'. That is to say: lost. Not World 1. Not World 2, or World 3. World 2.9, perhaps; or World 3.1. Somewhere in between. Beyond our reach. The Greater Cyberspace of which our paltry little electronic bit is just a tiny fragment. Here live the dead, the unborn, the never-conceived; the books never written, the love never made, the television broadcasts flung into the infinite ether. Here are the molecules, lost on the wind, of a lover's perfume, an enemy's breath, a last supper, a *déjeuner sur l'herbe.* Here are the ideas which never made it onto paper, here is the rubbish they give you to read in dreams, here is the longed-for reconciliation which will never happen, lost youth, missed opportunities, the golden age, the snows of yesteryear.

404.

Not found.

---

19 Except when it's gone from your account but hasn't got to the account of the person you've paid it to, despite the transaction really only taking a few milliseconds. Then, it's not in cyberspace. It's in your bank's sclerotic, greasy fingers – and they're lending it out to heaven knows who. You want to stick it to them? Try cash.

For this most documented of all ages, 404 is the Warhol Number: the sign that your moment of fame (or at least of your existence's being made available to others outside your immediate circle) is over. You typed out your story, your thoughts, your theory of conspiracy or ANGELS, your tales of triumph or defeat, laboriously, perhaps. You scanned in your photographs. You checked your links. You worked out how the hell to get the stuff into . . . cyberspace. For a while, you were, if not known, knowable.

Then something changed. Your account expired. You remarried, moved away, died; your Internet company went bust; a hyperlink broke; something. There is always something, the third man in the diabolical trinity: Death, taxes, and . . . something.

So you became 404: Not found. A blank where something once was. And in due course the web-crawlers, the spiders and the netbots will give up, and even the link to your unfound memory will cease to appear; presently you will become unfit for consideration and disappear into the void beyond the reach even of Google. World Aleph: the infinity of infinities.

Like all good taxonomies of loss, like all ways of vanishing, 404 has a history, a mythology, is impenetrable to the uninitiated, possesses an inexorable logic. The first '4' is the minatory voice of denial, appearing in cyberspace, much as one of our ancestors, bowing before Marduk in the fertile crescent of Babylon, might have hallucinated the voices of the gods who told him he was mistaken; that he was doing something wrong; that his petition would be denied[20].

If all had been well, the distant computer would have sent the code '200'. This, you would never see; just as you never see a healthy person in a health food store. But all is not well. But not well how? The '0' tells you that there is a 'general syntax error';

---

20 As in *The Onion*'s majestic headline of 15 June 2000: 'God Answers Prayers Of Paralyzed Little Boy. "No," Says God.'

the command was issued wrongly ('Please please let her love me again') or maybe even just misspelt.

And finally comes the terminal digit. It could have been '0', a Bad Request ('Let me be editor of the *Daily Mail*'). It could have been '1', Unauthorized ('I will ascend into heaven, I will exalt my throne above the stars of God; I will sit also upon the mount of the congregation, in the sides of the north. I will ascend above the heights of the clouds; I will be like the most High God') . . .

But it is not. It is '4'.

Denied. Syntax Error. *Not Found*.

The logic is inexorable; and there is no appeal. The myth says that the code was numbered in memory of the room at CERN in Geneva, where the World Wide Web was, in effect, invented. Sir Tim Berners-Lee, who, in effect, invented the World Wide Web at CERN in Geneva, says not. The Web was not invented in Room 404.

There is no Room 404.

Which would be a delicious note to end on, were it not for one remaining truth.

404 is not all there is. 'Not found': the phrase indicates a certain . . . uncertainty. Beyond 404 lies a further level of nothingness, a certainty of vanishing.

410: Gone.

But nobody ever sees 410. The best (or worst) we get is the defiantly uncertain 404.

As *The History of 404* puts it:

'410: 404?'

$107,000,000,000

The money lost by the George Bush administration in the fight to bring DEMOCRACY to Iraq? No. The increase since 1972 in the annual amount Americans spend on fast food. Then, it was $3 billion a year. Just over thirty years later, it was $110 billion a year. Think of all the democracy you could impose for that.

AAAAA

AAAAA Large White Chest for Sale. The lonely, the prurient, the neophiliac: men in dirty raincoats, gazing longingly into the drizzle-streaked windows of Soho tobacconists, where the scrawled postcards promise delights, transgressions, paradise on earth or just a simple end to the loneliness of sad rooms in big cities.

AAAAAAA Schoolmistress offers Private French 'tuition' BOX No. 132.

Why did they do it? The cards ('That'll be 2/6d for the week, dearie, minimum of one month, plus a pound for handling and 6d a letter if you want the accommodation address, most of our clients find that convenient, shall we say £5 down?') went into the window according to the tobacconist's whim.

No guarantee that *AAAAAAAAAAAAA Extensive Theatrical Wardrobe for Rent* would get pole position above a simple *AAA New Young Moddel* or *AAAAAAAA Lonely gent seeks freind's, interests art photography, plastic,* but still they went on with it, inspired, perhaps, by the newspaper small-ads or the classified directories, which were arranged alphabetically ('*1111A1AAAAardvaark Cleaning Services*').

Now the stranglehold – real or imagined – of the alphabet has been lost. The random access of the World Wide Web has seen it off. In an age where all you need to do is Google what you want, *AAAAAA* would be as foolish as indexing *Chambers Dictionary*. But the result has not been simplicity, but complexity. *AAAAA Large White Chest for Sale* may now be *www.sexyxenia4u.xxx*, but instead of a few letters of the alphabet, she has to hide on her website a comprehensive thesaurus of all possible depravity, so that, whatever you are seeking, Google will find her first.

They all do it, not just the New Young Moddels. And hidden

in the metadata[21], whether it's furniture or Schoolmistress, credit repair or Lonely Gent, is a humiliating lexicon of desire and the unattainable. But a lexicon it is. Words, words, words . . . them, we're stuck with.

Absurdity, Awareness of One's Own

What absurdities did you commit today? If you know the answer, you are probably wrong. Absurdities are like assumptions: they are the things we do not know we are making. But we can be as certain as death and taxes that we are committing absurdities and making assumptions.

You don't believe it? Imagine a Martian anthropologist: a little green man[22] comes down to Earth and (unseen) observes you throughout the day. When you go to bed, he goes back to Mars.

'How was it?' they say.

'Well,' he says, 'you're not going to believe this, but – don't laugh – the person I was watching really, actually, and with a perfectly serious demeanour . . .'

And then he tells them what you did. And it was indeed absurd. And we have no way of telling what it is.

To lose the sense of our own fundamental absurdity is a serious error. It might be argued – it might have been argued nearly 2,500 years ago, in the second (and lost) book of Aristotle's *Poetics* – that comedy exists to remind us of our absurdity, in much the same way that the slave would whisper in the victor's ear, as he rode in triumph through Rome, 'Remember you are only mortal'.

---

21 Which we might say is a concealed description, not of what they want to sell, but of what we're really buying . . .

22 Why are they always little? Why are they always green? And why (when it's the one thing that, whatever else they are, they aren't) are they always men? An assumption, and an absurd one.

It might, too, be argued that when we still had no option but to believe in GOD (or at least THE GODS), we also had no option but to believe in our own relative insignificance; in the face of which, our tremendous, earnest, grim-faced preoccupations with our worldly lives became clearly absurd.

Now we have options. The best of those options is to believe that we are here by happenstance, by a glorious and glamorous accident. No need to feel little; no need either, it seems, to feel astonishingly lucky that all the odds lined up in our favour and here we are. Instead, we seem to be feeling more and more earnest and self-absorbed. Everyone wants their rights to be respected. Everyone wants to be a celebrity. People find things 'offensive': a depressingly infantile response, being not a judgement but a whine. Now comedy is itself penned increasingly into a cramped corral where it cowers behind neutral language, terrified of giving offence to the men who control the money, who are in turn terrified of giving offence to those who *pay* the money. The cry is for 'responsible' comedy, as foolish a concept as 'safe' sex.[23] Even cartoons are not immune: *The Simpsons* has been attacked by the Fat Police who have counted – *counted* – Homer's doughnut intake, and want it cut down and replaced by – mmmm! – raw carrot snacks and healthy Lo-Cal yogurt.

And so, assailed by such absurdities, we have lost sight of our own. But the fate which awaits us is grim. Those who coldly condemn everyone else's absurdities while clinging to the notion of their own seriousness are destined to become politicians. (While those who do the opposite are fated to be satirists. Which, one might wonder, is the more absurd?)

---

23 'Virus-unfriendly' sex might be tolerable, but safe sex? As absurd as the tabloids' 'Sex Romps'. Has anyone ever had a 'sex romp' – presumably where everyone bounces on the bed a lot, and makes little witticisms, and remains good chums afterwards with no recriminations?

Accoucheur, Queen Charlotte's

Far from forgotten, Queen Charlotte's accoucheur, the great obstetrician and anatomist William Hunter (1718–83) is still remembered as a hero of his profession. His life was not without loss; as well as an estrangement from his brother John[24], he lost his great love, Martha Jane, when he was a young man. He had not long before moved from Edinburgh to London, and was living in the house of Martha Jane's mother, who was the widow of James Douglas (1675–1742), when Martha Jane died. Hunter never married, and so became another victim of lost love. Martha Jane's mother might have taken comfort in the reputation of her husband, which survived him for over 250 years in the form of the Pouch of Douglas, before finally itself being lost to the Advancement of Knowledge or, depending on how you look at it, the Dismal Progress of Fashion and Folly. Whichever it was, the Pouch of Douglas is no more[25]. A double disappearance, really, since it was always evanescent: perform a hysterectomy and (there being no uterus for it to lie beneath) the Pouch of Douglas disappears in the process. Gone; and gone again.

Acts, Second, In American Lives

UTU News is one of those must-read publications: published by the United Transportation Union of America, it announces itself as 'The Voice of Transportation Labor'[26], and who can deny its

---

24 Another medic, who once referred a patient to William with a note saying: 'The bearer is very desirous of having your opinion. I do not know his case. He has no money, and you don't want any, so that you are well met.'

25 It's the recto-uterine pouch these days; and see also ZELINDA PAMPAGLINI.

26 And never mind the missing 'u' in 'Labor'; we can leave that until we come to think about *spelling*.

claim? It is, too, an eloquent voice; in Volume 34, No. 4 of April 2002, it announces that:

> Scott Fitzgerald wrote, 'There are no second acts in American lives.' The story of intercity passenger railroading in America has proven him to be wrong . . .

It is one of Fitzgerald's most resonant quotes, cited in the most extraordinary circumstances in support of whatever you want[27]. There is a majestic incongruity in the words of the terminally elegant Fitzgerald being used in the oily, hard-hatted, gravelly world of trains; but the Union has got it partly right. Fitzgerald *was* wrong. Not for himself perhaps (there was no second act in his life, and he died before he could finish the book). But for America, second (and third, and fourth) acts were as common, and as easily attained as second (and third, and fourth) wives, though possibly less expensively. Pack your traps, saddle your horse (or gas up your automobile) and light out for the territory. The life of many acts was at the heart of the American Dream, the freedom to be whoever you wanted to be.

But that freedom is vanishing; the right of self-reinvention withdrawn under the twin demands of security and of the credit rating industry. Begin as an alien and America, it would seem, is your oyster; begin as an American, and your life is a one-act drama, and then the curtain falls. There is no salvation in this life, no purpose of amendment firm enough to defeat the fuzzy-logic and DNA databases, the sociometric loyalty-card profiling, the iris scans, the fingerprinting, the credit histories, the court and travel records, the purchase paper-trails, and the computers

---

27 Although you can be reasonably sure that most of the people who quote it have never read it in context, nor know where it comes from. You can tell that because it's usually introduced: 'As Scott Fitzgerald *famously* wrote . . .' In fact, it's from *The Last Tycoon* (1941).

which put it all together. No wonder America believes in God: only beyond the grave is there any chance of a new life and a fresh start. While one road to Damascus has been reopened with bombs and bloodshed, the other has been closed with data and stealth. Fitzgerald, at last, is right.

Adolescents, Envy of

From the Shulamite of the Song of Solomon, via the Beautiful Youth of ancient Greek poetry[28], to the twentieth century, with its clean-limbed heroes, its gods of the playing field and coyly bountiful goddesses of the Parisian hat-shop or Californian drive-in, and taking in every poetical and artistic venture between the two – the swoonful *amours* of Courtly Love, Juliet on her balcony, Donne's lethal love-bunnies, the intolerable posturing of the Romantics, big-chinned pouting Pre-Raphaelites and all the rest – a constant of our species has been its yearning envy of youth: the liminal land between childhood and the groaning yoke of adult life, when everything is possible. Everything, on the whole, meaning hope and passion.

Not any more.

The old envy was based on an ancient asymmetry: we gave you *all this*, and you repay the debt by being *younger*? By *outliving* us? By having opportunities which we have *lost*?

But the bargain has been broken, the debt called in. Look at the world we have left to the hapless adolescents of the early twenty-first century. A world of food fads and neuroses, of exploitation through mass media. The affectless uniformity of the Web. Danger lurking: perverts round every corner, terrorists in the shadows. A world where the sea kills fish, rain dissolves

---

28 Or pottery. Or both.

trees and sex means death. Of crumbling infrastructures, grid-lock, collapsing health services. A world where only a few will be able to afford a house. A world of McJobs or no jobs or insane jobs which eat the whole of life. Where illusions are buried, childhood torn short, innocence drowned. A world of gendering and relativism, of spyware and databases, of political correctness. A world where there is no right and no wrong, only data. A world of branding and expediency and the dullest, nastiest music in the history of humanity, but the poor little bastards *have* to like it because . . . because everyone has to like the music of their times or get *left out*, even though it is so *boring*, despite the rude words. (Bitch! Nigga! Ho! Aren't we baaad! Pee po belly bum drawers! Heeheehee!)

Hell of a world. As if adolescence weren't a hell of a world enough already. The *Observer* writer Euan Ferguson once drew a terrible picture of the Lynx-reeking, unspeakable-groined young male, hunched in its room, expressing itself in verse:

> Roses are red,
> Violets are blue,
> I hate my parents.

But the true horror is that they don't hate their parents, poor things. Most of them seem to quite like their parents, because their parents, realizing the world they will inherit, don't envy them any more. Almost the reverse. The baby boomers know that nobody ever will have it so good again, young (as they were) in the magical times between the invention of the Pill and the advent of AIDS: a two-decade **GOLDEN AGE**, a Saturnalia, where the laws did not run.

Poor adolescents. Bored by their music, stunned by their entertainment, living at home with parents who think of them-selves as 'friends', they are deprived of adventure, self-invention and the great treasure of being envied; and, worst of all, they are understood.

Roses are red,
Violets are blue,
My parents are okay really.

And so the world goes to hell.

Affordability

Once, affordable was easy: it meant you could afford it, and
GRANDPA BEANS knew damn well what *that* meant. It meant you
could pay CASH for it and still feed the family. Now it can mean
anything, depending on context, and it's almost impossible to pin
it down. Try a simple example: *Affordable Housing*. Does it mean
'subsidized'? Or does it mean 'Somewhere horrible, badly
designed and prone to condensation, but the rap music from the
next flat will take your mind off the mushrooms sprouting from
the blackened walls'? Or maybe it means 'Not actually affordable
at all, but if you take out a gut-wrenching mortgage and firewall
your credit rating – and always provided you don't go out or have
any sort of a life – you might just be able to get a foot on the
housing ladder, and, frankly, it's either that or an old age of
penury, because in the twenty-first century, houses aren't where
you live; they're where your MONEY is. Okay?'

A brief[29] search on Google for 'affordable' brings up over sixteen million different references, for everything from holidays to
motorcycles, dress hire to plastic surgery. Try 'affordable business
jet'; Google take 0.06 seconds longer – this is, after all, a tough
concept, verging on the grotesquely absurd – but comes up with
160,000 results. *Affordable business jets?* What we have here is a
complete loss of perspective . . . but at least it gives us some idea
of what affordable really means. It means: You are greedy and

---

29 0.26 seconds.

reckless. We are greedy and rapacious. But – hey! – let's not feel *bad* about it, right?

Age, Golden, The

Mundus, as we have said, *senescit*: the world grows old, and with its age comes decay and (often literal) diminution; there were, after all, giants in the Earth in those days, but they have gone the way of the snows of yesteryear and of the name of the rose. *Stat rosa pristine nomine, nuda nomina tenemus*: tough to get at the meaning out of the mediaeval Latin, but (close enough) the sentiment can be approximated as *when the rose has faded all we have is its name*[30]. Strange, perhaps, that the SILLAGE of a rosy scent should be a word . . .

And so to the Golden Age. Generations beyond number – certainly they were active when the Old Testament was being composed – have lamented that time when men were men and women didn't mind; when the air was cleaner, people stood taller, children obeyed their elders, food tasted better, wine left one mellow rather than crapulous, flowers were brighter, rain softer, animals more obliging, harvests richer and a hazy mellifluous peace engulfed the living world. Two millennia and more ago, Virgil, writing from the noise and stink and turmoil of Rome, yearned for his golden Arcadia where the farmers had decent values, NATURE rewarded them, their kids were tough and all was well. Two millennia and more later – What a coincidence! How time balances out! – London stockbrokers and Hollywood stars still yearn for the ranch or the manor house, though *rus in urbe* may have shifted from the back-garden vegetable patch to the

---

30 Though some versions of Bernard de Morlay's *De Contemptu Mundi* appear to offer not 'rosa' but 'Roma' – a gloss which changes the meaning (so far as we can translate it) from a lost perfection to a lost corruption. Even Gertrude Stein never thought to claim that a rose is a Rome.

more publicly visible, but strangely unmuddy, 4X4 or SUV. We might say that the clumsy, rumbling gas-guzzler is a mobile garden, an unequivocal sign that, though your money is in the city, your heart is down in some rural Arcadia.

It is not so absurd. The Golden Age was only ever a collection of symbols pointing back to a time when the world was, if not young, at least younger; and the assumption (easy enough to understand) was that, in a world of correspondence and degree, if we deteriorated as we aged, then so must the world. Couple with that the Jewish belief (spread around the world by that oddest of Judaic sects, Christianity) in the Fall of Man – the key to our inexplicable credulity about the WISDOM OF THE ANCIENTS – and it is easy to see why the Golden Age still exerts its fascination.

Yet its location in time remains uncertain. Just as the garden always looked better last week, just as the orgy was always the day before yesterday or down the road, so the Golden Age occupies a strange, shifting region of time; the opposite of the phenomenon observed by authors, lawyers and software engineers, the Constant Time to Completion effect. The Golden Age is always, and has always been, a little before we were born; perhaps when our parents were young. After all, it's they who spent our childhoods telling us how much better things were when they were children.

But there's the secret. The Golden Age is always, really, *us*. It's the memory of our own childhood. Not that it was necessarily wonderful; just that it was simultaneously us, and yet entirely foreign. Nobody can recapture how they thought as a child; how the world felt; how alert the senses were; how the world seemed to offer endless opportunity, unalloyed promise under the sun. The seventeenth-century mystic Thomas Traherne saw our lives beginning, as infants, in a condition of amazement, like ANGELS; and so the Golden Age is the angelic infancy of the world. No wonder we yearn for it.

Agony, Last

'Thus,' announced the sardonic jester at the end of Shakespeare's *Twelfth Night*, a comedy of perfect silver that glitters like the workings of a Swiss watch: 'Thus the whirligig of time brings in his revenges.'

It is one thing of which we can be certain. We may all lose time, but time itself will never be lost, and its revenges can be delicious. Reputations rise and fall, judgements are reversed, the guilty are exonerated and the once-lauded reduced to dust; the Romans were right to mistrust *fama* every bit as much as we now uncritically laud Fame. Riding on time's whirligig, even the lost can be found again.

Think of the seventeenth-century English composer, Henry Purcell. Once seen as the Kipling of music – a little dull, a little worthy, suspiciously jingoistic[31] – he has lately returned from the land of the lost, seen once more as a master, utterly *sui generis*, able to create the most astounding musical effects with an apparently almost insolent minimalism of means.

The most extraordinary of Purcell's accomplishments was his ability to pause time. The lament from his *Dido and Aeneas* of 1689 broke hearts, but when the chorus sang *Keep here your watch, and never part*, in the silences between the repetitions of 'never' it was not hearts which broke but all the clocks in the world.

Six years later, Purcell was to do it again. Queen Mary died, and for her funeral music he wrote a processional march of such breathtaking stasis that it is more like statuary than music. It may have been a piece of display for a great public occasion, but it was also the epitome of that private desolation and loss which we must all at some point feel in our lives; and the world stood still upon its axis.

---

31 My dears! Those *frightful* goose-pimpled Nymphs! And that *dreary* King Arthur!

Then, again, the choir sang the three *Sentences* from Cranmer's Book of Common Prayer, the last one ending:

> Suffer us not at our last hour for any pains of death to fall from thee.

The pains of death were the final test of faith. Fall away under their anguish, and you were lost indeed, not just to this world but to **GOD**.

You could – you should – argue that one of the greatest advances in the history of human suffering has been anaesthesia; and anaesthetists have moved out of the operating theatre into the ward, and out of the ward into the world. Pain used to be something to be borne bravely: the 'good' patient never complained, while the 'weak' patient bleated pathetically for analgesia and was sharply told there were people *much* worse off. Even the word 'patient', from the Latin *patior*, 'I suffer', implies both pain and its uncomplaining endurance. *Passus et sepultus est*, pronounces the Catholic creed: He suffered, and was buried. So it was for Jesus, so it was for the great Death-cult of Christendom; how on Earth (let alone in Heaven) should we even dare to contemplate an easier exit than that of God himself?

And so the dying, in their last agonies, were instructed that they were imitating Christ; that their sufferings were cleansing their soul; that it was an honour and a privilege to shriek with pain, to drown slowly in your own fluids, to suffocate slowly, to endure the hallucinating terrors of fever or the reeking horrors of the cancer that was eating you alive.

This was God's gift: that He included you, out of His great mercy, in the world of suffering that He had prepared for his only-begotten, and anyone who thought that that might mean God was either incompetent or rather horrible . . . well, they could suffer as much as they liked, but there was only one place *they* were going.

The monastic office of Compline, said immediately before the monks go to their beds, ends with the prayer *noctem quietam et finem perfectam concedat nobis Dominus Omnipotens*: Almighty God, grant us a peaceful night and a perfect end[32]. How many of us now pray for a good death? How many of us even consider the nature of our dying, unless it is to worry, in that most ridiculous but most universal of fashions, that when the time comes, we may not know what to do?

Very few. Most people, by the time they reach their middle years, have known someone close to them who has died. 'Well,' we say to ourselves, '*they* survived it,' and we take comfort: it can't be that difficult.

As for our last agonies, though: we don't expect to have them. As death approaches, we are confident that a friendly anaesthetist, someone with a soothing manner and a comprehensive MATERIA MEDICA, will take care of that side of things.

What does that mean for us? Do we somehow miss out on the contemplation of that most unimaginable and downright peculiar of all events, the extinguishing and permanent loss of our own actual selves? Or do we leave (nobody, after all, gets off the planet alive) more peacefully, being ushered out, not by admonishing prelates, but by the gentle detachment of the Specialist in Pain?

As someone once remarked to me in the intensive care ward where both our mothers lay gently dying[33]: 'If they'd had this sort of thing two thousand years ago, the Church Fathers would never have come up with eschatology.' That is now lost to all but the most devout (who, curiously, tend also to be those with the least access to the technological *finem perfectam*); which is one loss perhaps we need not regret too much.

---

32 The English loses the soft and telling resonance of the Latin: that *perfectus* itself comes from the verb *perficere*: to carry out, to finish or to complete.

33 Or possibly already dead, in all but the paperwork.

America, the Idea of

Once upon a time, America was our hope and our enchantment. We yearned for its manly men, its HATS, its deserts and its saloon girls; we yearned for its can-do culture, the rough shock of its cities, the smooth suits of its Mob, the sense of infinite possibilities in its violet dusks and blue, blue mornings. We yearned for its beer and jazz, its smoke-filled nightclubs, its Edward Hopper bars, the melancholy of rainy Manhattan Gershwin nights and the ring of its telephones; we yearned for the musicals, the high corn; we yearned for the prairie farmhouses and carried in our drizzled souls an inward, small-town Main Street to comfort us. We yearned for its big cars and, in our staid northern climes, we yearned, not just for its detectives, its soda fountains, its cold beer and sardonic desk-clerks, but for its *fun*.

Now we yearn for America to be, not itself – a greedy, domineering, isolated, stomping, hypocritical land of political correctness at home and blatant savagery abroad – but the self we always believed it to be. And *that*, more than anything else, is why we are so angry. We have been let down. The America we yearned for has gone. Did it ever exist?

Ancients, Wisdom of the

They were not. They were not wise. But one would have had to have lost one's wits entirely to believe that statement is enough; that one could say 'The Ancients were not wise', and everyone would say, 'Gosh, I suppose you're right, we'd better shut up with all this pyramids nonsense, all this rubbish about magic and secrets and holism and, God help us, GOD.'

That is not the point of the Wisdom of the Ancients, which exists as a massive quasi-philosophical Lost Sock, or the memory of vanished love: that's to say, as something which we once had

31

and, if we are very good and very careful, we might one day get back.

The Ancients knew little and understood less. They scratched a living and died like dogs. Gripped by an uncomprehending egocentricity, they believed that the world had been made for them, and they believed that by a process of crude extrapolation: when they needed something, they made it. Finding themselves in a world which suited them to a remarkable degree[34], they assumed that it had been made for them; obviously, by someone much like them, but much bigger. Unable to understand any laws other than the law of will[35], they assumed that when something happened in nature, it happened because NATURE commanded it. The river dried up because they had offended it; the volcano erupted because the Volcano Giants had not been placated; the harvest failed because someone – this is a bit of a leap of faith, but it leads eventually to Christianity, so it's all okay in the end – had not had his heart torn out and then been ripped limb from limb and his blood poured onto the soil.

In short, the Ancients spent what thinking time they had[36] trying to make phenomenological bricks without ontological straw. They were wrong about almost everything, hopelessly confused sequence and causation, left the scantiest record of their thinking, and croaked in short order.

So why do a significant number of people, even now, believe not only in the bits of the Wisdom of the Ancients that we know

---

34 Which of course it did, or they wouldn't have found themselves in it; an obvious point but one which is distressingly often overlooked.

35 As the Roman satirist Juvenal said, *hoc uolo, sic iubeo; sit pro rationem uoluntas*: 'I want it, so I command it; let my will take the place of reason.' He wasn't talking about the Ancients. He was talking about women. We have come on since then; ask any woman.

36 Not a lot, if you believe Julian Jaynes, of course. Between tilling the soil, groaning with sickness and malnutrition, dying in childbirth, being hacked to pieces in tribal wars, and being ticked off constantly by hallucinated admonitory gods, it is miraculous that the Ancients even managed to invent blood feuds and human sacrifice, let alone the rudiments of philosophy.

about (like astrology) but also that there is a huge corpus of lost wisdom which, if only we could find it, would guarantee us a future of bliss, with no wars or sadness or cancer ever again, a world of birdsong and crystal and . . .

. . . In our dreams. Specifically, in our dream that the world was created perfect, and has been drifting away from perfection ever since. 'The silver swan unlocks her silent throat' – the initiates will spot Orlando Gibbons's great madrigal, the others get a pretty image, everyone's happy.

Those who believe in the Wisdom of the Ancients disbelieve in any progress in human understanding. It is the intellectual equivalent of saying *There's nothing worth watching on the telly any more* or *This so-called music the young people listen to, it's rubbish*[37]. In truth, it is not the Wisdom of the Ancients that we have lost; it's any fathoming of their true Ignorance.

Angels

Jacob wrestled with one, Donne compared his girl to one, in advance ('So in a voice, so in a shapeless flame/Angels affect us oft, and worshipp'd be'), the mystic poet Thomas Traherne compared *himself* to one, when he was a boy and had his *innocence*:

> How like an angel came I down!
> How bright are all things here!
> When first among his works I did appear
> O how their glory did me crown!

But weren't they just a collective fantasy, an assembly of bits and pieces – fragments of the puffed-up Lucifer, detritus from the cherubim of Exodus, remembrancers of Athena Nike, the

---

37 Yes, yes, I know it *is* rubbish, but it's also rubbish to *say* so.

winged Victory, mere *putti* in the hands of the symbol-players of organized religion?

If *Reason* had triumphed, as we might hope it had triumphed, then the answer would be unequivocally 'yes'. Angels would have been lost to us for ever, except as a convenient collective fiction, something to aspire to or to be comforted by when comfort was (as so often) not to hand.

But we live, not in the Age of Reason, but in the Age of Relativism, a peculiar DEMOCRACY of the mind where nothing is true or false but everyone is entitled to his (or her) own opinion. And so we must acknowledge, not observation, but the poll. And a poll, carried out in 1998, tells us that seventy-one per cent of North Americans believe in angels[38].

Three years later, the number had risen. This time, seventy-seven per cent of Americans asked whether they believed angels 'in fact exist' said yes, they surely did; and seventy-three per cent believed they still came to earth[39]. Many claim to have seen them, and a distressing number have Internet access where they worry the question like a dog worries a sock[40]. Angels should have been lost to our belief centuries ago; yet in the heart of the richest and most powerful nation the world has ever known, they are still alive, if in the most mundane way imaginable – like the 'clean-cut . . . handsome young man' who helped a woman with her luggage at Dallas airport . . . and then, when she turned round to thank him, 'he had absolutely disappeared'.

---

38 Commissioned by the Chrysler Corporation, who were sponsoring a touring exhibition of Vatican artworks featuring angels.

39 The actual questions were 'Do you believe angels, that is, some kind of heavenly beings who visit Earth, in fact exist?' and that they 'still come into the world even in these modern times'.

40 In a marvellous conjunction of credulity and environmentalism, one individual sternly announces: *'DISCLAIMER: Please be aware that I believe in an Almighty God and that He and He alone created angels. I do not believe that when we or our loved ones die, that they become angels. If God had intended to recycle us, there would have been no need for Him to create angels.'*

Hard to argue with evidence like that, even if philosopher Paul Kurtz, founder of the Council for Secular Humanism[41], describes it as 'very disturbing, even tragic'. The only real explanation can be that this is yet another example of *lost wits*. But whose?

Appetites, Healthy

Yum yum! Meat and potatoes, and more meat and more potatoes, and some gravy with that? More mash? Go on, have some lard! It's Spotted Dick, your favourite! Custard and suet and stew and pie and pudding, puddings bursting with dried fruits and puddings bursting with steak and kidney and lard and oysters and suet and lard, *go on, spoil* yourself, have another **SHIELD OF MINERVA**, you know you can make room . . .

A healthy appetite was the thing. You cleaned your plate because there were starving children in Africa who would be glad of it[42] and because your parents would cause trouble otherwise. And if it wasn't trouble, it was concern, which was worse.

---

41 The irreligious kind, as opposed to the Renaissance kind which still believed in God but thought He had made a better job of things than *Genesis* would suggest, and that we weren't just rotten, disgusting, sin-shrivelled worms wriggling through the planetary filth on our way to judgement. On which point, I recall the doorman of the Central Park South, NY, apartment that I briefly occupied many years ago; on a perfect spring morning, he stood at the door (as doormen do), extended his arms to embrace the entire scene, and said: 'So what are you telling me? That God created all this just to *judge* it?'

42 Although this advice was seemingly contradicted by the duty to Leave Some For Mister Manners, the answer is probably that Mr M. was a pre-World War II invention. For Baby Boomers, brought up in the immediate post-war memory of rationing, more meant better, and good mothers bought Gold Top milk for their children, thus simultaneously demonstrating love and condemning them to coronary-bypass surgery at fifty-five. Another theory, put forward by the novelist Caron Freeborn (brought up in an East End Jewish family) was that cleaning your plate meant you were still hungry. Her partner, middle-class, had been brought up to eat everything. When she first took him home, he cleaned his plate. Her mother gave him more. He cleaned his plate. Her mother gave him more. Struggling manfully, he cleaned his plate . . . (See also THE ELEVENTH COMMANDMENT)

You were off your food. You were looking peaky. You couldn't go out to play. You might even have to have some terrible patent medicine and go to your room.

Now we live in an age where grown men eat lettuce, where women sit in expensive bars talking about how they look like stalks because they eat like birds, while drinking like fish. A healthy appetite symbolizes lack of self-control. Curvaceous women now describe themselves as 'BBWs'[43] and a manly belly, once the sign of power and prosperity, is something to be worked off by working out. Did they never read *Die Geschichte vom Suppen-Kaspar* in *Struwwelpeter*, the *Story of Augustus who would not have any soup*? Initially all is well:

> Augustus was a chubby lad;
> Fat ruddy cheeks Augustus had;
> And everybody saw with joy
> The plump and hearty healthy boy.

But then some dreadful anorexia strikes. Self-esteem issues? Psychosexual disaggregation? An occulted desire to remain a child? Peer pressure? The barbaric influence of evil *fashionistas*? Who knows . . .

> But one day, one cold winter's day,
> He threw away the spoon and screamed:
> 'O take the nasty soup away!
> I won't have any soup to-day!'

And the consequences are inevitable:

> . . . O what a sin!
> To make himself so pale and thin.

---

43 Big Beautiful Women – and quite right; no more than the truth; but would they say it if they really believed it?

[. . .]

> Look at him, now the fourth day's come!
> He scarce outweighs a sugar-plum;
> He's like a little bit of thread;
> And on the fifth day he was – dead.

The moral is clear: *scare your children*.

Ark of the Covenant

On the back cover of Graham Hancock's 1992 book *The Sign and the Seal*, an Ethiopian monk called Gebra Makail peers irritably into the camera lens. 'The subject of this book,' says the copy breathlessly, 'could constitute the single most shattering secret of the last three thousand years. This monk is the only man in the world who knows the truth.' The question is: is he the guardian of the Lost Ark of the Covenant which resides within the church of St Mary of Zion, Aksum?

Why this should be the most shattering secret of the last three thousand years is unclear. If you accept the proposition that God gave the Jews a written covenant which was kept in the Ark and then hidden away, the story is over. God did what God did, and everything else is unimportant. If, on the other hand, you believe that it's metaphorical at best and simply untrue at worst ('worst'?), then the search for the Ark is the hunt for a turnip-ghost. And if you believe that the Ark has magical powers which can be used for good or evil and gives the possessor dominion over all, except that if the possessor is himself evil, then the Ark will destroy him, then you already know where it is: in a huge warehouse Somewhere In America, where it was taken after Indiana Jones rescued it from the Nazis.

The most interesting thing about Ark-chasers – apart from the staggering lengths to which people will go in hunting their turnip-ghosts – is that they tend to demonstrate the peculiar principle that All Lost Secrets Are The Same Lost Secret. Hancock, in his various books, ravels up **ATLANTIS**, Mars, Comets, the Secret of the Pyramids, Lost Advanced Civilizations Ten Thousand Years Before Christ, the Knights Templar, the **ANCIENT WISDOM** of the Egyptians, Visitors from Outer Space, Genesis, Astrology and the **HOLY GRAIL**[44]. And he is not alone.

And yet, despite the implausibility and speciousness of their reasoning, despite the easy availability of the still-sharp Occam's Razor, despite the powerful arguments that we really *do* inhabit a WYSIWYG (What You See Is What You Get) universe, people still gobble up the most convoluted arguments to prove that the universe is really WYSCUAECBJAF[45] while shying away from the elegant simplicity of Darwinism. Following the trail of galumphing, mythical artefacts and lost 'wisdom' seems to hold a fascination that the *truly* shattering secret[46] – that complexity flows upwards, not downwards from 'God' – cannot compete with.

One reviewer on Amazon[47] writes: 'Sometimes after a first read too unbelievable, but after some thinking . . . you say "Yes of course!".'

No. Right first time.

And as for the Ark? The monk told Hancock to bugger off. So the most shattering secret of the last three thousand years remains hopefully lost for another three.

---

44 Or the Ark of the Covenant which, at one point, Hancock seems to believe (though it's hard to tell) is the Same Thing.

45 What You See Covers Up An Enormous Conspiracy By Jews And Freemasons.

46 Though it's not actually a secret. It's science. And that's the difference between science and religion: science doesn't keep secrets, and couldn't function if it did.

47 And the reviews on Amazon are as powerful an argument against **DEMOCRACY** as you could ever find.

Armchair, Favourite

'The unspeakable in pursuit of the uneatable,' said Wilde of fox-hunting; but the truth is that the unspeakable and the uneatable work together. Not, perhaps, on the hunting field, but certainly everywhere else. Both have the same job: to distinguish Us from Them, to mark who belongs and who doesn't.

The difference is that one works in space, the other in time. The uneatable is usually (or was originally) uneatable because the tribe next door ate it. The unspeakable serves to distinguish us, not from the people next door, but from the people who came before us[48]. And keeping up is a constant struggle.

We may delude ourselves that the Unspeakable is shrinking[49] as we become more open, more liberal, more, bless our souls, accepting of human diversity (while pretending not to notice it). But it is a delusion. Our forebears may not have been allowed to talk about sex, GOD or politics, but *we* have lost the right to make judgements, draw distinctions or observe differences. Yet any modern man, particularly a BACHELOR, who spoke about male friendship in the manner of his nineteenth-century equivalent, would be assumed to be a practitioner of the love that, then, dared not speak its name, but which is now, thank heavens, walking cheerfully about the place saying hello and introducing itself.

As always, the true pleasures are in the little things. GRANDPA BEANS had his Favourite Armchair and so did yours: green leather, uncut moquette, Naugahyde® or Parker-Knoll; adorned with an antimacassar or a brass ashtray on a leather strap; with or

---

48 Both, of course, also work in social class, even though relativism, egalitarianism and the telly may mean that we have lost our touch in determining what is or is not COMMON.

49 Though the Uneatable is having a boom, as anyone who has tried to feed their friends knows. 'Okay, we can't do monkfish for the fishetarians because it's not kosher, and the koshers won't eat red meat *either*, so cod will do for them, but what about the vegetarians, one of whom is wheat-intolerant and the other can't eat dairy . . .'

without a Smoker's Companion or a matching footstool: everyone had a favourite armchair. It was the guarantee of domesticity, the symbol of peace and power[50], the visible manifestation of order in the home.

Admit to a favourite armchair now at your peril. The concept may be publicly lost. But 'publicly' does not mean 'actually'[51]. The favourite armchair was once a bastion against the outside world, a bulwark against time, an unchanging absolute in the face of fashion. Now you can buy a favourite armchair – prefavoured, if you like – on the grounds that it is just like the one in *Friends*, on the television. A La-Z-Boy Oasis recliner, to be precise, with a built-in beer fridge in one arm, a 99-number memory phone in the other, a heated back, and a ten-motor electric massager. It's so uncool it's cool. Not comfy, but ironic. Not favourite, but iconic. A style statement for the 'bloke' with £1,000 to spare.

But its owners know the truth. It is as much a Favourite Armchair as anything your grandfather ever sat in. The only problem is this: can a single man have a favourite armchair? Probably not; because the whole point is that others must envy it, and want it, and plot to get it. The single man with a favourite armchair is like a child playing King of the Castle on his own: he may have gained the world, but he has lost his edge.

Artemis and Erinna

In the sixth century BC, at what is now Ephesus, a temple was erected to Artemis. It was one of the seven wonders of the ancient world, and was rebuilt seven times as earthquakes, Goths

---

50 Now replaced by the Thing. (It's supposed to be called 'the remote control' but everyone knows it's called the Thing, just like everyone knows there's a 'p' in 'hampster', and we might as well learn to live with it.)

51 Do we *really*, for example, believe that the Victorians knew nothing of drugs or buggery?

and Vandals destroyed it in their turn. But it took the Christians to deal with it for good: they dismantled what was left, and made off with the remains.

And so are the works of man scattered like Antipater's rooks:

> Brief is Erinna's song, her lowly lay,
>   Yet there the Muses sing;
> Therefore her memory doth not pass away,
>   Hid by Night's shadowy wing!
> But we, – new countless poets, – heaped and hurled
>   All in oblivion lie;
> Better the swan's chant than a windy world
>   Of rooks in the April sky![52]

Antipater? A Greek poet of the second century BC, whose list designating the Seven Wonders of the World has outlived all the Wonders except a pyramid, and outlived his poetry too; thus demonstrating that oblivion and loss are not the same thing, and that both are capricious.

Assumptions

When someone says 'I am going to make a few assumptions here,' disbelieve them. They are not talking about assumptions, because assumptions are the things that we don't know we are making. I am making them as I write. You are making them as you read. What are they? We do not know. They are lost to us. If we found out what they were, they would cease to be assumptions.

At least, we assume they would.

---

52 *Erinna*, trans. Andrew Lang.

41

Atlantis

So Poseidon[53], do you see?, waited until Evenor and Leucippe died (they were mere mortals, these **ANCIENTS**) and then married their daughter Cleito, and they had five pairs of twin sons, and Poseidon divided up Atlantis between them and *that* is all nonsense. And in 1665 the cartographer Athanasius Kircher put Atlantis in the middle of the Atlantic and made it bigger than Africa; and the extremely dodgy (one might almost say wilfully barking) American, Ignatius Donnelly, incorporated most of the ancient world into *his* Atlantis, and some say that records of Atlantis may be deduced from the Cretan Phaistos disc, and the wealthy nineteenth-century Hellenist and amateur archaeologist Schliemann thought he could deduce the location of Troy from Homer's *Iliad* (and how everyone laughed) . . . and Atlantis has been located variously in:

1. The Pacific
2. The North Sea
3. The Sahara[54]
4. Sweden
5. Southern Spain
6. Palestine
7. Cyprus
8. Crete
9. The West Indies
10. Peru
11. North Africa
12. South Africa

---

53 According to Plato (*Timaeus* and *Critias*).
54 Which would have made Plato quite unimaginably wrong, given that Atlantis was supposed to be an island. 'The ship: camel of the sea.'

13. Central America
14. North America
15. Spitzbergen
16. Australia
17. France
18. Sardinia
19. Israel
20. Lebanon
21. Malta
22. East Prussia
23. The Baltic
24. Siberia
25. Greenland
26. Iraq
27. Iran
28. Brazil
29. The Indian Ocean

Conversely, Atlantis has *never* been definitively located in:

1. Soho

Atlantis, in short, has provided harmless amusement for nearly two and a half thousand years and, despite having been so convincingly[55] and so often located, remains pleasingly lost.

Greatest of all the Atlantiarchs is certainly Donnelly. The British Prime Minister Gladstone was a great supporter, and wanted to finance an expedition to Atlantis[56]; and who can blame him, when even Donnelly's lecture posters are enough to

---

55 To those who have been convinced, of course.

56 Thus proving that Tony Blair is not the maddest of Prime Ministers, nor the most gullibly seduced into wanting to commit huge sums of money to insane and hopeless adventures; the difference is that Mister Tony, of course, got his way.

stir the blood while simultaneously reassurring his audience of his scholarship and high moral purpose:

LECTURE!
IGNATIUS
DONNELLY
AT THE OPERA HOUSE, ALBERT LEA
SATURDAY EVENING
MARCH 23RD, 1889
SUBJECT
WIT AND HUMOR!
MUSIC BY BRUNDIN'S ORCHESTRA

'This is a most entertaining lecture! And has everywhere been received with High Encomiums!'[57]

So far, so pleasantly silly, and no surprise when, in 1912, Schliemann's grandson Paul came up with coins and an inscribed plate, together with a vase inscribed 'From King Cronos of Atlantis', which had been left to him by his grandfather, on the basis of which he wrote a book modestly entitled *How I Discovered Atlantis, the Source of All Civilization*. Exactly what one would expect from a man whose grandfather had thought he could find the obviously mythical Troy from the obviously mythical *Iliad*, 2,600 years after the event.

Paul Schliemann's artefacts were bogus. Everything written about Atlantis has been at the very best entirely speculative. Nobody has found it. The whole idea of finding a lost metropolis – let alone a lost continent – from an anecdotal ancient account is absurd, whether it be Atlantis or Troy.

Except for one thing.

Using his *Iliad*, Heinrich Schliemann *did* discover Troy.

---

57 One may say, 'Where in this is Atlantis?' But Ignatius Donnelly was large; he contained multitudes.

There once was a time when people smelt of people[58]. Now we take one, two or, in extreme cases, three baths or showers a day without thinking much about it, and apply deodorant afterwards; but there are plenty of people alive who can remember when 'bath night' was a weekly occurrence, yet, strangely (if you believe the advertising), do *not* recall daily life as being unendurable because of the stench.

Our modern habits of bathing would have been seen as extravagant and unecessarily fastidious, or possibly even as evidence of an inner immorality. Bathing had echoes of baptism, which itself derived from the Jewish custom of the purification rite of *mikveh*; the religious overtones persist, for example, in Islam, where to keep a Muslim from his ritual ablutions is to interfere with his right to say his prayers properly. Taking too many baths was the mark of the irreligious, of those who had perverted a spiritual duty into a warm, slippery, fleshly indulgence, either for its own sake (dwelling too much on nakedness in the scented steam, who knows where the mind – or the fingers – might wander?) or as a precursor to more cooperative eroticism.

Public bathing was no better. The great *Thermae* of ancient Rome were as much notorious as houses of assignation and prostitution – the satirists Juvenal and Martial were particularly offended by this – where the aristocratic wife, stripped of the jewels and clothing which marked her rank, could fornicate[59] with a muscular nobody or even a satirist (who could later walk home railing against the corruption in which he had so recently wallowed). The Hammams of the Turks were associated

---

58 The argument for acceptability was, and remains, simple: as an anonymous French voluptuary put it, today's sweat, *oui*; yesterday's, *non*.

59 The word actually comes from the *fornices*, or arches, of great stadia like the Colosseum, in whose shady warmth the whores would ply their trade with punters overexcited by gladiatorial blood.

with the unspeakable indulgences of *odalisques* or, if that was your fancy, boys; the later, English incarnations of 'Turkish Baths' were resorts not just for the hung-over[60] but for buggeronies. And we are still ambivalent; the squeaky-clean Scandinavian sauna has become shorthand for a commercial masturbatorium, in which a man who merely wanted to steam away his aches and pains would be regarded with suspicion.

Reading texts written at a time when personal hygiene was what we would now call intolerable, and clothes were worn for months at a time without cleaning, our modern sensibilities are offended. 'By God,' we say to ourselves, 'they must have stunk. Or stank. Stinked? What the hell *is* the past tense of "stink", anyway? Whatever it is, they must have done.'

Maybe they did. Maybe they didn't. Maybe they noticed. Maybe they didn't. But in what was the perfect paradigm of modern advertising, Lifebuoy soap once ran a radio commercial starring a foghorn which rasped 'B.O.' The slogan: 'Your best friend won't tell you.' Sheerest genius. Invent a problem and offer to sell the cure. We couldn't tell we smelt, do you see? And our *best friend wouldn't tell us.* The only answer: bathing every day with Lifebuoy. Soon, Lifebuoy was not enough; first came deodorants, then antiperspirants, and presently the horrors of the early-morning train and the nine a.m. lift, overwhelmed by a cacophony of after-shaves and colognes and scented deodorants, until now an averagely well-groomed young urban woman can apply 400 chemicals (300 of which are synthetic) to her body *every day of her life.*

B.O. may have gone, but so has the natural smell of humanity. Some, noting that California and Scandinavia led the USA and Europe respectively in both 'personal hygiene' and divorce, have

---

60 In Russell Square, London, you can still see the directions *To the Turkish Baths*; not on an ordinary sign, but embossed into the paving stones. Presumably by the point at which the Englishman required a Turkish Bath he was already half-bent-over, either from drink or desire, and his gaze fixed below.

speculated that if we lose our smell, we lose our bonding ability.

But what *was* that smell? How did it seem to the people who smelt it? We know that, for example, pomanders were used in the sixteenth century, and judges at the assizes still carry ceremonial posies – but these were not for aesthetic but for (misguided) medicinal purposes, to counter the 'miasma' in which disease was thought to lurk. One of the great questions of history is: *what was it like then*? And all too often we can't answer it. Did the Romans' clothes itch? What did the outflow of the baths look like? Did mediaeval people shrink from kissing because of their foul teeth? Did our ancestors make love despite what we would consider their appalling hygiene, or did they simply not notice, or notice *and like it*?[61] Travellers' accounts refer to the hugger-mugger arrangements in inns and lodging houses, three-in-a-bed and damp straw, but nobody refers to the smell.

And we have no way of telling. One of the rules of history is that sources are full of ASSUMPTIONS: people simply don't mention the obvious. We can estimate the molecules in the air, but we cannot estimate the subjective experience of being there. It was too obvious to mention. And so the information, having never been recorded, is now lost for ever, volatile as bergamot, blown clean as a whistle by the winds of time.

Bachelors

Stereotypes, of course. Holmes and Watson: Watson married, it's true, but he was still a bachelor. Rooms. Landlady. FUG. Habits. No; not habits; *ways*. You know how they get. Tobacco in the slipper, needle in the arm, *bachelors*.

---

61 One of the world's great perfumes, *Je Reviens*, is not (as you might think) named after the promise of the wearer to return ('I'll be back . . .') but after Napoleon's sexy little message to Joséphine: *Je reviens; ne te lave pas*: 'Returning home. Don't wash.'

Or the Irish sort. Rooms; no, not rooms: DIGS. The landlady. The Brother[62], shady, all-knowing, up above there in the room, going quietly mad. Then there's the Bachelor Feline, exemplified by Uncle William Boot in *Scoop*, dreaming of rooms – no, *chambers* – in Jermyn Street, morning saunters between bootmaker, tailor and club, feline prowlings after dark. The Bachelor Dissolute (Madeira, Bentley, first editions and showgirls), the Bachelor Advantageous (James Bond, The Saint, The Toff), the Bachelor Despondent, shabby, pale, penurious. The Bachelor Academic, cloistered, collegiate and absent-minded. The Bachelor Spiritual: Jesus and all his celibate followers. And, of course, the Bachelor Comic: Morecambe & Wise, Matthau & Lemmon, Vladimir & Estragon.

We won't be doing with bachelors now. We suspect them. Sex has become so much the Greatest Good that we cannot conceive of anyone abjuring it without motive: nasty ways, inadequacy, small boys, little girls, simmering psychopathies. Those who have nothing to do with women we prefer to consider as closeted gays; sexual uninterest is beyond our hopelessly over-eroticized ken, and, perhaps, we so much fear and hate unfettered masculinity that we would rather it were corralled in the very homosexual relationships that a few generations ago we could barely imagine. Those same few generations ago, the bachelor, un-hamstrung by domesticity or the call of the bedsprings, was considered *more* of a man, freer to preach or fight or build or conquer.

Now, he is less. So much less that we cannot acknowledge him as such. He is denied a status, merely accorded a state. He is . . . *single*. And when he leaves the room, we glance at each other and the unspoken question hangs in the air. What, exactly, *is* he? He can't be just a bachelor.

---

62 For the perfect objective correlative of bachelordom, see 'The Brother' in Flann O'Brien (a.k.a. Myles na gCopaleen) in *The Best of Myles*. After a bit, you'll believe you were there. After a bit more, you'll want to hang yourself. Bachelorhood is a two-edged sword (but so are most swords, surely?).

Bakelite

A great step forward in the MATERIA MEDICA was Joseph Lister's use of carbolic acid[63] as an antiseptic. But if it didn't quite work, and the bugs got through, and you died[64], then formaldehyde would preserve your corpse for inspection by your relations or dismantling by medical students[65].

An odd pair of chemicals, then, to mix together; but that's what the Belgian chemist Dr Leo Baekeland did at the turn of the last century, while hunting for a non-flammable varnish for bowling-alley floors[66]. The result was a phenolic resin which, in the manner of the times, he named 'Bakelite'. It was a triumph, and in the early twentieth century became *the* material of Modernism. Mouldable, easily coloured (anything from pale golden ambers to deep woody browns and profound blues), its plasticity and cheapness brought experimental design to the masses.

Plugs, light switches, steering wheels, car cigar-lighters, telephones[67]. BOYARDS MAÏS smouldering in Bakelite ashtrays, racy women in Bakelite jewellery. Mad scientists twiddling Bakelite controls in underground laboratories. But perhaps Bakelite was best known for radios. Athlone, Allouis, Hilversum, Luxemburg: all came in via the Bakelite knobs of the Bakelite wireless, as did

---

63 Now known as phenol. It was still around in the 1960s in the form of pink, rough carbolic soap, to use in the shower after games. It may have worked on bugs but it was powerless against schoolboys.

64 Which you often did, if the bugs got through. Then, as once again now, hospital was a dangerous place to be.

65 No medic will ever forget the smell of formaldehyde, which penetrated the dissecting rooms like incense in a cathedral, except nastier and more eye-watering. They don't use it any more. Corpses, like everything else, have to smell lovely now.

66 Really. This is not a lie.

67 My paternal grandfather had the GPO Model 1/232 with Bellset 26 in his surgery. It had a little built-in drawer with a piece of paper on which you could write up to a dozen numbers. Who, after all, in the 1930s, would know more than twelve people with telephones?

the crackling transmissions from old aeroplanes, pilot peering into the fog as the radio operator said everything twice in the old phonetic alphabet. 'Charlie Baker Able Dog. Charlie Baker Able Dog. Do you read me, Croydon? Do you read me, Croydon . . . '

We only say it once, now, and only Charlie remains; his companions now are the pedestrian Bravo, Alpha and Delta. But the smell of hot Bakelite – and it *did* get hot; electricity was more capricious then – will live on in the nose of anyone who ever . . . I say . . . can you *smell* something? Quick, Father, stop the car! The cigar-lighter is on fire!

Bang-Bang, the Ripley

Strange, the potency of lost transports. When they closed the Mumbles Railway in 1960 (the world's first passenger railway) I cried; although I was too young to know what it was, I knew that something magical had vanished. The strangeness of the Métro, with its characteristic smell of Paris and its huge mad barriers slamming shut and its seats reserved for the *mutilés de guerre*, still haunts me, even though it has long since become Scandinavianized, just like everything else, clean and affectless. The trolleybuses of my childhood, gliding like dancers in a nimbus of ozone (the trolley coming off the wires, and the conductor standing in the road with a special pole to hook it on again) are a memory as sharp as pine, as filled with promise as an old frost moon. I dream of an imaginary Underground, based on the incalculable strangeness of the first time, aged seven, that I saw the London Tube on a school trip.

And of steam trains we need say no more. Hardly surprising that the most compelling magical transformation in recent fiction involves, firstly, a hidden platform, and, secondly, a gleaming scarlet steam engine: the Hogwarts Express. Steam trains are like STOCKINGS, potent and arousing even to those who never encountered them before. Seeing one recently, casually pulling out of Paddington without ceremony, provoked such dislocation in my crowded, ordinary train that the passengers alighted in silence, shaking their heads.

For my father, though, it was the Ripley Bang-Bang which caught his memory: a boneshaking, rattletrap tram which ran from Nottingham to Ripley, clattering through the 1920s streets (factories, men in mufflers and heavy overcoats, Tin Lizzies and snow on the pavements) in a shower of sparks and a screech of steel tyres, bell ringing and bicyclists wobbling in the vanguard, terrified of getting their wheel stuck in the tramlines.

Aged six, he persuaded his mother to take him on the tram. They rattled up Derby Road, clattered along through Nuthall and Kimberley, and finally reached Eastwood, roughly the halfway point, when my grandmother said, 'Right. I've had enough.' 'And,' said my father, 'we got off, crossed the road, and caught the tram in the other direction and went *all the way home*. I remember it still!'

Who will remember it for him, after he's gone? And will there come a time when all transport is lost, after the oil runs out and we have done nothing to find another way even though we had all the warning in the world, and we remember jet planes and motor cars and all the casual travel and all the distances we shrank as being just another lost world?

Banks, Proper

Never mind Internet log-on and CALL CENTRES, credit cards and direct debits and customer service hosts; let us recall Mr J.G. Harding, Manager of the Midland Bank. He wore his MISTER like a hard-won honorific, and J.G. could have been anything; Jehosophat Galitzine, possibly, though John Graham is perhaps more likely.

Mr J.G. Harding seemed (though he may not have been) portly, a man of overwhelming substance, pinkly shaven, grim-suited, the epitome of *gravitas* as he steepled his fingers across his virgin blotter. To reach him – in response to a summons, in which he invariably expressed disappointment[68] – you crossed the marble-floored, mahogany-countered, high-ceilinged, ecclesiastically hushed Banking Hall; were admitted through a locked, bolted door; walked along further corridors being eyed with speculative contempt by financial *illuminati* glancing up from their ledgers, and finally into the Manager's Office.

This was *proper* banking, and all Banks were like it. Not the phony gravity of modern parodies, the so-called 'premium bankers' designed to make *arrivistes* feel important; these were not so much the cathedrals as the criminal courts of money, and we were not so much customers as defendants. Everyone eventually left school; but as long as you had a bank account, you would be a schoolboy for the rest of your life.

Now, like parents, the banks want to pose as our friends; until, that is, we need to talk to a human being, at which point we realize that they have entirely resigned control to their computers, and all of them, *all* of them, are in the end helpless before the software.

But then . . . then, they were run by inhuman beings. *Proper* Banks. Banks which, unlike the claims of their sillier modern counterparts, liked to say 'No'.

And how much harm, how much incalculable harm, did they, with their Properness, do? The economy we have now is built on the decisions of those Proper Banks three or four decades ago. You can answer the question yourself.

Bayko

See **MECCANO** if you don't know what Bayko is. This isn't about Bayko being gone (though Bayko *is* gone). This is about the *experience*

---

68 It was not until many years later that I realized that, though he may have written 'I am disappointed to note . . . ', he was not actually disappointed at all. He didn't give a damn. It was just what bank managers said. But why did it work? Why was one so keen not to disappoint a man who treated one with such frosty disdain?

of Bayko having vanished, not into oblivion but into worse-than-oblivion: the area of memory where you don't know whether you're remembering the thing itself, or the last time you remembered it[69].

I now remember myself playing happily for hours with Bayko: slotting the little rods into the little base, sliding the little bricks and doors and windows down the little rods, watching my little buildings taking their little shape.

But at the same time, I also *know* that I spent my Bayko time *hating* it. Hating the rods which got under your fingernails. Hating the bricks which fell off the rods when the rods splayed in their little holes. Hating the incomplete buildings, the lost *bits*, the sheer desolate *tedium* of Bayko. Of childhood. Of having to *play with toys*.

Which is true? What we remember? Or what we know? And how can we tell? Or has it just . . . gone?

Beadle, the

You'd know him if you saw him. Fat, smug, several overcoats, silly hat. He'd know you too: a minor official, it was his job to keep order at the parish sermon. We don't need him now; nobody goes to the parish sermon so nobody needs to keep order. Then, perhaps, he was a bouncer, an enforcer. Harbour Albigensian thoughts? Secretly unpersuaded by the resolution of the *filioque* controversy? Watch it: the beadle would *know*.

Now that the *Vicar* would prefer you to call him Ken ('Don't call me Vicar; call me Ken') and GOD is on his uppers, the beadle is redundant, and has been for over a century. Where you find him, his function is purely ceremonial. If he lives on in function as well as name, it is only in the Punch & Judy show; which itself is dying out, condemned for its misogyny and violence, perfectly reflecting the lost world inhabited by the beadle.

---

69 It's the last time you remembered it, actually. Always. That's how memory works.

But he survives in spirit. He is privatized now, a skip-tracer or council bailiff, an underpaid enforcer in thick-soled shoes, lacking title and dignity, bothered by his haemorrhoids as he burps over his lunchtime pie, parked round the corner, with his mobile, in his van. How the world moves on.

Beans, Grandpa

My maternal grandfather is four ways lost.

- He is dead.
- He was a man of Monmouthshire.
- He was a steel man.
- He was an industrial craftsman.

You don't get much more lost than that. Leaving aside being dead (which can hardly be said to be an injustice, happening to him in his eighties), Monmouthshire, once a proud border county between England and Wales, was subsumed into the peremptory-sounding 'Gwent'[70] by politicians, either pursuing votes or (which they are equally fond of) pointless reorganization.

Steel, too, has nearly gone from Britain, driven out by all those things (cheap foreign labour, expensive domestic labour, industrial unrest, union strangleholds, an admirable British idleness after the mad frenzy of the nineteenth century followed by two pan-European wars) which in the 1970s allowed Margaret Thatcher to come to power and finish the job.

No more steel.

No more – or precious few more – industrial craftsmen, either. Grandpa Beans[71] was a Master Roller in Number 1 (Hot) Mill.

---

70 Which itself sounds like a particularly final mode of vanishing. 'I don't know; he just upped and gwent.'

71 Not telling you.

They made sheet steel, spring steel, steel rod, anything you could do with white-hot steel and Gargantuan rollers, except they were not called rollers; they were called 'rolls' and the 'Rollers' were the men who operated them.

What other men did with a micrometer, Grandpa Beans[72] did with his thumb. When I was five, he took me to see the mill on a night shift. It was a place of titanic drama, a controlled Vesuvius, and my grandfather bestrode it like a safety-booted Vulcan. Men wore caps to doff them to him, not for reasons of class but from respect for his Mastery. Smoke blared, fumes shone, steel whirled like angry snakes along the floor, captured by men with giant long-handled tongs. Grandpa Beans[73] walked unperturbed, stopping every now and then to run his micrometric thumb along a roll, adjust a control, ask a question in his Monmouthshire rumble which penetrated the cacophony of the mill.

Machines do it now. Everything is computer-controlled, and the craftsmanship of the Master Roller has, like all other forms of industrial craftsmanship, become reduced to tapping on a computer keyboard. Everything is viewed through the screen, so that TEXTURE has become so homogenized that we sometimes cannot tell the difference between television and anything else. Our world is a world of glowing pixels. In the post-industrial world, a man must type or die.

There was a Number 2 (Cold) Mill, with its own Master Roller whom Grandpa Beans[74] very slightly patronized, because his steel was cold: it could slash you, crush you, tear you or engulf you in its coils, but it could not burn you. The danger was slightly less, and

---

72 No, it wasn't his real name.

73 It's *private* and I have my dignity.

74 Very well. It was when I was two. He was eating baked beans. So was I. I finished mine. I wanted his. '*Grandpa* beans,' I said, '*Grandpa* beans.' And Grandpa Beans he became. I wonder if as a young man, strutting in his virility, his pretty girlfriend (soon to be my mother's mother) on the back of his Brough Superior motorcycle, he ever thought that one day he would be Grandpa Beans? And that he would *like* being Grandpa Beans?

so, therefore, was the level of **MASCULINITY** required to master it.

And there was Old Man Bledlow (let us call him), the mill owner and top banana. Old Man Bledlow had a nice but dim son, who helped him; Stan and Frank, the salesmen who went out and sold steel; and Muriel in the Back, who typed and did the books. And there was Malcolm Chemistry and his assistant Dai **GLOVES** (because he always wore them), who did the metallurgy. Between them, these people – two Master Rollers, two salesmen, two metallurgists and three people in the office – ran the whole great enterprise and saw no need for more.

Eheu fugaces. Go to your local railway cafeteria or in-house (but out-sourced) catering facility and you will see the symptoms on the menu as clearly as the crumbling conk on a syphilitic's face. There will be a pickle-'n'-bean potato bake; a chicken tikka wrap; a tuna & cheese melt.

'Melt'. 'Wrap'. 'Bake'. These are *processes*. You melt something, you bake it, you wrap it. But we have turned these processes into *products*, and if there is any transformation which epitomizes our times, this is the one[75].

Walk the streets of your city. Look into the office windows. (Keep your mackintosh well buttoned, lest you are mistaken for a peeping Tom and carried off by a policeman.) What are they doing, in there?

They are . . . *managing*. Management used to be a process by which you kept the company doing whatever it was meant to be doing. Now it has become a product. Most companies – whatever they tell the world, through their PR people[76] – exist to create, maintain and expand management. Management is their

---

75 Only slightly undermined by the fact that there's an **ANCIENT GREEK** word for the, excuse me, process: 'Anthimeria': the rhetorical device of using one word class for another, an overwhelmingly popular principle in the United States of Anthimeria.

76 And mostly what you tell the world through your PR people is either (a) nothing or (b) untrue.

product. Management is what they do. And if they have to employ people – terrible, unpredictable, stroppy, irrational *people* – to do primitive things with steel and furnaces, with drills and hammers and swarf and grease in order to justify that management, then they will. Reluctantly; but they will.[77]

You might have thought that, as the (bogus) 'science' of management (not to mention all those bone-crushingly fatuous books on the subject) grew, the need for management would decrease as they finally started getting it right. You'd have been wrong. Who would have imagined it?

Not Old Man Bledlow. Not Muriel in the Back, nor Malcolm Chemistry nor Dai Gloves nor Stan and Frank; none of them. Nor Grandpa Beans. All gone: lives, crafts, industry, county. Only management remains.

Beer, Keg

The Elizabethan Age was founded, directed and maintained by people who were, to judge from records of their consumption, permanently drunk. Sobriety was potential death; they might have lacked any microbial theory of disease, but simple observation showed that plain water was filthy: brown, scummy and evil-smelling. So, of course, was the beer, but the beer was meant to be, and didn't kill you; so, since we had to drink or die, we drank beer.

Progress and public works have perfected the water in much of the world[78] but, for a while, it looked as though the same forces

---

77 At least there's a bright side: if you have to employ all these buggers, at least you can skim off their pension funds.

78 A useful – and grim – dividing line of rudimentary civilization is between those people who have ready access to clean water, and those who don't. 150 years after John Snow took the handle off the Broad Street pump and stopped a cholera outbreak, 1.1 billion people have no access to clean water; two billion have no sanitation; and two million die each year from water-borne diarrhoea. They're lost, too.

were destroying the beer.[79] What we now know, thanks to the agency of large-bellied men from the Campaign for Real Ale, to be horrible, gasified water free of flavour, complexity or, damn it, any goodness at all, was passed off as 'beer' having been squirted, stone dead, out of kegs under the pressure of carbon dioxide.

Yet such is the perversity of humanity – especially youthful humanity – that those who were brought up in the days of Double Diamond, Red Barrel and the inexplicable Harp Lager[80] had an absolutely wonderful time on the stuff.

The apogee of Keg Beer, though, was the Pub Experience At Home offered by giant beer-cans holding roughly a gallon of the stuff, epitomized by the Watney's Party Seven. The platonic teenage party (platonic in the sense that it was the ideal party of which all others were mere imperfect copies[81]) involved a rented room, a trestle table, a Dansette Bermuda or maybe even a proper discothèque (two Dansette Bermudas and a flashing light), some girls, and a supply of Watney's Party Seven.

It was impossible to get into, requiring a special tool which

---

79 A decline attributed, by Dr R.E.W. Fisher (calling himself Paddy Ryan), to 'the man, the very fat man/ That waters the workers' beer', an early exemplar of the anti-globalizers' bogeyman who doesn't 'care if it makes them ill,/If it makes them terribly queer/I've a car, a yacht, and an aeroplane,/And I waters the workers' beer.' ('The Man Who Waters the Workers' Beer'. Paddy Ryan. © Workers Music Association)

80 Asked what it was that people liked about it, the marketing manager of one of the Harp-style innocuous lagers – think Bud Lite without the depth, the bite or the bouquet – reportedly said, 'It's not that anyone particularly likes it. It's more that nobody can find anything to say *against* it.'

81 Platonic, too, of course, in the sense that nobody actually had sex, although in theory one might be lucky enough to encounter a compliant girl, herself a sort of Party Seven, eager for love, who would make herself available under a table – sometimes under the very table on which the Watney's Party Seven was resting – for prolonged kisses and wandering hands; a sort of *Paradise* seldom recaptured in later life. The trick was to wait until her accomplice had disengaged to go to the *W.C.* or to get more beer (the two activities being almost synonymous and often indistinguishable), then duck under the table and take his place. This is mere hearsay, but, whoever she was, I hope it all worked out well for her in the long run. Such women were a benison in the sensual aridity of youth and deserve eternal bliss.

sliced (appropriately) the Mount of Venus on the way in, showering the operative with sticky foam like waterborne Horlicks. It poured at random, got everywhere, and always ran out. But in its benign gleam, the music sounded better, the lights were softer, the girls more beautiful and potentially yielding, oneself manlier, one's friends friendlier, the night darker, the stars brighter, the moon fuller, the air warmer, the hour later, the future brighter, the present aching with that particular adolescent promise which does not need to be fulfilled to make it miraculous.

Filthy stuff, keg beer; but such stuff, filthy or not, as dreams are made on; brewed with a magic that the earnest Men of Ale, the micro-brewery mavens, the stout-sniffers and specific-gravity experts can never hope to reproduce for all their honesty and skill.

Sometimes, better can be worse.

Bierce, Ambrose

There are, on the Internet – where else? – people who will tell you how to disappear and never be found. They are telling lies; it is not possible – except, perhaps, by being sucked into a cult, where nobody will ever find you.

Some might say this is a violation of our fundamental right to reinvent ourselves, the right, even, to make mistakes and leave them behind. Now, everything you have ever done will follow you for ever, and it will only get worse; we have traded freedom for

---

82 Whatever the mendacious, crazy, whoreson drafters of the US Patriot Act may claim.

83 The bantam is a creature which has lost comfort in the face, first of evolution, then of husbandry. Chickens evolved to their natural size, and laid eggs the right size for their little chickeny selves. Then we came along and grew them littler. But there was no evolutionary pressure for their eggs to get smaller to keep pace with their new, compact bodies. Anyone who has ever seen a bantam laying an egg will immediately understand that evolution is a one-way process and has no interest at all in what happens to its products, whether bantams or us.

technology[82] and, like the bantam's egg, can never go backwards[83].

There was a time, though, when one *could* vanish. The American Ambrose Bierce led the sort of rackety life most of us (docile little cits, even if we believe ourselves to be free spirits) can only try to imagine. Born in 1842, he fought for the Union in the American Civil War, prospected for gold, worked as a journalist for William Randolph Hearst[84] and, in 1906, published *The Devil's Dictionary*[85]. His cynicism was not unprovoked: the goldfields' addictive cycle of hope and despair[86], the inevitably coarsening effects of journalism[87], the forensic nightmares of war, in no matter how deeply held a cause; this, and the suicide of his son, and the estrangement from his wife, and her subsequent filing for divorce, and her suicide a few days later in 1905: all these would drive any man to a depth of alienation in which he might take any action to get away and to seek a SECOND ACT in his life.

And so he did. Rather casually mentioning that he was off to the wars in Mexico, Bierce headed south in 1913 and was never seen or heard of again. All attempts to trace him failed. But then, in those days, there were no credit rating agencies. Now, though Interpol and MI5 may be baffled, Visa, AmEx and the mobile-phone company will effortlessly track you down and, even in the wildest place on Earth, you will have no choice but to ring the CALL CENTRE and speak to Tracey.

---

84 The model for *Citizen Kane*, as everyone knows. What some people don't know is that 'Rosebud' wasn't his sled. 'Rosebud' was his name for his young mistress's pudenda. The moral? Never trust a man who uses pet names for private parts.

85 Originally published in 1906 as *The Cynic's Word*. It didn't become *The Devil's Dictionary* until 1911; then, as now, there's more money in devilry than cynicism.

86 The mechanism of all addictions, of course, whether sex, drugs or (I cannot speak of rock 'n' roll, which, for me, goes straight to despair, bypassing hope altogether) gambling.

87 Which I *can* speak for.

Billy

Billy was my friend. Billy had a rubber head. Billy was a toy soldier with a little stuffed body and a little uniform with braid and buttons and a rubber head, and Billy's rubber head perished one day and almost came off: sticky and simultaneously friable, Billy's rubber head simply would not do; and when your head will not do, nor will you. That is how lives are lost: not by death (which merely completes them) but when your head will no longer do.

There is a suit hanging in a tailor's shop in London, held together with white thread, so that at the whim of the tailor the arms can be pulled off and the lapels torn away, like a comedy suit. It is a work of art in fine Lumb's Golden Bale worsted; a work-in-progress which will remain so for ever, because the tailor who was making it for me suddenly found one day that his head would not do. It had perished; become sticky and simultaneously friable, so that some ideas would not go away – he sat sewing imaginary thread, smoothing out imaginary cloth – and some would shatter and crumble. Non-existent chairs; walls that he could not see; outings he was going on with people who were not there. The one constant was his DOG. He missed his dog, though he called it by his previous dog's name.

They had rung up. 'Your suit is ready for a fitting,' they said. I didn't order the suit. I discussed it with him, knowing that I didn't have enough money at the time. But he went ahead anyway, without demanding fifty per cent deposit. That was the first sign of his head beginning not to do.

'I'll go in next week,' I thought. Next week, I thought 'I'll go in next week.' Then the telephone rang. He had been taken into hospital. They did not know what was wrong. It was grave. He would not get better. The padded cell was for his own safety.

The man who makes your clothes is like a latter-day MOTHER. He even knows your shape; suck your belly in as you may, he can stand there holding his tape-measure longer than you can stand there holding your breath. When his head won't do, it is far worse than, for example, when **DUNN & CO** closed down for ever. It is a little death, the end of a small civilization.

And the suit on the hanger in the shop, held together with white thread, never to be fitted and assembled and lined and handed over to be proudly worn at triumphs and sadly at funerals and grudgingly at weddings and bar-mitzvahs[88]: an admonition against procrastinating.

My mother threw Billy away when his head went, but I kicked up hell. 'Billy! Billy! Billy! Billy!' I explained in my eloquent four-year-old way; 'Billy! Billy! Billy! Billy!' and my father went off to the rubbish depot and *got Billy back*. A bad lesson for life. Things can't be got back.

Perhaps I should pick up the suit anyway. Frame it. Hang it on the wall, a moral tableau done in Pure New Wool. I could call it Billy. That's what I shall do.

Tomorrow.

Blower, the Double

Or *Doppelbläser* according to the description of Dr P.J.B. Previnaire[89]. This unpleasant-looking device (in its shagreen-lined, fitted wooden case, complete with tubes and bottle) was, of all lost *cures*, perhaps both one of the strangest and most ambitious, being a cure for Death. Or, at least, for apparent death, something which vexed our forebears no end.

One might think death was unequivocal. The heart stops, breathing stops, the victim ceases to take an interest in his sur-

---

88 All that horror, other people coming along and having *their* turn.

89 See his *Arten des Scheintodes* of 1790, all about how to revive the apparently dead by giving them tobacco enemas. Essential reading for the apparently dead. (This, of course, was when tobacco was still good for you, a period continuing well into the twentieth century; even I remember advertisements saying that doctors recommended Craven A cigarettes because they were good for your throat.)

roundings and presently a deterioration in personal hygiene makes his fate obvious.

Far from it. Death has always been a liminal matter, straddling the tideline between this world and the next. Our confidence in the present judgement of doctors is only skin-deep; all the brain-death tests may be carried out conclusively, yet it still takes a strong head or a profound philosophical calm to watch without qualms an organ-harvesting operation. How much worse in 1790, when the *Doppelbläser* came into being! There were no electronic monitors then; you were dead when you appeared dead, and the mythical air was still rife with tales of the vampire and the *vrykolokas*, of ghouls and the risen (un)dead, of hasty burial and frantic scratchings at the silk-lined coffin-lid.

One cure for, if not death itself, at least the semblance of death, was the *Doppelbläser*. In would come the doctor, out would come the bellows, tube and nozzle, and tobacco smoke would be blown up the seemingly deceased's (see **BABY'S BOTTOM**) bottom. If you weren't dead, you would be (so it went) resuscitated. Whether it was the holy herb Nicotiana or merely the thrusting nozzle that did the trick isn't recorded. But we can guess[90].

Books, the Terrible Flammability of

Demetrios of Phaleron was the first, appointed by Ptolemy I, 'The Saviour', in 330 BC. Then came Zenodotus, Callimachus, Apollonius of Rhodes, Eratosthenes, Aristophanes of

---

90 Smoke – not just tobacco smoke – has an ancient lineage in medicine; the ancient Greeks used it to address the issue of hysteria, which, then as now, was used to describe any woman who wasn't behaving as she should. The problem was attributed to a wandering womb, and fragrant smoke would be wafted around her nether parts to attract the womb back into place; or, if it was thought to be wandering downwards, heading for the outside world, noxious smoke would be wafted to drive it back up again. It is extraordinary to see that this example of the **WISDOM OF THE ANCIENTS**, has not yet resurfaced in the pages of the *Sunday Times*. But it will.

Byzantium . . . the Librarians of Alexandria. Over 700,000 scrolls there, and it is thanks to the Librarians that we have as much ANCIENT GREEK literature as we do. And yet the flames and destruction came. Fire struck in 97 BC; it recovered itself. Theodosius I ordered it destroyed in AD 391; again, it survived, weakened. Then at last the Arab conquerors burned it down in AD 640. Much remains, dispersed around the world. But what have we lost for ever? And how can we ever tell?

Boson, Higgs's

And the Earth was without form, and void; and darkness was upon the face of the deep. And the Spirit of God moved upon the face of the waters . . .

For the devout, and for the born-again fundamentalist, the world makes sense. Perhaps the rest of us have lost that world in the face of a complex science which seemingly requires just as much to be taken on faith as religion, but is harder to grasp.

But what can we do? Attempts to yoke together the models of science and the poetics of the poor bloody ANCIENTS are doomed to discord at best, embarrassing fatuity at worst. The most hapless victim is poor Werner Heisenberg, whose Uncertainty Principle has been prostituted for almost eighty years by novelists and dinner-table pundits as proof that, well, life, right? You never can tell and even science is uncertain, right[91]?

---

91 Not really, no. Heisenberg proposed that when an electron is examined, 'the more precisely the position is determined, the less precisely the momentum is known at that instant, and vice versa'. The proposition is *about* uncertainty – the uncertainty inherent in the very nature of the electron – but it is itself certain. This seems hard to grasp, but isn't. After all, if we don't know something, we can say *with certainty*: 'I don't know.' (There are, of course – as Donald Rumsfeld said, with absolute clarity – 'unknown unknowns: the [things] we don't know we don't know.' This beautifully precise expression of an unassailable truth about ASSUMPTIONS earned Rumsfeld (or more probably his speech-writers) a Foot In Mouth Award from the Plain English Campaign, which rather reassuringly suggests that the awards committee of the Plain English Campaign is collectively stupider than the American Secretary of Defense.)

But if there ever were a scientific proposition which seemed to demand – and deserve – metaphorical status, it is Higgs's Boson. Predicted in 1966 by Peter Higgs[92] of Edinburgh University, this elementary subatomic particle occupies a near-mythical position in the Standard Model of current physics, close to that occupied by the Spirit of God at the beginning of Genesis – so much so that it has been fancifully called 'the God Particle'.

The problem with the Standard Model is, simply, why anything weighs anything. Nothing, according to the model, should. We ought, by rights, to be occupying a sort of PYECRAFT Cosmos, though, like Pyecraft, we are guilty of a slight euphemism, because it's not *weight* as such, but *mass* – the quality which allows gravity to produce what we experience as weight – that's unaccounted for.

And that is what Higgs's Boson is said to do: it imparts (if it exists) mass to everything else, like a kindly Dickensian BACHELOR philanthropist, shepherding the young ones into happy-ever-after marriage, prodigal with its purse (115 giga-electronvolts will enable a particle to do a lot of good in the world).

But why should this most peculiar and beautiful thing exist? It is, if you will, an implicit consequence, not unlike John Donne's 'ordinary nothing':

> If I an ordinary nothing were,
> As shadow, a light, and body must be here
> But I am None . . .

Like the physicists hunting down Higgs's Boson, Donne is trying to deduce what *is* from his observations of what is *not*. Like the theologians attempting to erect the structure of GOD by means of logical reasoning from a small set of initial assumptions, the

---

92 Who later is said to have got fed up with all the fuss and refused to talk about the bloody boson any more; and who can blame him?

physicists proceed a step at a time: and so we end with alchemy, love, the Nicene Creed, Higgs's Boson.

And in each case we risk trying to find what is not; a nothing which is; something lost because it can never be found. In the spring of 2004, a question was posed in *Nature*: 'Has the Higgs boson been discovered?' We immerse ourselves in the mysteries, not of love and loss, nor of creation and redemption, but of hypothetical lattices, electro-weak interactions, spin-$\frac{1}{2}$ fermions and quantum loop effects, like the lost worlds of our *dreams* where reality flashes and tunnels, things pop into glittering existence and wink out again, where it is possible to be in two places at once and the interconnectedness of all things is a reality. And the answer? Has this missing, last, lost piece of the puzzle been found?

The answer, mercifully, is a definite 'maybe'.

Bottles, Water, Hot

The furry ones. The ones marked *Property of the Royal British Hotel Do Not Remove From The Room*. The Suba-Seal ones with the finned, push-in stopper and the snap-over cover. The Suba-Seal 'Airflow' ones with fins all over the bottle surface; you could play with them with your toes; the fins would undulate satisfyingly, in their warm rubbery way: impossible to burn yourself on a Suba-Seal 'Airflow'. Toasty toes in a cold bedroom; bedrooms *were* cold because that was *good* for you, and everyone knew that people who slept in warm bedrooms (with the windows closed) turned to politics and homosexuality in later life, and grew moustaches and had more than one wife and *showed off*, even though nobody was looking at them. (Who did they think they were? They weren't on stage at the Old Vic *now*.) And that was what happened to people whose bedrooms were too warm. And don't talk about electric blankets. Parkie-Nanny Parkin knew someone who went to sleep with the electric blanket on and was *burned to death*, just like she knew someone who said 'bum' near a church and was *struck down*! By GOD!

There were covers, too: pink candlewick covers and furry tigerskin or leopardskin covers, and blue velveteen covers, and you had to fill the hot water bottle *no more than half full* and then fold it over so that the water rose to the neck before you screwed the stopper in *or there would be a vacuum as the water cooled*; it was never explained why that was a bad thing but the word was enough: just as **NATURE** abhors a vacuum, so a vacuum abhors *us*, and as the water cooled in the night, Something would Happen to it, then Something would Happen to *you*.

Thus was comfort – not just the furry cover or the pre-erotistical fins, but the hot-watery plosh of the womb-y, wibbly *flollop* and the *smell*, the lovely, warm, rubbery, foot-y, beddy smell of cold nights, frost-webs on the morning windows, long nights with the stomach-ache and a fresh hot-water bottle when your groans awoke your parents, and the heavenly peace when the stomach-ache finally went away – mixed, as always, with fear. The archetypal fear of childhood: that Something would Happen.

Central heating did away with all that, just as duvets did away with Lan-Air-Cel blankets with magic holes that kept you warmer than a blanket *without* holes[93] and puffy eiderdowns with specially slithery satin chintz covers so that they'd slide off the bed in the night and leave you freezing . . .

Doesn't matter, though. We're warm now, and hot-water bottles are no more. Or, rather, they are now made of plastic; which amounts to the same thing.

Bottom, Baby's

As great a Lost Comfort as you could yearn for, this one will undoubtedly provoke instant outrage, both from those who live

---

93 Why, then, didn't they do a blanket which was *all* holes, just *one big hole* and a thin, woolly, satin-bound rim? They could have charged a fortune.

in a perpetual bristle of potential paedophilia[94] and those, more recherché in their understanding, who even now will be banging the table and shouting about benzpyrenes, oat cells, metastases and carbon monoxide. Let us leave them to it and meditate briefly[95] on the lost comforts of tobacco smoking . . . because it is that of which we speak.

Baby's Bottom[96] takes its place in that vanished (or vanishing) litany of ease, along with John Cotton's Number 1 & 2 Mixture Medium; Balkan Sobranie Flake; Ogden's Rich Dark Honeydew; Cope's Escudo; Cut Golden Bar; Blue Book cigarettes; PWE Burma cheroots; Sullivan Powell Sub-Rosa Turkish; Sullivan Powell Khedive cigarettes . . . It would be a small-minded, a cheese-paring, an anxious, teeth-gritting, Puritanical man who had never dreamed (as a pimply adolescent jiggling from foot to foot on the threshold of perplexed MASCULINITY[97]) of being let loose in a tobacconist. Once, Ezra Pound could write:

> O God, O Venus, O Mercury, patron of thieves,
> Give me in due time, I beseech you, a little tobacco-shop,
> With the little bright boxes
> piled up neatly upon the shelves
> And the loose fragrant Cavendish
> and the shag,
> And the bright Virginia

94 No cross-reference to that, of course, the thing itself being as worthy of demonization as is the grim tendency to see it around every corner and in every family snapshot . . . though Lost *Innocence* might be appropriate.

95 While, on my part, lighting my pipe: an old meerschaum by Sommer of Paris, of a sort no longer available since the Turks declared monopoly on meerschaum, and the whale oil needed to cure it is politically incorrect beyond description. But mine is seasoned with whale oil and I am glad, do you hear me? *Glad.* So? Come and get me. I am calm.

96 'As Smooth As . . .' is the gag here, although anyone in possession of the Y-chromosome, the genetic harbinger of MASCULINITY, who claimed to have any idea of the smoothness of a baby's bottom would find themselves in pokey before you could say 'Eheu fugaces'.

97 Whatever *that* may be, and *q.v.*

loose under the bright glass cases,
And a pair of scales not too greasy
And the whores dropping in for a word or two in passing,
For a flip word, and to tidy their hair a bit.
O God, O Venus, O Mercury, patron of thieves,
Lend me a little tobacco-shop,
or install me in any profession
Save this damn'd profession of writing,
where one needs one's brains all the time.

Now, all gone, or almost gone. A Briton introduced the tobacco habit from the New World to Europe. In 1612, John Rolfe first planted West Indian tobacco varieties in Virginia, and so saved the Colony (though over twenty years too late to save the Lost Tribe of Roanoke). America grew rich on it and spread the habit through the world. Then, in a strange symmetry, a Briton, Sir Richard Doll, proved the link between smoking and lung cancer, and Americans turned against smoking as enthusiastically as they had once taken it up. Where America leads, the world follows, and we shall undoubtedly live to see tobacco outlawed: so bringing to an end the era begun almost four centuries ago.

Bottom, Mozart's Little

How we yearn to commune with the great lost figures of the past! Just to be in the presence of Mozart; the *young* Mozart. But now, with a little technological ingenuity, we could. This invention is the fruit of the fertile brain of Stephen Fry, who bought himself a piano which recorded onto, and played back from, floppy disks: like playing a pianola, but without requiring the same dexterity or musicianship.

We admired it for a while, then he put the floppy disk in the slot and it began. Mozart juvenilia. Miraculously, the keys went down as the notes were played. 'The keys!' we cried excitedly.

'The keys! They are going up and down! It is as if little Mozart himself, though long dead and gone, were seated at the piano, performing juvenilia.' Fry grew reflective, and gazed speculatively at the piano stool. 'It would not take much in the way of electromagnets,' he said after a bit, 'and some simple programming, to make the upholstery go up and down in time with the music; as if Mozart's little bottom were seated there, invisibly, like a revenant.'

Boyards Maïs

If there was one central component to the proper SMELL OF PARIS it was the Boyards Maïs: a thick-as-your-finger industrial-strength cigarette wrapped in yellow paper, harsh as an Iron Curtain arrest warrant, stuffed with throat-scouring black Caporal tobacco; it was said that a true expert (a true Boyards expert being, generically, a half-pissed bloke in *bleu de travail* up a telegraph pole in the rainswept Pas de Calais having Ideas about someone else's wife) could smoke the thing up one side and back down the other . . .

Not any more, he can't, because, like Bruce Chatwin's precious **MOLESKINE** notebooks, *la vraie cigarette Boyards n'existe plus*. Rumours abound: the French tobacco monopoly found them unprofitable; the owner of the factory burnt it down (thousands of Frenchmen gathering round the flames to inhale one last time); the machinery broke and could not be replaced; health laws banned them (it being discovered that even asking for a packet in the *tabac*[98] was enough to bring on lung cancer). Forty a day is one thing. But forty Boyards Maïs is heroic.

---

98 France being what it was, the *tabac* licences were allegedly awarded as a sort of under-the-counter reparation to war widows.

Boys, Five, Fry's

A novelty bar from the Quaker firm of confectioners, Five Boys was first introduced in 1885 and might be said to be the world's only performative text made out of chocolate. In a (perhaps unwitting) gourmand's parody of the road to salvation, each piece had a boy's face moulded onto it, running through the canonical expressions of 'Desperation[99] . . . Pacification . . . Expectation . . . Acclamation . . . Realization . . . it's *Fry!*' though probably most customers would have realized it was *Fry!* at the point at which they asked for it in the sweetshop.

Confectionery is the plaything of fashion, just like everything else, and Fry's Five Boys has joined the list of vanished sweets along with Spangles, acid drops, Cherry Bitter, pineapple chunks, strawberry bonbons, Beech Nut chewing gum, kali and whatever the Fry's chocolate bar with multicoloured (and sort of – but only sort of – multi-*flavoured*) fondant filling, all, magically, in the same bar[100] was called. But perhaps its disappearance was more than simply the caprice of the market. Perhaps it wouldn't play any more in these sophisticated times. Never mind the faint undertones of pederasty; to be a truly contemporary sweet, it would have to be Fry's *Six* Boys.

And the sixth boy?

Disillusion.

Boys, Scouting for

You'd not get away with it now. There'd be cries of paedophilia, parents up in arms, boys refusing to go. Healthy, clean-living,

---

99 The facial expression being achieved by holding a rag soaked in ammonia under the hapless boy model's nose.

100 Not to mention the drinking straws with a strip of felt running up the lumen, impregnated with a flavour – strawberry, banana, chocolate – which turned any glass of milk into a *real milk shake*, amazingly *just by sucking* . . .

spoor-tracking patriotism? Dying for your country? Camping out in the damp? All that woggle business, and garter business, and ropes and knots and forked sticks? No. Most children grow up without ever *seeing* a forked stick, let alone boiling a **BILLY** that hangs from one.

Not so in 1908. Then, Robert Baden-Powell, author of *Scouting for Boys*, was a hero, a rugged man introducing healthy ways to clean-limbed boys and all the better for it, even if he did (according to his editor) use perfumed soap in the bush, even if he did think the Zulus (jolly good chaps, if black-ish) called him 'Grey Wolf who never sleeps' when there weren't any wolves round those parts and what they were actually calling him was 'The Hyena', which wasn't necessarily an insult, or at least not *only* an insult . . . and even if he did claim to tell a man's creditworthiness from how he wore his **HAT**[101], and insist on honour and thrift and declare that *A Scout is a Friend to All, and a Brother to Every Other Scout, no matter to what social Class the Other belongs* and that *A Scout is a Friend to Animals, even if it is only a fly – for it is one of God's creatures*, and, worst of all, insisted that *A Scout Smiles and Whistles* which offers a fairly alarming and cacophonous picture, all these young shavers in woggles and shorts and big **HATS**, grimacing and tooting . . .

His observations and prejudices seem enchanting, if naive, through the vanishing-glass of time. 'I was once accused of mistrusting men with waxed moustaches,' he observes. 'Well, so, to a certain extent, I do. It often means vanity and sometimes drink.' He is keen on *MAKING THE SKIN PERSPIRE to get rid of dirt in the blood* and insists that one must *MAKE THE BOWELS ACTIVE to remove the remains of food and dirt from the body.* Important exercises include *Body Bending*[102] and *Kneading the Abdomen* and, of course, a *regular daily 'rear'*[103]. Travelling through Natal, he comes

---

101 If worn on the back of the head, the man was 'bad at paying his debts'. Well, of *course* he was.
102 Shh. Stop it.
103 I said *Shh*.

72

upon a roughly furnished hut. But there are 'several tooth-brushes on what served as a wash-hand stand, so I guessed that the owner must be a decent fellow, and I made myself at home . . .'

His reading list, too, is a delight, encouraging boys to immerse themselves profitably (when they're not immersed in a healthy cold bath) in:

> *Thrift* by Samuel Smiles
> *One Hundred and One Ways of Making Money*
> *Do It Now* by Peter Keary
> *Rabbits for Profit* by J. Brod
> *Esperanto for the Millions* 1d. (Stead, 29 Whitefriars Street, London, E.C.)
> *Work Handbooks* series. 1s. each. On Harness-making, Tinplate, Pumps, Bookbinding, Signwriting, Beehives, etc.
> *Rafia Work* by M. Swannell
> See also 'Papers on Trades for Boys' in *Boys Brigade Gazette*

But it is not all fun. Baden-Powell's ad hoc morality informs every page, whether in parable:

> Two frogs were out for a walk one day and they came to a big jug of cream. In looking into it they both fell in.
>
> One said: 'This is a new kind of water to me. How can a fellow swim in stuff like this? It is no use trying.' So he sank to the bottom and was drowned through having no pluck.[104]

or exhortation:

---

104 The other one kept trying and trying until his kicking turned the cream to butter and he climbed out. Just in case you were worrying.

Don't be disgraced like the young Romans, who lost the Empire of their forefathers by being wishy-washy slackers without any go or patriotism in them.

or by example:

The boys of the International Anti-Cigarette League bind themselves not to smoke, in order to make themselves better men for their country – that is the best reason for doing it.

None of this would seem particularly sane or comprehensible to the boy of the early twenty-first century, brought up to be entertained, exhorted to celebrity, told from all sides that the unacclaimed life is not worth living. Least comprehensible of all, though it was daring at the time (PUDEUR being what it was) to even mention it, was his attitude to the sin of Onan:

You all know what it is to have at times a pleasant feeling in your private parts, and there comes an inclination to work it up with your hand or otherwise . . . The practice is called 'self-abuse'. And the result of self-abuse is always – mind you, always – that the boy after a time becomes weak and nervous and shy, he gets headaches and probably palpitations of the heart, and if he still carries it on too far he very often goes out of his mind and becomes an idiot.

A very large number of the lunatics in our asylums have made themselves ill by indulging in this vice although at one time they were sensible cheery boys like any one of you.

The use of your parts is not to play with them when you are a boy but to enable you to get children when you are grown up and married. But if you misuse them while young you will not be able to use them when you are a man: they will not work then.

. . .

74

Just wash your parts in cold water and cool them down. Wet dreams come from it especially after eating rich food, or too much meat, or from sleeping with too warm a blanket over you or in too soft a bed or from sleeping on your back. Therefore avoid all these.

Alas, Baden-Powell's argument falls apart. Continence now, he seems to suggest, will lead to self-control later; the alternative being too many children begotten by uncontrolled fathers. But if you don't control yourself in your youth, you may be unable to control yourself in (married, of course) adulthood, so it won't matter because 'your parts [. . .] will not work then'. So no excess children, either way. Yet his heart was, perhaps, after all, in the right place. No knee-jerk feckless working classes for him; at the end of this homily, he walks around 'with some of the unemployed to see if they were really anxious to get work'. They were.

Then one of them made the remark which seemed to me very true. 'There's not enough work to go round. The truth is there's too many of us in this world.'

Now, it all seems strangely risible, simultaneously naive and dodgy. Still, it is always dangerous to laugh at one's forebears and their ASSUMPTIONS, and not just because of the prevailing historical sin of retrojection[105], but because, as the culture declines (how one yearns for the GOLDEN AGE), *Scouting for Boys* may, like the HATS themselves, be due for a renaissance.

---

105 Judging the past by the standards of the present: that is to say, what they do on telly.

Breakfast, Proper Cooked

What was once an act of love is now a demonstration of indifference. Succour has become lethal, nurture clogs arteries, yesterday's caring is today's cholesterol. The great cooked breakfast – bacon and sausage, black pudding and kidneys and suicidal eggs (with a splod of baked beans to elevate the whole on a cloud of methane[106]) – is a minority, and shrivelling, treat. Gone with it, too, is the morning essay in COMMENSALITY. No more toast rack, no more coffee pot; no more father, grumbling behind *The Times*. Once, breakfast was a time when families cohered, gathering their strength for the looming day; now, only new lovers linger over the breakfast table, negotiating their futures, and, even then, the breakfast table is probably in public, owned by a conglomerate.

Once, breakfast was a wifely morning gift, an advance against the hocks and rabbit skins brought back each evening by even the most pallid and weedy of CLERKS. Now, in motorway service stations and through the steamed-up windows of drizzling caffs, you can see men on their own, lorry men or men in company cars, eating their illicit All-Day Full English with the guilty pleasure that other nations reserve for whoring[107]. Breakfast is now fragmentary, swallowed on the run if at all; and yet it still retains its potency as a symbol of familial love, its absence a marker of isolation, as in John Betjeman's 'Business Girls':

---

106 Heinz will not admit that beans make you fart; 'There is no truth in it,' one of their scientists assured me, 'and we have an entire team working on it as we speak.'

107 You may judge a country on what its name stands for. French, Greek and Spanish, for example, are sexual tropes, while English is a pork orgy. (And nobody has ever gone into a brothel and said 'Do you do Welsh?') (And if they did, it would probably consist of a slap, a ham tea and an anecdote about the sudden death of someone they'd never heard of.)

From the geyser ventilators
Autumn winds are blowing down
On a thousand business women
Having baths in Camden Town.

[. . .]

Rest you there, poor unbelov'd ones,
Lap your loneliness in heat.
All too soon the tiny breakfast,
Trolley-bus and windy street!

Somerset Maugham once observed that *To eat well in England, you should have a breakfast three times a day*. But he's dead.

Brut, the Great Smell of

Karl Mann's peculiar creation for Fabergé is still around, though a watery shadow of its former self. A good thing, really, for Brut was the archetypal men's cologne of the 1960s and early 1970s. If Old Spice made you think of your father, and Mennen Skin Bracer made you think of suicide, Brut was *it*. Not so much butch, despite the name[108], as aggressively suave, with an unctuous oiliness as smooth as a seducer's leer; women, it was said, were ineluctably captivated by its smell. It may simply have been that what they were *really* captivated by was a man who didn't smell of **B.O.** or even the idea that a man who – gosh! – wore *scent* might possibly show some interest in the less usually regarded internal organs of a female; like, for example, her brain.

---

108 How could it be butch? Butch would smell of testicles and baked beans, policeman, gun oil, acne and White Van; Brut smelt of anise and basil, geranium, jasmine, ylang-ylang, oakmoss, vanilla, tonka bean, and they kept that VERY quiet from the punters . . .

Brut is still with us. What has been lost is women's response. Now they don't turn their heads when they catch a whiff, unless it is to confirm their olfactory guess that here comes a querulously valetudinarian dotard in a polo-neck jersey[109]. And it always is.

A pity, in some ways. Brut, despite its preternatural smoothness, actually smelt rather good. But then smell has never had much to do with it, really.

Brylcreem

Between the Second World War and the 1960s, a 'little dab of Brylcreem' was the final, decisive touch which guaranteed the attention of women, all anxious to run their hands through the wearer's hair (and come away with a thin slick of emulsified oil, like inedible mayonnaise, on their fingers). Now, though Brylcreem itself is still hopefully marketed, its traditional mode of use has all but vanished. Once, Brylcreem was used to slick back the hair in a greasy, weighty quiff; then came the 1960s, longer hair, and the daily shower replacing the weekly tub. Any and all hair-grooming products fell out of favour, and Brylcreem (or any of its fellows, like Vitalis, Silvikrin, Palmolive Hair Cream, Trumper's Eucris[110], Macassar Oil, Yardley's Lavender Brilliantine, Vaseline Hair Creme, and more, far more, than you

---

109 So important to cover the neck after a certain age, of course.
110 Not to mention Trumper's Coronis, Special Lotion ('An excellent dressing prepared for ridding the scalp of dandruff without leaving the hair parched'), Lazy Scalp (with hormones, 'prepared in conjunction with trichologists and dermatologists, to provide a light effective scalp stimulant'), Floreka (green and amber), San Remo and Fernil – all designed, in one way or another, to deal with the hair without being *common*, so that the trained eye, confronted with two identical heads of identically slicked-back, glossy hair, could tell at a glance which had been slicked by Trumper and which by any other, less acceptable, product; and, by extrapolation, which of the two head-owners was beyond the pale and which was, until proven otherwise, a sound sort of chap.

could shake a clogged and greasy comb at) became a marker of the dysfunctional. 'Still using that greasy kid stuff?' demanded the Vitalis ads, pugnaciously, but the truth was that *any* stuff was out of favour.

Then, all of a sudden, they came back. Fish Wax, Black-and-White (with Genuine Pluko[111]), Dax Wave 'n' Groom, Fudge Moulding Putty, Kiehl's Shine 'n' Lite[112] . . . a list even longer than our fathers ever dreamed of.

But now they are used, not to create the impression of perfect, irreproachable grooming, but of *no grooming at all*. Young men (and men old enough to know better) will stand endlessly in front of the mirror[113] to achieve the effect of having just got out of bed after a terrible, sweat-soaked night of hallucinatory sex and bad drug nightmares. And why? It is what they do. It is all they *can* do. Despite the best efforts of the cosmetics pushers, make-up for men just won't catch on. The all-pervading male gaze (which has made young men now as miserably self-conscious, as prone to anorexia as any teenaged girl *and* as compulsively gym-pumped as any ancient Athenian *eromenos*[114]) draws the line at slap.

And yet they've pulled off something rather clever. All young men want to be like their fathers, while simultaneously wanting to be nothing like their fathers at all. The answer, traditionally, has been to cleave to your grandfather, who (a) doesn't boss you about and (b) bossed your father about, which, on the venerable principle of 'my enemy's enemy is my friend', makes him entirely worthy of loyalty and devotion. But being like your grandfather

---

111 Though you'll look in vain for it on the ingredients list.
112 Not to mention a solid grooming aid from Kiehl's, called 'Kiehl's Solid Grooming Aid' and wouldn't you have liked to be a fly on the wall at *that* product-branding meeting?
113 Stand, not sit. Sitting in front of the mirror would be womanish.
114 The 'beautiful boy' of classical Greece whose main qualification for desirability was that he did not fancy the older man who, given half the chance, would be on him like a duck on a June bug.

would make you *old*. It's a tricky nut to crack, but the answer is found in reinterpreting the calcified old jar of Brylcreem on grandad's bathroom shelf. You use the products, but you entirely subvert their function[115]. Kinship and difference established in one smooth dip into the pot of scented grease. It's masterly.

Buggers, Silly

They were Bulgarians originally. Bulgars. Suspected of all sorts. *You* know. The buggeronies, down at Mother Clapp's Molly-House. Quite so.

Then they became just . . . *silly*. People's fathers said it. 'Don't play silly buggers, old chap.' Could have been anything:

1. Proposing to marry beneath one's station.
2. Proposing to give up reading for the Bar and join circus.
3. Proposing to marry above one's station.
4. Driving recklessly fast.
5. Driving deliberately slowly.
6. Smoking nasty aromatic foreign muck instead of decent British **BABY'S BOTTOM**.
7. Not getting hair cut.
8. Getting hair cut too short.
9. Appearing ready to depart for church/synagogue/Masonic lodge/court appearance/ trip to pub wearing floral tie.
10. Suggesting socialism had a core of sense to it.
11. Proposing to marry exotic dancer.
12. Proposing to marry some dashed darkie[116].
13. Coming out.

---

115 So successful has the process been that kids are now starting to call these products by their generic and antique name: *pomade*.
116 'It's the children I feel sorry for, neither one thing nor t'other.'

Silly Buggers have joined the list of things which are simply no longer said: Great Scott, dashed awkward, dashed *anything*, actually, bad show, *good* show, jolly good, what?, rather fun, damned pipsqueak, rotter, cad, bounder, jumped-up, no can do, *won't* do, tickled pink, bad sport, good egg . . .

But, of course, we don't need them any more. Like a high-speed computer with a Reduced Instruction Set Chip, we can do all that with a few basic commands. 'Like', 'fuck', 'fucking', 'fucker' and 'you know'. Silly buggers? Fuck, it's like so fucking, you know, like, fuck.

Pipsqueaks. *Bad show.*

Bus, Lost on the, Actually Not

The two immutables in life (though not in physics) are cause and effect. But sometimes the tiny, grand peculiarities of quantum mechanics leak into our everyday existence. Cause and effect become reversed (*ante hoc ergo propter hoc?*) or tucked into each other like a rolled-up causal STOCKING. Ravel, for example, really did lose his manuscript in THE SHOP but found it again; Eric Satie, on the other hand, didn't leave the manuscript of *Jack-in-the-Box* on a bus, but lost it. Or, rather, assumed it was lost, told everybody it was lost, and so it *was* lost. But it was nothing of the sort. When he died, in 1925, they went through his flat in Arceuil and, behind the piano, found a notebook. It was the manuscript.

Cancer, Not Worrying About

Shortness of breath, sweating, irregular heartbeat, nausea, an overwhelming sense of dread and imminent dissolution. Could it be *carcinophobia*, the irrational, persistent and abnormal fear of cancer? It could. And not only do you feel terrible about the chance – no, the *certainty* – of getting cancer, but, thanks to

modern marketing, you can now feel terrible about carcinophobia, too, as snake-oil salesmen tell you how it's ruining your family
life, upsetting your 'loved ones', and getting in the way of business
success. They want your money. You want not to get cancer. But
that used to be free. There were so many other causes of death
now fallen into desuetude that cancer hardly got a look-in.

Now that things have got so much better that it's quite hard to
die of anything else, cancer is all the fashion. Everything gives it
to you, except, inexplicably, reading the *Daily Mail.* And the odd
thing is, just as you've got used to the fact that something gives
you cancer (smoking, HRT, meat, gin and tonic, sunshine), it
suddenly stops giving you cancer.

So can you then stop worrying? No. Because there's something else waiting in the wings. All you can do is yearn for the
GOLDEN AGE when nothing gave you cancer. And between carcinophobia and yearning, the time will just fly by, and before you
can say 'Oh **GOD**, I'm going to die', you'll be comfortably dead.

Cane, The

Yaroo! Oww! Leggo, you rotters! The Fat Owl of the Remove[117] takes
another whopping from the *corpus praefectorum* as his howls (more of
outrage than of pain) echo along the Gothic corridors of
Greyfriars School. Nor is this some class gimmick; the creaking,
skull-like Teacher of Bash Street was every bit as prone as black-
winged Quelch of Greyfriars to wield the cane, and reality was no
different. Slob Peters (hist.) had his Walking Stick of Damocles,
Chalky White (gym) had his plimsoll[118], Noddy Aspin (Lat.) was a

---

117 Or 'morphologically different' as he'd now be called, in case his self-esteem
    were damaged. Back then, in the lost world of SCHOOL STORIES, self-esteem
    was something that was flogged out of you. It was straightforward esteem
    you were after; and that came from others.
118 Inexplicably called 'Little Willy'.

dead shot with a blackboard eraser, Sandy Powell (Fr.) ditto with the chalk – both could send a missile whistling through the hair-parting without touching the head beneath – and Fez Parker (Phys.) had the entire resources of the physics department at his disposal, a sort of extremely Non-mutual Assured Destruction which, like its *Weltpolitik* counterpart, was never actually used. And The Duke – the natty yet dignified headmaster, K.R. Imeson – managed to put his shoulder out caning the entire Classics Sixth whom he had caught in a pub one lunchtime.

Did we live in fear? No; we were respectful but wryly entertained. Did we regard our schoolmasters as sadists? No. It was a mark of their idiosyncracy. Was the punishment meted out fairly? Not invariably; I copped six stingers from one of The Duke's whippier accoutrements for 'pulling faces during prayers'[119]. The Cane was just another way in which grown-ups were boring, and the (minimal) physical invasion it generated was more than compensated for by the clear boundary it drew: not of behaviour, but of clan. On one side were Them. On the other side were Us. The sanction of what is now thought inappropriate assault served as much to exclude Them as to discipline Us. We inhabited our own country, and the presence of an occupying force with superior firepower simply served to enhance our own sense of a secret inviolability, just as men are said never to be happier than when faced with a common enemy.

Now the schoolteachers (not 'masters', not *ever*, that would institutionalize a power-imbalance) want to be their students' friends. Nobody asked the students whether they would prefer the occasional missile whistling past their ear in a vapour trail of

---

119 To be fair, in later years he admitted that the memory had stayed with him ever since. 'You'd have been all right,' he said, 'if you hadn't tried to claim you were not pulling faces but were moved by religious ecstasy. "Right," I thought, "I'm going to cane the bugger." And I did. Marvellous. Spring in the step. Quite set me up for the Governors' meeting. Absolute despotism: one of the great perks of the job.'

chalk dust, or the enforced chumminess of adults who attempt to claim both the licence of friendship and the superiority of command. But perhaps they never asked because they know the answer already.

Canford Cliffs

There were SnoFrute ice lollies and SnoCreme ice lollies and banana SnoCreme were best, a Platonic banana of which the real thing was a mere imperfect copy. There was a beach hut, in a sort of tribal village of beach huts, each with a spirit burner for the kettle and the smell of meths and creosote and hot plastic curtains and Ambre Solaire oil, a smell so redolent of the long-lost English seaside holiday that any woman who dabs a little behind her ears will be able to captivate any man over the age of forty whom she chooses but the price she has to pay is that he will become a child again, dancing on the shoreline. There were tomato sandwiches gone soggy in their wrapping, and Kia-Ora orange squash, and hardboiled eggs with a little twist of salt, and buckets and spades in multicoloured rubber, and panelled beach-balls like anaesthetists' ventilation bags, and there was a girl you fell in love with at the hotel who was older than you – seven? eight, even? – and the dining room smelt of seaside-private-hotel dining room, a mixture of frying and stew and sideboard and landlady, and the owner went mad every now and then and would chase his wife along the clifftops by the light of the full MOON, brandishing a hatchet. And the bedroom had chintz and a dark-stained Utility wardrobe, left over, and the pipes went *kerchuggachuggachuggaDONK* in the night, and you had to go out after breakfast and *not come back*, and there was a tap to get the sand off your feet down at the bottom of the chine but it didn't work because there was still sand when you put your Clarks sandals back on, with the crepe sole and the punched-out daisy pattern in the toe, and your mother said *Don't play there* and then she said to your father *What is it about the drain outfall that draws him like a magnet? You tell him, he takes no notice, take him out in the little inflatable boat or something*, and there was a Lilo made of rubberized fabric which was soft and warm and you didn't slip off and you could pretend to be the ferry, which was also *real*, a ferry with an *engine* and a man *working the engine* and you could *watch* him, and there was seaweed and the cliffs crumbling and the ferry ran on chains and you sang all the way up the chine and once there was a *snake!* and the earth around the pine trees was friable and fibrous and the geography was always slightly mystifying but *Look! Look! The SEA!* and sometimes you went to the other hotel where the owner didn't chase his wife but there was a *pirate ship* in the grounds and a red-headed girl in a bandanna who lisped and told everyone what to do and you fell in love with her, too, even though she was ten and really grown-up, and you wore ruched yellow swimming trunks even though what you really wanted was a pair of JANTZENS, and one evening you went to Christchurch and saw the boats and another evening there was a *tree-walk!* and you walked *high up*, in the *trees!* and there were fairy lights and music and you kept thinking that maybe the red-headed girl in the bandanna would be there but she wasn't, and then it was time to go and it's all gone now anyway, or is it that we've all gone now, but there were SnoFrute ice lollies and SnoCreme ice lollies and banana SnoCreme were best.

Cash

A rum thing, cash; its cover blown, its probity knackered, it now only excites suspicion or pity, depending on the sum. Deposit the dodgiest cheque ('Luca Weasolio Enterprises (Cocaine) Ltd') and no questions asked; unpeel a fat roll of banknotes and there will be whispered conversations, messages passed to dyspeptic men in Compliance Divisions, black marks raised. Conversely, go into a supermarket and pay for your small order with cash, and not black marks but eyebrows will be raised[120]. Cash means you have no cards; no cards mean you have no *credit*; no credit means that you are on the margins, on the busk, a criminal, a bogus asylum-seeker[121], an underclass hoodlum, on Drugs, a ticking bomb about to burst into tattoos and erupt at the checkout counter in a flurry of laaaaaaaager, swear words and screaming children.

There was once an advert which claimed that the American Express card said 'more about you than cash ever can', and so it does. Cash says nothing except 'Here is the money', and we don't like that. Curiously obsessed with provenance, we find anonymity distressing. There is no added value to cash. All you can do with it is pay. Soon it will be confined to liminal transactions with hookers, crooks, Latvian navvies on the lump. The wedge of fifties is now a mark of failure, not just anonymous but, however big, finite. With a black AmEx, nobody can tell how much you have left. Cash cannot bullshit. Cash tells no lies. And so we no longer trust it, and so it must go.

Casinos

Once it was James Bond, immaculate in midnight-blue Savile Row. A mysterious countess, deep-plunging cleavage, diamonds glittering in a SILLAGE of Shalimar. A bullet-headed villain; a minor aristocrat, dissolving himself; the click of chips, the rattle of the roulette ball, the whisk of cards from the shoe, and a blue haze of Monte Cristo No. 1. Now the casino has lost its glamour, more likely to be the refuge of deracinated Chinese waiters on their afternoon off, uncertain women in tottering heels, bewildered Saudis on a sad razzle. The casino owners are mobsters no

---

120 Yet imagine what would happen if you changed your name and identity as often as your bank changes its.

121 They are *all* bogus. Don't you read the *Daily Mail*?

more, but large companies with head offices on rainswept ring roads, corporate branding, gilt-plastic lighting and Draconian rules (no drinking, no credit, no mysterious countesses . . .).

Hardly worth bothering any more, if it ever was. Just find a cheap pub at closing time, be refused a drink, then wad up your CASH and stick it in an ashtray. At least it might be put to some good use.

Centres, Call

As nasty an example of Lost Meaning as you could shake a stick at. (To obtain your stick, please call 0890 918 228 2727 18801 between 0900 and 1600 New Delhi time where all our agents are currently unavailable, you are held in a queue and your call will be answered as soon as possible, pling plunk whinn[122] your call is important to us pling plunk all our agents are currently unavailable pling plunk this office is now closed please call later beeeeeeeeeeeeeeeeeeee.)

Lost meaning? Yes. Not in the word 'call' because you can, by God, call as often as you like, and even if you get through to someone it will be to no avail; they will not do what they said they would, they will not understand your question, they will have no authority to do anything about it, you will not be able to speak to anyone who does have authority, and if you call back (and call, and call, and call) you will only have to go through the whole thing again.

'Call' is valid. But 'centre'? These things, these instruments of torture, these cheese-paring, moronic bastard children of the sclerotic brains of purse-lipped accountants and the madness of perpetually pre-adolescent computer programmers, are not central to anything except their companies' urge to save money.

---

122 The sound of *Nessun dorma* being played on a harmonium by a revenant.

They are in truth purely peripheral, to the extent of often being thousands of miles away from where the actual business is located. They are conceptually peripheral, too: all the people who work there can do is read things off the computer screen. And all the computer screen does is reiterate the 'information' which made you call the bastards in the first place. 'I'm sorry, sir, but according to our records . . .'

And, of course, 'I am afraid we have no record of your earlier call/calls/outburst of weeping/letter/solicitor's letter/suicide attempt' . . . and therefore, it doesn't exist.

We have moved on from the days of personal service. Now the centre is at the periphery, and powerless. Big business is leading by example. Because where do you think they want you, the customer?

Yes. At the periphery.

And powerless.

Just like the poor people who work in call centres. Be nice to them; it is not their fault, and (while they are working there, at least) their *lives* are lost.

Chap, Old

An oddity, Old Chap; a curiously English construction, suggesting intimacy without actually suggesting intimacy. You can see why the English would need such an honorific.

To call a man 'old chap' was shorthand for what would otherwise take far too long to express. But we can try. What it, at least in part, meant was:

'What I am about to say presumes upon our acquaintance to the extent that to address you as MISTER whatever-it-is would be unbecomingly stuffy. Yet I do not wish to embarrass you with a self-conscious use of your first name. The matter that I am about to raise also temporarily (it may even be permanently, but I do not want to assume that) obliterates any fine gradations of rank or differences in income between us, yet although I am addressing you as what might, to Johnny Foreigner, appear to be an equal, I am nevertheless retaining the upper hand in the conversation which is to follow. I am probably going to give you some advice, which you may find unpalatable; alternatively, I may be about to make light of something which you find serious to the point of being unbearable; or it may be that I am about to give you bad news, and my old-chappery is an indication that, while I am obviously sympathetic to your plight, I most certainly do *not* feel your pain, and I would be frightfully obliged if you could at least give the impression of not feeling it either, or we may face the possibility of embarrassment. Whether I have been having regular and passionate sex with your *wife*, leading her to heights of gratification which she never experienced beneath your clumsily uxorious advances; whether I have been advised by your commander-in-chief to suggest that suicide is your only honourable course; whether I am about to tell you that you have **CANCER**: the fact that I am preceding it with an old-chapping (and possibly sprinkling some further old-chappery in the conversational interstices) is advance warning that you must neither show feelings nor use pronouns in what follows. That is to say, you must not say 'I take your point.' No no no. That 'I' is *far* too intimate and makes it somehow . . . well, *personal*. You must say 'Hmm. Take your point,' or, better still, 'Point taken, old chap.' Do you see what I'm driving at, old chap? Course you do. Good show.'

How the hell can we say that, now that 'old chap' has been for ever lost? We can't. And so we don't. Instead we go in for all sorts of un-Englishness – first names, sharing, emotional honesty, hugging, stuff *bordering on intimacy* – and then we wonder why Johnny Foreigner no longer looks up to us and the world is going to hell. Bad show. Blame the women. And that dashed Viennese fellow, said everyone wanted to have a pop at his **MOTHER**, you know the fellow, trick cyclist, jabber jabber, dreams, cigars, face dropped off, won't do, old chap; won't do at all. Thin end of the wedge. Do you know what I think, old chap . . . hello? Hello? Are you there? Hello . . .?

Chilblains

We address ourselves specifically to the Very Reverend Roger Dawson, Dean of St Mary's Anglican Cathedral, Caracas; and particularly to a sermon he preached in the summer of 1999 in which he recalled dozing, aged thirteen, in his Scripture classroom, shoes off and feet on the radiator while the snow lay thick outside. 'All the boys in the class were falling asleep,' he recalled from the pulpit, ' "And early in the morning" the teacher droned on, "Jesus came towards them walking on the water and that, Roger Dawson, is how you get chilblains." '

The Dean's schoolmaster was theologically wrong but medically less so. Out in the cold goes MOTHER on her bad legs (never been right since she had Our Kevin), out in the cold with damp shoes and wet cotton stockings. Back she comes with her shopping bag, sliding on the icy pavements, the yellow afternoon lights coming on and trolleybuses schussing along on their crackling ski-poles. Key in the lock, down the passage into the kitchen, throws open the stove doors (that MICA never lets enough heat out) and feet up in front of the glowing coals. All the little blood vessels in her toes will dilate in the heat – mmmmmm! toasty-warm! – and before you know it, ooh, her chilblains are giving her gyp. Itching! Red! Burning! Swollen!

They once were endemic in the colder northern climes. But we have central heating now, and shoes are better, and we don't walk to THE SHOPS but drive in the car. And so chilblains are dying out, so our feet don't hurt any more, and we can walk to the shops in the cold; except we don't. Which is why chilblains are dying out, so our feet don't hurt any more, so . . .

Chivalry

'Chivalry,' she said, 'now *that*'s gone, for sure.' So it has. The Knightly Code. Opening doors. Tipping his HAT. Holding her chair for her to sit down. Walking on the outside of the pavement (mud splashes). Going into public places ahead of her (rapists, with drawn swords). Paying. Driving. Making the first move. *Not* making a fuss. Being loyal when dumped. Stammering a little.

The knightly code: a matter of indenture and power. Men with big swords, banished from the gene pool and into battle or the woods. At the heart of it all, not women, not the fey russet-tangled adorables of Pre-Raphaelite fantasy, but horses. *Ritter*: a rider. *Chevalier*: a horseman. The Romans had their Equestrian class; men who rode. It was the great division: men who rode horses looked down on those who walk[123]. Odd, really, an animal so stupid you have to sit on it to take it for a walk; but there it is. Chivalry: the cult of the horse. Men who treated horses as gods and women as goods.

All over now. Now, we have the car. Once there were 'knights of the road' but it never caught on. Now men sit in their cars, looking down on those who walk. And treat their cars as gods, and women as *stupid* bloody *women drivers* for *God's* bloody *sake*, darling . . .

Chord, the Lost

First of all, it's not. Adelaide Ann Procter's horrible poem is 'A Lost Chord'. Just the one. There may have been others. We must hope not.

> Seated one day at the Organ,
> I was weary and ill at ease,

she maunders

---

123 Just as cavalry regiments look down on others, even though cavalry regiments no longer ride horses but sit in great big vulgar tanks. Even the memory of a horse, it seems, is enough.

> And my fingers wandered idly
>> Over the noisy keys.

An odd organ, this. Usually you have to bang quite forcefully to get the keys to rattle; mere idle wandering won't do it. But still:

> I do not know what I was playing,
>> Or what I was dreaming then;
> But I struck one chord of music,
>> Like the sound of a great Amen.

Beginners' luck, obviously, or possibly a hallucination (Procter was obviously in a funny state, quite possibly on her TONIC). It just doesn't happen. Yet 'A Lost Chord' struck such a note with the sentimental Victorian public, particularly after Sir Arthur Sullivan's truly horrid setting of it in 1877, that it has some claim to have been one of the most popular songs of all time. Every self-respecting tenor recorded it, but to get the full effect nothing quite beats Kenneth McKellar's 1963 recording[124], on which it still sounds as hateful as it did on the day it was composed.

Allegedly, Sullivan wrote it seated at his brother's deathbed, and subsequently, in a deliciously Victorian yoking of sex and Death, bequeathed it to his mistress, Fanny Ronalds.

But is it possible there was more – and something nastier – to it than met the ear? Certainly Procter was suggesting some inherent theological component of the chord

> Which came from the soul of the Organ,
>> And entered into mine.

and the proposition becomes spookier when she frets that

---

124 *The World of Sir Arthur Sullivan.* Kenneth McKellar, cond. Bob Sharples (Decca LP, SPA-548, 1979). You were warned.

> It may be that Death's bright angel
> Will speak in that chord again . . .

Could she be having us all on? Could this particular Lost Chord –
only, remember, *A* Lost Chord – be none other than the tritone,
the augmented fourth, the *Diabolus in Musica*: the Devil in Music?

It's a strange story, this satanic interval allegedly forbidden by
musical theorists. 'Allegedly', because the truth is harder to come
by. Some suggest it simply sounded harsh, a 'wolf': to mediaeval
ears accustomed to smooth *organum* lines of fourths and fifths, an
interval that came halfway between the two was neither fish nor
fowl . . . but may prove to be as good a red herring as the argument that the *Diabolus* was in some way blasphemous because it
represented the Holy Trinity[125].

Actually, there is plenty of evidence to suggest that the *Diabolus*
was not the horror later generations claimed that *earlier* generations believed. Jacobus of Liège, writing in the early fourteenth
century, gave examples of its being perfectly acceptable.
Monteverdi deployed it with foxy cunning. Gesualdo (as you'd
expect from a man who did his wife in, and her lover, with a
dagger) loved it. The tritone, in short, was never the Lost Chord.

So what *was* Procter thinking of? We will never know. One sug-
gestion is that a rather odd Viennese 'philosopher' called Arnold
Keyserling not only spent most of his life searching for it, but actually found it. Keyserling was said to be descended from the Count,
Hermann Carl Keyserlingk [*sic*], who was in turn said to have
commissioned Bach's *Goldberg Variations*. The story is charming:
the Count was supposedly an insomniac and commissioned Bach
to write a set of variations for his harpsichordist, the young vir-
tuoso Johann Gottlied Goldberg, to play to comfort him in his nights

---

125 Which neither holds water theologically nor musically. All to do with the
     Doctrine of Correspondences, probably, the idea being that the three perfect
     intervals symbolise the Trinity *built upon the lower note*, which doesn't make
     sense, and in any case the damned interval is a fourth, augmented or not.

of lost sleep. The story is disputed, though fiercely defended by another descendant, Robert Henry (Bob) Keyserlingk.

If it is true, the Count's musical ear was not inherited by his Viennese kinsman, who, in 1975, announced that he had discovered the lost chord – or, rather, the entire Lost Scale. He had built a special electronic instrument to play it on, and had christened the result 'Chakra Music' (that old WISDOM OF THE ANCIENTS again), and the instrument itself a Chakraphone. The result is an early form of New Age Ambient, but without the excitement, the tension and the complexity. If there was a Lost Chord, Sullivan's setting, oozing hot, occulted, saccharine sensuality like syrup spilled on a red velvet sofa, was closer. But the manuscript will never be seen again. It is lost for ever, buried with Fanny Ronalds in her grave.

Chronics

They were there when you arrived, asking what was wrong. They were there when you got back from the theatre: their hoarse, confidential voices whispering in your halothane-blurred ear, tales of men who had died, in *agony*, in *that very bed*. And they were there when you left, walking gingerly so as not to pull the stitches.

They were the chronics: a carefully graded hierarchy of heroic sufferers, men with wheezes and backs, men with a Leg and men with an Insides, men who had baffled the experts ('The experts is baffled'), for whom the top men could do nothing ('I've had top men look at me. Nothink they can do'), men who should, by rights, not be alive ('They said I shun't be alive, by rights').

Knackered by war and gas, by asbestosis and silicosis, by the LONDON PARTICULAR and crap sanitation, by bugs and consumption and damn-all MATERIA MEDICA, they chuffed and shuddered, tottered and creaked, reduced to a small but soothing life of lurching between ward and sluice, out on the balcony sucking on a PARK DRIVE in the sooty London air, hawking and

SPITTING in their grim little sputum cups, joshing the nurses ('You watch out, darling, when I'm back on my – *arckk! hhhrft! aaaaaaaarckk!* – feet again'), nattering with the porters.

Hospital was their final home. They'd done the army, rubbed along, knew the wrinkles: where the tea things were, the extra blankets, how to get round the Sisters who could be got round, how to spot the ones who couldn't, who was sleeping with whom (everyone, with everyone else, it seemed).

Not a bad way to end up. But inefficient. Not cost-effective. Clamp down. Stamp it out. And out they went, back on the out, with new drugs for their wheezes and borborygms, no longer venerable on the pyjama'd wards, but feeble, hopeless, and buggered in the trouser-and-flannel-shirted reality.

The PROPER DOCTORS are all dead, and the new experts are hardly ever baffled. But the hospitals . . . somehow, when the chronics went, so did some of the spirit of the place.

Church

Gothic tracery, nave and steeple, vestries and alleys and archiepiscopal shade: how they'd like to be shot of the whole lot of it, in favour of something in the municipal council-meeting-room style. And, slowly, they're ditching them, flogging them off for restaurants and flats and recording studios.

Not unreasonable. Nobody goes any more, and we may want them as monuments, but we don't want to pay.

But it's not just churches; it's architecture as a whole, which no longer can encompass any human grandeur of aspiration. Its only two models for any sort of ultramundane dignity are the Municipal Utilitarian and the Executive Hotel. Mixed in varying proportions, these two styles can produce any type or function of building you can name, and, worse, they have.

What have we lost, that this is what things have come to? Perhaps what we have lost is the model for our being. Once, we could ourselves aspire to grandeur, and the individual human being could do great things; now, our highest aspiration is efficiency, a lubricated electronic smoothness, a flatness of affect. Once we aspired to the condition of GODS. Now we aspire to the condition of computers.

Cigar, Brunel's Disappearing

Iconography? We can't be doing with iconography, particularly when it might give the wrong message.

So we should not be surprised at what happened to Isambard Kingdom Brunel's cigar. The Portsmouth school named after him decided that their device, which showed the great engineer with his habitual stogy crammed into his mouth, was setting the children a bad example. And so *damnatio memoriae* it was. Brunel was effaced entirely, and replaced with some cogs.

It is tempting to say *sic transit gloria mundi* but that's LATIN, elitist, and almost as bad as smoking. Let's just say that in art, as in life, Brunel's cigar took him off.

Clerks

What has become of the Little Man? The clerk was once a cleric: a churchman, literate, possessing the secret of temporal power contained in writing: the ability to be in two or more places at once. Presently he evolved into the pen-labourer of commerce, since he who trades must reckon, and reckoning came cheap. The armies of clerks who poured over London Bridge each morning have now gone, superseded by computers; yet still they pour in, hundreds of thousands; still you see them backlit in their offices on autumn evenings. What are they doing now? What are they *for*? Clerks they are not, because clerks have gone. So *who are they*?

Not, for sure, what they seem.

Commandment, the Eleventh

The strangest of all the Commandments, this one simply says: 'Thou shalt not.'

You never heard of it? You never saw it? What did you expect, in a book of lost things?

But – come, come – it is not hard to deduce its existence from the pronouncements of churchmen, of moralists, of politicians. 'Thou shalt not.' It's obvious, once you know.

Commensality

The noblest of human institutions; that which separates us from the beasts. All good flows from the common table, all goodness of talk, all sharing and generosity, all community. The mark of humanity is that we sit down to eat together; without that, we are fragmented, solipsistic, unmannered.

Now we browse the fridge or cram greasy burgers into our gobs in the street, and we grow fat and uncouth, and serves us right.

Common Prayer, the Book of

One of the most powerful impulses of the lover is to have the world understand his love[126], and one of the greatest extended love letters in human history has been the LATIN liturgy and its extension into English in the Book of Common Prayer. Cranmer's masterpiece informed written and spoken English for over 350 years: not only the great set pieces like the General

---

126 'His', because women, in general, seem more concerned that the *beloved* understands their love.

Confession, the Creed, the Litany and the jewel case of tiny prayers and Collects, but its numinous poetry, its cadences and, above all, the way in which it discovered or invented a perfect register for addressing what those who believed in its purpose must also have believed was a Power by definition beyond our understanding.

All that has been lost, abandoned in favour of a collection of protocols which read like EU directives for the harmonization of turnip radii, and once the tone of voice reserved for addressing the Almighty[127] had been replaced with a register more suitable for addressing a platoon of community-care workers, the mystery of faith was obliterated, and in its place stood a poor sort of vision, neither formal nor demotic, but rather the language of the business conference, the corporate meeting or the entreaty to the cold impersonality of the CALL CENTRE.

The religious of all persuasions are encouraged to believe that God is, by his very nature, unfathomable. That, not pardoning, is his true *métier*. In attempting to address the unfathomable in what passes for 'MODERN' speech, the Church of England has not only made a stylistic error as grave as a middle-aged man sporting an out-of-date cheesecloth shirt and a medallion – in which he is neither appropriate nor modern – but a graver category mistake: that a GOD who can be comprehended in the language of the suburban estate agent is not a God at all.

That is what they think of their God: an ordinary fellow, just like you and me. That is what they think of their congregation: a collection of prosaic lummoxes with no power to apprehend mystery.

Serve them right if their prayers were answered, and answered appropriately: 'Your prayer *is* important to Me. You are being held in a queue and will be answered shortly . . .'

---

127 For surely nobody believes, or ever did believe, that the average Englishman in the seventeenth century spoke like that to his friends?

Common, Don't Do That, It's

Rock music is of course by its very nature common. It makes a fuss. It uses language[128]. It draws attention to itself. It mentions, or at the very least hints at, private parts. It is appropriate, then, that the idea of commonness is as hard to pin down as life itself, at least according to the late Frank Zappa. Zappa is remembered for his observation that 'There are more love songs than anything else. If songs could make you do something, we'd all love one another.' But one rock journalist offered an alternative: Zappa, interviewed on his premature deathbed and asked how he felt about his early demise, allegedly said, 'Well . . . you do your best, and you look after your family and the people you love, and you end up in this situation, and it makes you think. And what it makes you think is: "What the fuck was *that* all about?"'

We could say the same thing about Commonness. It has gone now. Telling children not to do things because they're common is now common, so that people who were brought up to worry about whether things are common can no longer transmit that philosophy: a majestic loop of negative feedback.

The curious thing about being common is that actually *being* common was not, in itself, common. The list of things not to be done because they were common was always capricious, but, equally, consistent across the social classes, and was to be distinguished from (a) Snobbery and (b) Class Markers. Snobbery is now almost entirely confined to the *Daily Mail*-reading classes, and so beneath our notice, and Class Markers are constantly

---

128 As defined by the outraged parents who, in response to their child's being taught Philip Larkin's poem 'This Be the Verse', wrote to complain that they did not 'pay school fees in order for our child to be taught *language*'.
(Happier, perhaps, was the medical student who told me that he had heard that Larkin was a miserable bugger but didn't see why; hadn't Larkin written a rather kindly poem beginning 'They tuck you up, your Mum and Dad . . .'?

being subverted as soon as the people they are designed to keep in the dark actually cotton on[129].

Common, for example, would include:

- Not holding doors open for women
- Making a fuss about religion
- Making a fuss about food
- Referring to bodily functions
- Snoring
- Drawing attention to things
- Drawing attention to oneself
- Inability to hold one's drink
- Eating with mouth open
- Talking with mouth full
- Putting on make-up in public
- Wearing too much make-up
- Sleeping in make-up
- Saying 'Thank you' after sex (male)
- Saying 'Better now, darling?' after sex (female)
- Saying 'Have you done yet?' during sex (both)
- Groping
- Burping
- Pushing in
- Whining
- Showing off
- Living beyond one's means
- Snatching
- Gobbling
- Going to the toilet

---

129 A good example is 'pardon'. As soon as the middle classes discovered that the upper classes thought 'pardon' was common, and so started saying 'What?', the upper classes started saying 'Pardon?' – at first in ironical quotes, then without them. As usual, the middle class was left feeling uneasy and out of sorts, without quite knowing how.

- Shrieking
- Doing facial expressions
- Enthusiasm
- Lack of generosity
- Over-cleanliness
- Pursing the lips
- Not standing one's round
- Too much perfume
- Brylcreem
- Laughing too loudly
- Sponging
- Sulking
- Retching
- Flouncing.

All these, and many more, behavioural *topoi* are now commonplace and form the staple of our main 'leisure' activity, television. If TV producers were suddenly to ban being common on telly, ninety-five per cent of programming would vanish on the instant. Partly because of television's influence, partly because of the prevailing culture of relativism and 'diversity', which opposes the noticing of differences[130], 'common', as an unarguable proscription, now lies spent and inert.

And do we care? Of course not. That would be common.

Crowns, Three

Some things should never be found. So it is with the legend of the Three Holy Crowns. The Kingdom of the Angles was first ruled from Rendlesham; a silver crown was buried there, together with one at Dunwich and another at a place unknown.

---

130 And quite right too; it's common to notice things.

As long as they remain undisturbed, England (so the legend has it) will never fall to invasion. The Rendlesham Crown was, perhaps, the sixty-ounce silver crown unearthed in 1687, and melted down before it could be examined. The Dunwich Crown was swept into the sea. One left, then, its location unknown, and every weekend the fields and beaches alive with treasure hunters, their metal detectors clicking and bleeping . . .

Daaaaaaaaaaaaaaaaaaaaaaaaaa-NUH

Once the streets of London were so rich and varied that composers like Orlando Gibbons would set them to music, and nobody else could hear themselves think . . .

> Hot pudding pies hot.
> White radish, young white radish.
> New oysters, new.
> New plaice, new.
> Will ye buy a mat for a bed?
> Have you any work for a cooper?
> Hard onions, hard.
> Dame, dame, give me an egg for the worship of Good
> Friday.
> Pips, fine.
> Buy a fine washing ball.
> Will you have any small-coal?
> Good gracious people for the Lord's sake pity the poor
> women. We lie cold and comfortles night and day on the
> bare boards in the dark dungeon in great misery.
> Old doublets old doublets old doublets, have ye any old
> doublets?
> New mackerel, new.
> And a potting-stick with a dildo . . .

And now? All gone. Only the evening-paper seller remains, with his cry of Daaaaaaaaaaaaaaaaaaaaaaaaaaa-NUH! And even he is becoming rarer. Most simply stand and wait. And the cries of London are silenced. (But still they lie cold and comfortles night and day.)

Dead, Methods of Disposal of, Fallen into Desuetude

The municipal crematorium with its puzzled PARSON and its piped organ music is a poor way to end our life on Earth. Time, perhaps, to reconsider some of the alternatives we've lost sight of:

- Perpendicular burial, as in the case of Ben Jonson in Westminster Abbey.
- Perpendicular burial, on horseback, upside down, as in the case of Richard Hull on Leith Hill.
- Smoke-curing in one's best clothes, as in Haiti.
- Tying together the ankles of a dead virgin with white ribbon, as in Corsica (the reasons are fairly obvious).
- Placing a stone or prayer book in the corpse's mouth to stop it chewing its way out of the grave.
- Burial with the head chopped off and placed between the feet, to stop the corpse coming back to life and terrorizing the living.
- Stakes through the heart, ditto.
- Entombment in a sarcophagus, which is Greek for 'flesh-eater' and refers to the marble of which they were made.
- Burial of the dead man's boots on the shore between high- and low-tide marks, to stop the corpse from walking.
- conversion into useful products as in the alleged German Cadaver Utilization Establishment, a commercial enterprise where battlefield corpses, 'neatly tied into

bundles', were passed from process to process, including (it is said) retorts for the production of gas for lighting.

- Best of all, perhaps, the ancient funerary rites of the Siamese Kings, who, once dead, are seated in a special throne over a golden jar and filled up with mercury. Then a gold mask is put on the face, and the jar is daily emptied, with great ceremony, into the river. Once the corpse is dry enough, it is left in a giant urn for a year, while a 300-foot catafalque of sandalwood is built. Finally, the body is brought in a tremendous procession and placed on top of the pyre, and after seven days of public games the pyre is lit by the heir, the body burned, the ashes collected and mixed with clay and distributed to the people as souvenirs.

How one would love to be a souvenir. It would almost be worth dying for.

Democracy

Democracy? *Lost?* Surely not. We are, after all, in Eye-raq at the time of writing, *bringing democracy*[131]. Democracy is the ultimately unarguable good. Whatever anyone says, *there is no alternative to democracy*. Do you have that straight in your mind? Or would you rather be . . . persuaded? Repeatedly? By dogs? Through a hood? That, in the free world, is your choice. Choose wrong and die. Democracy in action.

But look back two and a half millennia to the strange city-state of Athens, where democracy, in what classicist Simon Goldhill describes as 'a fundamental and shocking innovation', was born.

---

131 And if the bastards don't accept democracy, we'll by God send highly trained elite forces over to pile them into human pyramids, and take their clothes off, and point, smirking, at their genitalia until they *do* accept it.

The ANCIENT GREEK system involved a democratic judiciary without professional judges, the Council of Five Hundred, a supreme *Ekklêsia* or assembly; all of which were composed, not of professional politicians, but of citizens – a 'level of political engagement', says Goldhill, which 'is strikingly high'.

Now our democracy consists in perhaps half, perhaps less, of those eligible wielding their vote once every few years (and, if they can't get out of it, doing jury service once or twice in a lifetime). Between elections, power is handed over to increasingly unaccountable professionals, bankrolled by corporate wealth, and relying on appeals to the 'trust' of the electorate or protestations of their own religious (or at least 'good') faith; none of which would have gone down well with the Athenians.

Suffrage may have widened magnificently – in ancient Athens, it was confined to the citizenry of enfranchised men over the age of eighteen; no slaves, foreigners or women[132] – but the implementation of democracy has been weakened and corrupted almost beyond recognition. 'Democracy,' wrote E.B. White in the *New Yorker* in 1944, 'is the recurrent suspicion that more than half of the people are right more than half the time.' Or, as his compatriot H.L. Mencken put it: 'Democracy is the theory that the common people know what they want and deserve to get it good and hard.'

Tom Stoppard, in *Jumpers*, was more trenchant and less facetious: 'It's not the voting that's democracy, it's the counting.'

The United States Supreme Court disagreed in 2000. The people's right to have their votes counted, it ruled, was less important than deadlines[133]. And so George W. Bush became President, democracy continued to be exported by lethal force, and the world became safe for naked human pyramids. One wonders if

---

132 Who were not even Athenian citizens, but 'women of Attica'. (Goldhill 190–1).
133 Indeed, it went further, declaring that there was no Constitutional right to vote for President.

the Athenian courts, under the reforms of Cleisthenes, would have reached the same decision.

But one does not wonder for long. The core of democracy, for its inventors, was participation. You not only voted, you served in office when called upon. Now, perhaps, a gentleman might think it poor form to discuss politics; his Athenian forebears would think it idiotic not to. Literally idiotic: those who 'kept out of politics' were risible, contemptible, 'The Selfers', *idiôtes*, foolishly self-absorbed and out of the swim.

And still are[134].

And were they peaceable, the people of this first democracy? Did they knit their own muesli, with a kind word for trees and a pacifist smile? No. They frequently went to war. They voted themselves into battles which they themselves fought. Not the poor. Not hired mercenaries[135]. Themselves. But at least they didn't have to wait to see what Halliburton wanted.

Let us end by reminding ourselves of Solon's three great innovations, made around 590 BC and paving the way for Cleisthenes:

First, he ruled that it was illegal to raise money on the security of one's body: an end to the bond-slavery of the poor to the rich.

Second, he declared that a third party could bring a legal action on behalf of a victim.

Thirdly, he declared that all citizens were equal under the law: specifically, that they had the right of appeal to a court.

How do we think we are doing now, in the twenty-first century? And before you decide, think of this: modern visitors to Athens, drinking from the *fons et origo* of our culture, visit (if

---

134 If the price of freedom is eternal vigilance, the price of democracy, for the Athenians, was permanent participation. 'We do not say that a man who takes no interest in politics minds his own business; we say he has no business here at all.' So (reported by Thucydides) Pericles, in his panegyric over those fallen in the Peloponnesian War; or, to translate it another way, 'We do not say he is unambitious; we say he is useless.' Children of all democracies, real, pretending or aspiring, should perhaps learn this great oration.

135 Or 'private contractors' in the language of Bush and Blair, so that we think of jobbing builders, perhaps, or air-conditioning repairmen.

nowhere else, as they scuttle back and forth from their cruise ships, moored in Piraeus harbour, or pass through on their way to the islands) the Acropolis, seat of power and wealth, and gaze misty-eyed at the Parthenon[136]. Solon made his great declarations from the Pnyx, some ten minutes' walk to the west, across the valley, addressing the crowd. The Pnyx: Mob Hill.

But then, he didn't have to ask permission from Halliburton, either.

Deprave or Corrupt, Tendency to

The British – and, more specifically, the English – have spent the last hundred and fifty years in a bit of a fret about depravity and corruption. Not, of course, the ruling class. No, no; place, *degree*, power and privilege have a shielding effect upon the morals, which anyone with any experience at Cabinet or boardroom level will instantly refute.

It was the *people* who had to be protected. Specifically, protected from anything to do with people inserting portions of their body into regions of other people's bodies, and *specifically* specifically if both bodies had the same number of X-chromosomes.[137] This was something the British were dreadfully worried about. And they went about it in a very British way.

---

136 'Why do we weep at the Parthenon?' asks the historian of the ancient world Mary Beard; and the answers are not flattering.

137 For the non-specialist reader: females have two, while men, bless us, have to rub along with just the one. Which makes all the difference to the morality of body-part insertion. As the MP Nicholas Winterton announced in 1998, with all the certainty of the uninformed: 'If God had intended men to commit sodomy, their bodies would have been built differently' – an argument lost upon one sodomite of my acquaintance who cheerfully pointed out that he had never found it a problem; and which inspired the great political sketch-writer Simon Hoggart to note in the *Guardian* that Winterton had perhaps hit on 'the "skeleton key" theory which, it struck me at the time, would make incest all right'.

Other, pragmatic, nasty, *thinky* sorts of nations like the French – and we all know what **PARIS** used to smell like – would have thought it through, and said: 'Right. No publishing obscene stuff. And this is what obscene stuff is,' and gone on to make a clear and helpful list. Which is precisely why the British wouldn't do it. The list would be helpful. It might help people who wanted to publish things which weren't on the list, but just because they weren't on the list didn't mean they weren't obscene, even if the list *was* a definitive guide to what was or was not obscene.

Clear? No? Remember, then, the founding principle of British public life, which is this: *If you don't know already, then I'm certainly not going to tell you.*

Which is why, instead of a list, the British had the Tendency to Deprave or Corrupt. The phrase was originated by Lord Chief Justice Cockburn in 1868 and enshrined in the Obscene Publications Act 1959, which is all very well but for the definition. How do you define an Obscene Publication? Why, it has the Tendency to Deprave or Corrupt. But *what* has the Tendency to Deprave or Corrupt? Why – for heaven's sake – an *Obscene Publication*, of course.

This led to wonders of convoluted logic. Censorship was, of course, necessary; but who would want depraved or corrupt censors? Yet if the material they were censoring was judged depraving or corrupting, then they, by being exposed to it, were either too depraved or (or maybe even *and*) corrupted to make a judgement, or they remained resolutely undepraved and uncorrupt; in which case, the material was not depraving or corrupting. Attempts to get round the law's woolliness[138] were often majestically creative, such as the Plain Blue Background, alleged to strip any hint of titillation from the

---

138 And woolliness is not necessarily a bad thing in the law, just sometimes a silly thing.

activities displayed in front of them[139], and the Mull of Kintyre Guide, which suggested that you'd be all right if you refrained from publishing any photograph of a penis at a steeper angle than the well-known dangling Scottish promontory[140]. The zenith of the genre was the magnificently barking *caveat* issued in the 1970s by the short, rich David Sullivan, in which readers of his publications – aimed at the pre-literate amateur gynaecologist, and in which women were photographed in a condition of such amazement at their own pudenda that their immediate response was to push things inside themselves with startled expressions – were informed that they were being sold as medical equipment to prevent 'brain strain' by saving men the mental effort of having to make up their own fantasies.

But, in truth, the Tendency to Deprave or Corrupt really began to die in 1960, when Penguin announced that, despite the ban which had existed since 1928, it intended to publish *Lady Chatterley's Lover*.

Five years before, a bookseller had been sent to prison for selling the book. The Director of Public Prosecutions had little choice but to test the new law by prosecuting.

He lost.

Conventional opinion had it that the case was lost when the

---

139 A distinguished British journalist, who began her career as a stylist on a well-known 'men's magazine', once said that the true obscenity lay not in the artfully soft-porn professional photo sets, but in the stuff readers sent in. 'You got blasé very quickly,' she said, 'but you never got used to the terrible *wallpaper* or the awful, awful *sofas*. You'd be minding your own business and someone would say "My God, look at this *nest of tables*" and you'd go over and blanch in horror, completely not noticing the bloke's wife splayed like a plucked turkey in the foreground.'

140 Then, as always, it was the male organ which had the power to Deprave and Corrupt. The female pudenda were considered relatively innocuous, leading to a whole genre of BritPorn featuring pallid women, on their own, gazing at their splayed pudenda with an improbable mixture of astonishment, bewilderment and glee, like people whose BREAKFAST had come suddenly to life.

hapless prosecuting counsel, Mervyn Griffith-Jones, asked the jury: 'Ask yourselves the question: would you approve of your young sons, young daughters – because girls can read as well as boys – reading this book? Is it a book that you would have lying around the house? Is it a book you would wish your wife or servants to read?' But the truth, dug up by author Alan Travis forty years on, was that the authorities were simply unable to find anyone to take their part. Anonymous civil servants from the DPP's office paged through the book, writing down mucky words, crawled through libraries looking for negative comments about Lawrence[141], begged academics, bishops, authors and critics to support their side. The response was a resounding and unanimous snub.

In the end, Griffith-Jones called just one witness, the hapless policeman to whom, in legal terms, Penguin had 'published' the book. The jig was up, and the jury found Penguin not guilty.

The public credibility of the Tendency to Deprave or Corrupt has never recovered, although it still lies on the statute books. But while Britons might sometimes yearn for an American-style constitutional right to freedom of speech as a central platform of a **DEMOCRACY**, they might equally well reflect that it was not in Britain but in California that, in the spring of 2004, a nineteen-year-old Canadian girl contracted HIV as a result of being simultaneously buggered by two (unprotected) men, during the making of a pornographic film. The wages paid for her flesh and her future were $800, and the Obscene Publications Act would not have helped her. After all, it speaks of a Tendency. The pornographers behind the camera and the chequebook had been depraved and corrupted long before.

---

141 For an example of civil service lit.crit.: 'pp 177–185. Connie goes to the hut the same day after tea. Intercourse unsatisfactory to Connie to start with but all right the second time (full details and four-letter words) [. . .] This language has everything. The presumption of the man thinking that it takes him to fly in the face of convention. If this is not shocking for shocking's sake, what is? Just letting out his own miserable ego.'

Dials, Analogue, Proper

The human tendency to do things because we *can* do them is nowhere shown better than in (a) war crimes and (b) digital controls. Digital controls, and displays, for things which are not digital – time, temperature, volume, speed – are absurd. You only have to think of the old microwave (twist the timer knob and off you go) compared to the new microwave (select the mode, adjust the minutes, adjust the seconds, adjust the mode, adjust every other bloody thing so that by the time it eventually grumbles into action you have no idea what the hell it is going to do, but that doesn't matter because you have lost your appetite anyway) to see the problem.

And the problem is that we think we're so clever when in fact we've lost our wits.

Digs

Who lives in digs, now? There aren't digs; not digs with BACH-ELORS in, run by a landlady with a parrot and, somewhere (dead, shed or drunken) a possible husband, but by and large not; there aren't digs with a communal table and a favoured tenant ('An extra egg, Mr Ghoste?') and a disfavoured tenant ('Ai don't know what he's doing up theah but it hes to stop or Ai'll hev words with him') and Rules of the House; there aren't slightly spiffier digs of the Sherlock Holmes sort; there aren't digs, period. Nobody would live in them. Now, everyone must own or at least rent their own home and the lack of privacy[142] in the old-style digs puts them beyond the pale. Now, instead, there are bed-and-breakfasts: chipboard sties run by crooks for the defeated – battered wives, single mothers, asylum-seekers, people whose

---

142 Illusory, of course; never in history have we had less privacy.

lives might warn us that sometimes things may go so irrecoverably wrong that there is no way back. Digs were once cosy: the familiar habits, the lamplight warm on the rainy street. Now they are gone, and what replaces them is a glum destination, the sad terminus of hope.

Disney, Honeyed Meretricious Sentimentality of

What happened to Disney? Surely Disney was once the articulator of childhood creativity, making manifest the gorgeous particoloured miracle of the unfettered imagination . . . and then didn't it all go wrong, and the thing become corporate pap, a sort of cowardly, sentimental porridge, every enterprise reduced to a slick, odourless lubricant of flattened affect and mass acceptability, all complexity and ambiguity ruthlessly suppressed in the name of increased market share? Isn't that what happened? And then the corporate battles, and the septuagenarian Roy Disney, nephew of the great Walt – Walt *was* great, wasn't he? – locked in an embarrassingly public bout of fiduciary name-calling and hair-pulling with CEO Michael Eisner? Isn't *that* what happened?

And shouldn't we be glad that it's happened, because Disney sprayed and deodorized and infantilized – that was the trick, that was how they epitomized the Great American Dream: infantilizing their audience – and puréed and blanded everything it touched, from the crypto-egalitarianism of *The Jungle Book* to the vicious peculiarity of *Pocahontas*? Shouldn't we rejoice that it's gone?

Not as such. It was always more complex. Did we *like* Disney? Not really. *Fantasia* mystified and scared us by turns. *Dumbo* was just downright peculiar. Uncle Walt himself was a white-supremacist, commie-fearing, obsessional weirdo. And as for the damnable mouse . . . when I was about four, my mother in hospital having trouble while expecting my sister, my father rented a Mickey Mouse film which he showed (after all the usual fuss with trying to find the screen, failing, pinning a sheet to the wall, getting the film on backwards, tripping over the projector-flex) just before bedtime.

Mickey had been left alone to mind the children, just like my FATHER[143]. There was trouble with the feeding-bottle, during which Mickey got the teat stuck on his nose. He pulled and pulled and pulled; at last, the teat came away, leaving him with a hideously extended snout like Pinocchio.

Some time later that night, I woke screaming.

'Mickey!' I howled. 'Mickey! Mickey Mouse with the long nose! Mickey with the long nose and he's *under the bed*!'

'Don't be silly,' said my father. 'There's nothing to be frightened of.'

'Under the bed! Under the bed with the long nose!'

'No,' said my father, 'he's not. Look. I'll look for myself and that'll *prove* he's not' – he bent down – 'under the *OH MY GOD OH MY GOD IT'S MICKEY WITH THE LONG NOSE*!'

Eventually I calmed down. But I never forgot. And many years later I reminded him.

'Oh, for God's sake,' he said irritably. 'Look. You've got a four-year-old child who's having nightmares because he thinks Mickey Mouse is under the bed. It's the opportunity of a lifetime. What would *you* have done?'

I saw his point. And I think, too, that I saw Uncle Walt's point. The man was a genius. Not as an animator; not as a weaver of lovable coochie-coo butterscotch and twinkle; but as the inventor of a way of scaring the hell out of children without their parents having a clue. So on the grounds that one can forgive anything if it's done from genuine malice, let us forgive

---

143 Each night I would creep into his bed around 11, and he would tell me a story. They usually began: *It was a dark and stormy night, and the black-caped horseman rode through the rain, past the gibbet where the corpses hung in chains, blood squirting from the torn stump of his neck where his head should have been . . . BUT WAS NOT!'* Curiously, after these tales, I would sleep like a baby.

Disney his eponymous Land, the Mouse, Tinkerbell and all those terrible Fred MacMurray movies. Malice in Wonderland? What else is there?

Doctor, the Non-

'Vibration is Life' yelled the 1910 advertisement in *Modern Priscilla* magazine[144]. 'The secret of the ages has been discovered in Vibration. Great scientists tell us that we owe not only our health but even our life-force to this wonderful force. [. . .] Vibrate Your Body and Make It Well. YOU Have No Right to Be Sick! . . . It sends the rich, red blood leaping and coursing through your veins . . . it makes you **fairly tingle with the joy of living**.'

If the pictures of bulky ladies Vibrating the small of their back or the top of their head (or indeed the pigeon-chested, rather weedy man in his braces apparently Vibrating his belly-button through his shirt) made you so keen to fairly tingle with the joy of living that you sent off for the whole colossal kit (complete with imagination-stretching vibratodes and a massive wooden box), the Lindstrom-Smith Co. of Chicago would throw in a vibrating chair and endless bliss was yours right up to your LAST AGONY.

We may sneer now – the new! improved! version of the Rampant Rabbit[145] is advertised in the high-street windows of Ann Summers, with no doubt at all concerning its function – but not that many years ago things were very different. Then, the height of electro-vibratorial blood-leaping was to be had from

144 Reproduced in Rachel Maines's *The Technology of Orgasm*: a wonderful work which women will read with a knowing smirk, and men with a sinking heart.

145 Men: if you don't know what the Rampant Rabbit is, you need to work on your relationship a little because she's keeping something – probably a Rampant Rabbit – hidden from you.

the celebrated Non-Doctor, a name which, in the slippery way that it started to yield up its meaning only to slide skittering away again, suggested a Japanese hand in its conception[146].

Those of us who reached sexual maturity in the 1970s will immediately see the Non-Doctor's image before our inner eye: its black, torchlike barrel; its thick metal band; the four attachments (only one of which had any obvious function); and, best of all, the picture of the woman in the advertisement, her lips parted, her eyes shining, an expression unequivocally suggesting that she was fairly tingling with the joy of living, and, wonderfully, the Non-Doctor plainly visible . . .

. . . held to her face.

That's what it was for. It was for *Vibrating the Face*. No wonder it sold so well: all those women, for all those years, thinking, 'Merciful heavens, if only there were something to *vibrate my face* . . .[147]' And then came Non-Doctor.

It's the innocence that's touching. No; not the innocence. We all knew perfectly well what it was for; we merely colluded in the pretence, while buying the things by the thousand. Historians of the future, when sex has been replaced by something more cost-effective, may marvel at the outbreak of neuralgia in the 1970s ('I bought this for you, darling; I thought your cheeks looked tired') but we know better.

Yet though the Non-Doctor has been lost, the PUDEUR has not quite gone away. It still lives on in all those stories about women whose Rampant Rabbits turned themselves mystically on

---

146 This was, after all, the nation which gave us Japlish, exemplified by a T-shirt which announced 'Big Shopping God Stick', and a carrier bag which was decorated with cartoons of little cats showing various expressions: inexplicable until you read the legend on the bag. 'Little Cats Various Expression,' it explained.

147 Just as one imagines all those people who, after their first toot of cocaine, experiencing a moment of pure epiphany as, finally, they have found something to *numb the inside of their nose*. Thank God! No wonder they get addicted.

during meetings, or fell out of their luggage and squirmed across the check-in floor. The shock! The delight! *Women Like It, Too!* Oh, the sheer *cheek* of it.

Doctors, Proper

You go along and you are, to be frank, worried sick. Worried *and* sick. And there's the doctor: someone you would ideally like to be a cross between **GOD** and an old-fashioned **PARSON**, but instead it's some disgruntled but caring person who has been on courses about empathy and body language and non-judgemental ungendered relativism, and speaks with a soothing voice while sitting next to you instead of behind a desk like a *proper* doctor, and calls you by your first name, when you are feeling (*vide supra*) worried and sick and you want to be called **MISTER** at the very least, possibly even Sir, or, if it's *cancer*, '**OLD CHAP**'. 'Old chap' will do very nicely, as in 'Well, old chap, I'm afraid your number's up. Can't say when, but my advice is, don't worry, but, equally, don't start any long books. Short stories and an early night – oh, and try to keep your bowels open.'

You won't get it. It's all about collaborative consensual patient-care programmes (or, probably, 'programs') and, above all, non-paternalistic. But still one yearns. Many years ago, the British Medical Association held a conference on 'The Doctor/Patient Relationship'. At the end, the chairman, a patrician old chap called **ELSTON GREY-TURNER** – triple-breasted, five-piece suit, watch-chain, white moustache, looked a bit like Mr Pastry, for those who remember Mr Pastry; for those who don't remember Mr Pastry, see **MR PASTRY** – stood up and said: 'Well, it's all been very interesting, particularly for those who are concerned about the doctor/patient relationship. For my own part, the doctor/patient relationship has never troubled me overmuch; I look across my desk and think, "I'm the doctor, he's the patient."'

Things now are infinitely less simple, nor as benign as one might think. Medicine – particularly general practice – will soon be a profession dominated by women, and these women will not have been hardened and made cynical by their training, but rather encouraged by (possibly well-meaning) sociologists to empathize with their patients. Whether one wants one's doctor to empathize is debatable; perhaps a latter-day Galen or a Dundreary-weeper'd Victorian medical man would be a little too much, but while *sympathy* is certainly desirable, do you really want a doctor who *feels your pain?*

No. And the doctor who *does* feel your pain . . . what of her? The endless assault of the lonely, the weary, the anxious, the dispossessed; those with no organic illness who are nevertheless simply *tired all the time*; the poor or inarticulate caught in the dumb hopeless soul-sucking coils of bureaucracy; the addicts, descending into crime and degradation through the grotesque policies of prohibition; the solitary and old, with no family, no friends, no resources and the slow drip of cancer ebbing away their lives: do we expect our doctors to feel all this pain and still survive? The old-fashioned Proper Doctor, having done all he could with his lamentable **MATERIA MEDICA**, could close up his surgery and, protected by watch-chain, dignity and heavy black serge, sleep easy in his bed. His modern counterpart may instead draw a more irrevocable curtain of self-prescribed medication about her and seek a more permanent quietus.

Dodo, L'Estrange's, the Perishing of

In 1638, the English theologian Sir Hamon L'Estrange, walking in London, saw 'the picture of a strange fowle hung out upon a clothe' and, with a few friends, went in to see it. They found:

> . . . Kept in a chamber [. . .] a great fowle somewhat bigger than the largest Turky Cock, and so legged and

footed, but stouter and thicker and of a more erect shape, coloured before like the breast of a young cock fesan, and on the back of dunn or dearc colour. The keeper called it a Dodo, and in the ende of a chymney in the chamber there lay a heape of large pebble stones, whereof hee gave it many in our sight, some as big as nutmegs and the keeper told us that she eats them (conducing to digestion) . . .

The fate of L'Estrange's dodo is as sad as that of the species as a whole. According to Errol Fuller[148] it was stuffed and placed in the famous museum established by the naturalist and gardener to Charles II, John Tradescant. In 1659, the dodo, along with the rest of Tradescant's collection, passed to the Ashmolean Museum in Oxford, where Elias Ashmole's Statute No. 8 reads: 'That as any particular grows old and perishing the keeper may remove it into one of the closets or other repository; and some other to be substituted.'

The dodo – named from the Portuguese *doudo*, or simpleton – lived in Mauritius where it had no natural enemies. And then we came along. The result being that this magical, clumsy, guileless creature has become a synonym for the lost, the vanished, the obliterated and the extinct. As dead as a dodo . . . and so they are, every last one. The last record of a living dodo comes from a 1681 account of a visitor to Mauritius, and is with hindsight more eloquent than its author could have imagined:

'The bird's flesh is very hard.'

And so, in the fullness of time, the Asmolean's dodo, which L'Estrange and his friends had watched peaceably eating stones, grew old and perishing, and was cast away. But there was none other to be substituted, not anywhere in the world.

---

148 *Extinct Birds* (2001).

Dog, The

The dog it was that died.

Well, of course it was. That's what they do. The dog is dead. Not the current dog, perhaps, but *the* dog, the dog who you thought was your friend, the dog you had when you were little, the dog that occasionally struck you as miraculous – it was warm, it moved of its own accord, it was alive, *you were bigger than it was*; most of all, it *existed* – that dog, *the* dog, is dead.

That is what it was for. That is what dogs are for: they are there to die. It was not always like that; the dogs of mythology were other creatures altogether, minatory hunters, with teeth. Think of Odysseus's Argos, of King Arthur's Cabal; think of Anubis and Cerberus, of Sirius, Xoltl, Garm and Angrboda. Now, though, the dog's job is to die on our behalf, making death into something manageable. An old, wise doctor once told me of a man, a farmer, whose wife of over fifty years died suddenly. He showed so little emotion that the doctor was beginning to worry; modern post-Freudian psychology, which views the human mind as a sort of cistern or boiler, believes it is bad to 'bottle things up' and will, if necessary, arrange counselling until one bursts.

But then, a few weeks later, the farmer's collie died. The man was distraught, howling and wailing and beating his breast. 'It wasn't for the dog,' said the doctor, 'it was for his wife. It was just that the dog was in a way small enough for him to mourn.'

Kipling, in 'The Power of the Dog', asks:

> We've sorrow enough in the natural way
> When it comes to burying Christian clay.
> Our loves are not given, but only lent,
> At compound interest of cent per cent.
> Though it is not always the case, I believe,
> That the longer we've kept 'em the more do we grieve;
> For when debts are payable, right or wrong,
> A short-time loan is as bad as a long-

119

So why in Heaven (before we are there)
Should we give our hearts to a dog to tear?

There, perhaps, is his answer. We send them on ahead to test the waters of Lethe, and they reduce to manageable dimensions life's endless cycle of loss.

Dogs, Mad

Once, all strange dogs were mad. Until proven otherwise? No. You didn't let them get close enough. They were all mad. Hydrophobia. *Rhabdoviridae*, genus *Lyssavirus*. A bullet-shaped, enveloped, single-stranded RNA virus of 75–80 nanometers in diameter. Do you see? *Rabies*. Mad dog, he'd take one look at you, *whup*, teeth would go in, die in agony, twitching, unable to drink: why, even the sound of someone pouring water in the next room would throw into spasms. Nanny Parkin knew a little boy who petted strange dogs even though his mother had told him not to. This was when they were at the seaside. At CANFORD CLIFFS! And they had to put him to bed and he died in spasms – *spasms* – brought on by the reflection of the sunlight off the sea on the ceiling of his room. Even that was enough! To throw him into spasms!

Folk memory. One case of mad dog in 1969. Before that, towards the end of the Great War. Gone, as near as anything like that is gone. But still the British remain terrified. All those notices at seaports. All those precautions: Passports for Pets or it's Mister Woofy-Woo holed up in quarantine like a recidivist, six months, no parole. *But what if he forgets us? What if he pines?* Should have thought of that beforehand, Madam: the smug, bulging yawp of the official since time began.

And meanwhile, in Europe? Speaks for itself. Carry a flask and glass wherever you go, you'll never have to stand on a train again. Just start pouring and half of them will be on the floor, in spasms. *Spasms!*

Proves the point. You may think Mad Dog is just another cause of **Death** fallen into desuetude but better safe than sorry. Look before you leap. Best of all: don't leap.

Domitian, Emperor, Hair, Care of the, Guide to

The Emperor Domitian ruled for fifteen years and four days, stabbed to death in his bedroom at the age of forty-four, on 18 September AD 96. His fingers were slashed and mangled from grabbing at the knives that killed him. Afraid of assassination, he kept a dagger under his pillow. But that night he found only its hilt. The blade had been removed. His wife Domitia was part of the conspiracy.

Roman history divided its emperors into two sorts: good emperors, and bad emperors. Domitian was a bad emperor. You could tell as much from the contents page to the translation of Suetonius's *Twelve Caesars* made by A.P., Gent., in 1692[149].

> A Dwarf stood always at his Feet . . . most Cruel and Inhuman . . . His cunning and surprize in his Cruelty, His ways to get Money, From his Youth uncivil and dis-obliging, confident and presumptuous . . . He was Impatient of Labour, He neglected all manner of Liberal Studies . . . His great addiction to Venery . . .

Indeed so. While he was *at the beginning of his Reign Mild and Gentle*, curbed the viciousness of the magistracy and stamped down on judicial corruption, he was not to be remembered as a reformer.

The seeds had been sown young.

---

149 A tricky time to publish a work dwelling on the bad ends of Emperors, just forty-three years after England had beheaded her own king. She had then tried the Cromwellian republic, restored the monarchy and was still convulsed with a collective disquiet about the right form of government, and a collective guilt about what she had done.

He misspent his youth. He was said to have prostituted himself to Nerva, who succeeded him. He stole his wife from her then husband, divorced her for sleeping with an actor called Paris, took her back again, shut himself up for an hour a day to stab flies with his pen-point, kept a dwarf as a confidant, made an artificial lake to stage sea battles, held races of naked virgins, banned comedians, had the High Priestess of the Vestals buried alive for debauchery and her debauchers whipped to death, treated sex – 'Bed-Wrestling' – as if *it had been a kind of Exercise*, would personally *smooth and depilate his Concubines, and swim among the most notorious Harlots*, killed one of Paris's pupils for looking like his teacher, and crucified his accountant.

So far, so grotesque; and we so much expect grotesquery from bad emperors that this catalogue of transgression fails to bring Domitian to life. That task must fall to his appearance. He was tall, ruddy-faced, with large (but weak-sighted) eyes, *handsome and well proportion'd in all his Limbs, even if he later grew Swag-belly'd and Gouty-legg'd*. But he had a secret sorrow:

> . . . His baldness troubl'd him to that degree, that he would take it as an Affront put upon himself if any Man offer'd to call another Bald-pate, either in jest or in earnest. Yet in a small Treatise which he dedicates to one of his Friends, entitled *Of the care and preservation of the Hair*, he inserted this, *as well for his own as the Consolation of his Friend*.

The 'small Treatise', as the hair that prompted its composition, is now lost, and no trace remains.

But there he was: a bad emperor; and no youth driven witless by power, like Nero, nor an old roué, like Tiberius, swimming in his pool at Capri with children – his 'minnows' – trained to pluck and nibble at the Imperial crotch, but a man of intelligence in his middle age, gifted with an imaginative and predatory sadism and the absolute power to indulge it. And yet brought so low by the baldness of *the imperial head* that he had to apply his fly-stabbing pen *for his own . . . Consolation, announcing sadly that I am forc'd with patience to endure my Aged Locks in the midst of my Youth.*

As men have discovered since the beginnings of time, there is no power that can stop the hair from falling. Wigs, grafts, comb-overs, lotions, thickeners: all look *wrong*. All say *bald*. Was Domitian, to himself, in the privacy of his bed-(and later his death-)chamber, the Greatest, the All-High, the most powerful man in the world?

Or was he just . . . *bald?*

The answer, of course, is not so much lost as never known. And Domitian is remembered for what he lost: his hair, his book, his dagger, his life. But how very, very much one would love to read the Emperor Domitian *On the Care and Preservation of the Hair.* And how very, very much he would have loved Minoxidil.

Dungeons & Dragons

Orcs and kobolds and wizards, shapeshifters and oubliettes, phosphorescent moss and an extravagant but bogus Gothick: Dungeons & Dragons was once the epitome of the lost life, reality subsumed in fantasy, pale people on sentimentalized Arthurian quests at the roll of the dice. You could even play it in real dungeons: I went to one, in Cheshire, and my chest was caved in by Orcs. No wonder it had to stop. Perhaps the devotees simply grew up, paired off, and started going to other dungeons, on other quests, where the dress code was no longer a latex head but a latex *bustier*, and nipple-clamps cast an entirely different spell.

Dunn & Co

Dunn & Co was the quintessential 'gentlemen's outfitters', whose half-timbered mock-Gothic stained-glass-clerestory windows blighted the sartorial lives of countless men in every town and city in England until they mercifully went out of business. There were other chains, but none approached Dunn & Co as the absolute epitome of the English middle-middle-middle-class man of the 1950s and beyond. Destitute of dress sense, vanity knocked out of him, terrified that any tentative approach to 'style' would result in the immediate dropping-off of his testicles, the Englishman took to Dunn & Co like a dog to its vomit.

And dog-vomit was the defining colourway of Dunn & Co. A greeny-brown-yellow shade of lumpy dysentery could be had in desperate trousers, grim tweedy HATS, grimmer corduroy ones, stiff jackets in hairy tweed, woolly ties, even 'car coats' and, nadir even of Dunn & Co, the elastic-sided dog-vomit PlastiCap with jaunty button: this was the world of Dunn & Co.

That, or grey.

When the French today sport what they call *le 'look' Anglais*, they are mistaken. *Le* real *look Anglais* came from Dunn & Co. It will never be recreated.

Epilogue, the

You know, I was thinking only today about the Epilogue, and it occurred to me that, in a very real sense, it's very like life itself. The bright, new morning, the long day's work, the well-earned evening's rest, thrilling to all the manifold glories of the television set; and then, just as you are feeling tired, a representative of **GOD** comes along, has a quiet word for a moment, and then everything shuts down. Time for a long sleep, as life dwindles to a tiny white spot, and then . . . darkness. Everything must come to an end, and we none of us know when. Why, even the Epilogue, which for so many years rounded off every evening on the BBC, would one day just c—

(plink.)

Fathers

What the *hell* happened to fathers? A father's job used to be easy: when in doubt, say no, unless he were a lone father, in which case, as explained by the writer Simon Carr, a simpler policy was recommended: When in doubt, say yes. Fathers wheezed and grumbled. Fathers were rigid in their habits. Fathers regarded their children as playing SILLY BUGGERS unless proven otherwise. Fathers had to pause for a moment to remember who their children were. Fathers went out to work and came back and their children had *absolutely no idea* what happened in the interim. Fathers were men. Fathers were as perpetual as the sea, reliable as rocks. Fathers were not their children's friends; they were their *fathers*.

Then fathers got into trouble. Television programmes, gender politics and advertising diminished them; their authority was eroded; their functions questioned. The female model became the only moral high ground, men squirming in the mud below. Diminished at home, flayed alive in the divorce courts, condemned to bedsits and cheap takeaways, denied access, or alternatively failing to see what the deal actually *was* and just bailing out and buggering off (almost invariably to repeat the mistake; see all those brow-furrowing elderly fathers outside any expensive prep school at going-home time), fathers became an endangered and reviled species.

No wonder we have lost our easy belief in GOD; we no longer have fathers to base it on. But now the orthodoxy is changing. Fathers may be men, and therefore corrupt and corrupting[150], but they have, perhaps, some redeeming characteristics. But how will the next generation learn how to be fathers? What will they do? A father is more than a mother with testicles, but the trick of it may have been lost, and it will take more than BRYLCREEM to bring it back.

---

150 The new mark of the beast is no longer 666 but the Y-chromosome.

Finisterre

Finisterre. *Finis terrae*: the end of the earth. Gone. It was there for ever, or so it seemed, introduced by the trite, comforting MELAN-CHOLY of 'Sailing By'. For cosy landlubbers rocked in the arms of the bedclothes or cradled in the seats of their warm cars, the Shipping Forecast is as glamorous and as soothing as the sound of a gale howling outside a warm bedroom: the marker of a world outside, dangerous and capricious, from which the listener was mercifully protected.

It keeps curious, almost liturgical, company, not chanted but almost intoned in an ageless rhythm: Viking, North Utsire, South Utsire, Forties. Cromarty, Forth, Tyne. Dogger, Fisher, German Bight . . . Humber, Thames, Dover; Wight, Portland. Plymouth, Biscay, Trafalgar, Sole; Lundy, Fastnet, Irish Sea. Shannon. Rockall; Malin; Hebrides, Bailey, Fair Isle, Faroes, South-east Iceland.

A litany of imaginary places drawn by the spirit of meteoro-logy moving upon the face of the waters; an occulted prayer for they that go down to the sea in ships, that do business in great waters: These see the works of the LORD, and his wonders in the deep. For while it may be Radio Four – zippy, businesslike, numerate, MODERN – the rest of the time, on the Shipping Forecast, it is still the BBC Home Service, and Britain still a great maritime nation; the LORD is in his heaven, looking down upon a nation in handknitted jerseys, a pipe-smoking, MECCANO-building, hobby-practising nation built upon decency and the cadences of the BOOK OF COMMON PRAYER. And the Shipping Forecast a secular compline, a *Collect for ayde, agaynste all perils*, recited liminally, through the air, between land and sea: *Lyghten our darkenes, we beseche thee, O lord, and by thy great mercy defende us from all perilles and daungers of thys nyght* . . .

And so we move from the end of the Earth to our end on the Earth. But Finisterre, which once stood between Biscay and Sole, vanished in 2002, replaced by FitzRoy, just as Heligoland was driven out in 1956 to give way to German Bight. It is appropriate; Admiral FitzRoy introduced the first weather forecasts in *The Times* in 1860 and was a notable inventor of barometers, celebrated for his 'special remarks' advising on how to predict from their readings:

> When rising: In winter the rise of the barometer presages frost. In wet weather if the mercury rises high and remains so, expect continued fine weather in a day or two. In wet weather if the mercury rises suddenly very high, fine weather will not last long.

We cannot grudge FitzRoy his late, nocturnal celebrity; but it comes at a cost. In its sound as well as its meaning, Finisterre epitomized the sea, literally the end of the Earth. Now it is only commemorated in SNUFF, and in the last lines of Carol Ann Duffy's *Prayer*:

> Darkness outside. Inside, the radio's prayer –
> Rockall. Malin. Dogger. Finisterre[151].

Fishing rods, Built-Cane

The bottom two sections were split cane, but the top was built cane. Built cane was better. It had to be *built*, not just split. The result was ... better. Better than what? It didn't say, but you could have entire fishing rods made of built cane and they were the best.

It lived in a green canvas bag which presently took on a unique odour of maggots and maggot bran and groundbait and aniseed and fish, but not much fish because there weren't many

---

151 *Mean Time* (1992).

fish to be had in the river, by the power station, just downstream from the New Bridge. But that didn't matter. Fish weren't the point. The point was that the fishing rod went in its green canvas bag, and the other things went in their old canvas holdall – the maggots and the groundbait, the plastic wallet with hooks and floats and rubber bands, the disgorger (in case there *was* a fish) and the keep net (to keep the fish in, if there was a fish, because you wouldn't eat these fish; they tasted of mud and bones) and the little folding stool, and the transistor radio which your father had sent up for[152].

And that was it. Sometimes the river was high; sometimes, low. There were rules about what fish did in either case, and what they liked to eat, and how to catch them, but you didn't know those rules because they were for people who went fishing, and this was not about going fishing. This was about sitting on the embankment, by the power station, just downstream from the New Bridge, and thinking 'Here I am: fishing.'

Now the rods are fibreglass or carbon fibre, and anglers speak of elastic return and bearings and low-drag rings, and there are fish-finders and strike-alerters and bait-casters and a thousand bits of technology designed to take your money from you, and the old pleasure – 'Here I am: fishing' – has been taken away, replaced with a new, edgier one: 'Here I am: dissatisfied with my technology, and wanting more of it.'

Built-cane rods? Forget it. What would you want one of *them* for?

---

152 It was called a 'transistor' radio to draw attention to the technology, because this was the late 1960s, when there wasn't much technology around. On the other hand, sex didn't kill you, especially if you weren't having any because you spent your time with your fishing rod or playing the organ. And it was 'sent up for' because that was what you did when there was something special you wanted, like a transistor radio. 'Mail order' wasn't special enough. You *sent up for* things. Let there be no mistake about that.

Flour

If ever there were a symbol of contented domesticity, it was flour. Good wives were always lightly dusted in flour; the better the wife, the higher up the arms it reached. Floury kisses betokened licit married love, as opposed to the lipstick and scent of the illegitimate liaison; no mistress or courtesan knew what flour even *was*. A house without flour was no home. Flour sustained explorers and stockmen; flour moved us from hunters to agrarians, and thence to villagers and, presently, citizens. Once, it came in sacks; fortunes were to be had from milling it; the miller himself was a potent symbol of aspiration and the misuse of power (think of Schubert's *Schöne Müllerin*).

Now it is tucked away in supermarkets in little bags barely enough to flour a decent woman above the wrists. Where are the sacks? Where are the millers? Where are their yeasty, floury daughters, bosoms rising like well-proved dough? The dogs bark, the caravans move on, and even for those of us who aren't gluten-free or on the Atkins diet, flour lives, like everything else, in factories, computer-controlled by executives. And *they* never get their hands . . . clean.

Found

You'd expect more of it, but you're getting less. As the Web grows larger every picosecond, so your chances of finding what you *really* want (as opposed to what the search engines *think*[153] you want) decrease. Google may have become a verb and another tool in frustrating the advances of perves, shills, dweebs and

---

153 Or, more likely, *decide*; they are, after all, commercial organizations with commercial pressures which aren't always obvious but are always there. Did you think you got your store loyalty card for being loyal?

bunny-boilers ('I Googled him and he'd done time for rodent offences') but try finding something you need. You'll spend hours sifting through endless lists from shopping sites, all saying the same thing, and equal hours sifting through porn sites which work by inserting a key word from your search into a randomly generated Porn Word Thesaurus ('Hot wet Medtronic Octopus®4 tissue stabilizer cuties! We have best hot moms Medtronic Octopus®4 tissue stabilizer MILF bestiality barely legal teens sexing Medtronic Octopus®4 tissue stabilizer animal sex fondle gaping Medtronic Octopus®4 tissue stabilizer gang-bang Viagra enlargement').

There were alternatives; the best of them was also one of the first, the Alta Vista search engine. Its searching was extraordinarily powerful and flexible, and once you had spent the five minutes to find out how to use it, you would never get a false cheating wives $$$$ clear bad credit rating now!!! search again.

But the punters didn't have five minutes, or so the wisdom said. The punters are low-rent, undiscerning, Windows®-using, herd-following mouse potatoes who just want to type one word ('Donuts') in their Googlebox and find naked teen Donut nirvana.

So Alta Vista was bought up, amalgamated, and, as from All Fools' Day 2004, no longer found. Gone **404**. All one can say is 'Oh sexy suspenders Medtronic Octopus®4 tissue stabilizer *blast!*'

Fretwork

The Modern Boy's Book of Hobbies is before me as I write. Not in reality, for it, too, is long lost; but in my mind's eye it is as clear and vivid as the day I was given it.

It was already old when I got it: published in 1937, it is a curiously obsessional volume, prepared to tolerate the occasional excursion into the recondite but invariably return with almost indecent speed to its Great Theme: *fretwork*.

As Europe moved inexorably towards war, the picture of the

Modern Boy's life was seemingly one of a now entirely lost innocence. There sits the Modern Boy, in his grey flannel shorts, his grey knitted jumper, and – *at all times* – his tie. Set out before him are his wood, his patterns ('available by post; send a Postal Order for 1/3 to receive the FULL SET') neatly arranged, his new supply of wood graded and stacked, his cheeks red with anticipation as he prepares to use, for the first time, his Deluxe No. 3 Model Treadle Fretsaw (£1/2/6). Beside him, in his grey flannel trousers, his maroon knitted jumper, and his tie, his cheeks red with paternal pride, stands his **FATHER**[154], his pipe held aloft to signify irrefutably the sexual maturity of which his paternity alone is not proof enough. In the background, somewhere, is the shadowy figure of chintz-frocked Mummy, a touch of pomade in her hair, a touch of salve on her lips, but the bottle of oh-so-shocking *Schocking* firmly stoppered in the dressing-table drawer; only *that sort of woman* would wear scent every day. (Sometimes Mummy isn't even there, signified solely by the aroma of beef or baking from the kitchen[155].)

But the innocence, the familiality, the *peace* is an illusion. Soon the air will be torn by the shriek of the fretsaw, the reek of hoof-and-bone glue, the suppressed curses of Modern Boy ('Gosh!') and Father ('I say, dash it!') as wood splinters and cracks, and the cries of Mummy ('Sawdust all over the rug!').

Eventually, things will improve ('I say, **OLD CHAP**, you're getting the hang of it!') and then it will be full speed ahead to Fretwork Hell. Mirror frames, picture frames, pipe stands, match stands, nameplates, spectacle-cases. Pipe-racks, letter racks, stamp racks, stationery racks, key racks, plate racks, magazine racks: so many things in the 1930s home needing racks – and fretwork racks, by their nature, so flimsy and evanescent – that other hobbies simply had no time to flourish in the frenzy of rack-fretting.

---

154 Fathers got a capital letter in the 1930s. Or else.
155 And how they managed to get that onto the printed page, I don't know. But they did.

131

And then came war, and fretting changed for ever. After which, nothing was the same. Who does fretwork now? What Modern Boy has a fretsaw, yearns for balsa (practice) or mahogany (the real thing), or capitalizes his father?

None. All gone. Vanished into air, into thin air. And left not a rack behind.

Fug

When did you last encounter a good fug? A good fug requires pipe smoke, **B.O.**, a **LONDON PARTICULAR** outside, the windows tight shut, cabbage boiling on the stove, and the memory of earlier cabbage boiling, and boiling, and boiling, and beef roasting, and the cabbage *still* boiling, and everyone in front of the coal fire, getting **CHILBLAINS**, and central heating just will not do. It was cosy, a good fug; it was reassuring, and comforting, and safe; it was depressing and claustrophobic and your head ached and the oxygen was sucked out of the air and, for a child growing up in the days of the good fug, it was Sunday teatime every day and everything that was worst about being grown up, and then you died. A good fug? No such thing as a *good* fug, and never was.

Gadgets

The Ghost of Christmas Yet To Come was only partly right. As the computer programmers would say, concept fine, implementation sucks. Look around your room. What have you got?

Me first. No cheating. Only what I can see. 20Gb flip disk, Logitech wireless trackball, Olympus digital voice recorder, a two-colour pen, three three-colour pens, a four-colour pen, a Porsche pen made of hydraulic-line steel braiding (won't distort under high pressure), a joystick, a Spyderco Delica lock knife, three wristwatches, a Palm Pilot, a Sony Clié, another Olympus digital voice recorder, a CD walkman, two pairs of noise-reducing earphones, a USB hub, an Airport wireless base station, two USB pen drives, a laser-printer, three electric razors (Philishave, Braun, Grundig), a C-Pen text scanner, another C-Pen text scanner, a Gaggia espresso machine, a vibrating head massager, a Post-It dispenser, another one, another one, another one, a Leica camera, a Canon camera, a Sony camcorder, a digital camera (broken), a plastic reindeer which defecates candy, a plastic computer which plays 'Frosty the Snowman', a pair of clockwork sushi, a Parthenon snowstorm, a rubber penguin, eleven disposable lighters (not disposed of), a Ronson lighter, several hundred CD-Rs which have I don't know what on them, and a computer.

A PowerBook G4 1.33GHz computer.

A PowerBook G4 1.33GHz computer running OS X 10.3.3 (upgraded only yesterday) on which there is software: NoteTaker, Mellel, DEVONthink, Tinderbox, Bookends, Safari, Mail, Voodoo Pad, DEVONagent, Grokker, NewsWatcher, Pyramid, OmniGraffle, OmniOutliner, Reference Miner, NovaMind, CMap, Ulysses, StickyBrain, Sonar Professional, Cindex, iTunes, Papyrus, Palimpsest, EndNote. Microsoft Office is there somewhere, though I hate it, just as an uncountable number of others hate it. More stuff is there, too: stuff I have tried and not liked or not used or can't be bothered with: Boswell, Butler, Final Draft, Final Draft AV, In Control, MacJournal, MTLibrarian, Nisus Express, RagTime, Reference Worker, Scribe . . .

Gadgets.

And there is probably more that I just can't see; or, rather, that I *can* see but just can't process.

Gadgets, which eat time. Time to earn the money to pay for them. Time learning how to use them. Time caring for them. Time worrying when I abandon them. *Time deciding which one to use, then changing my mind.*

The Ghost of Christmas Yet To Come does not appear clad in

austerity with a shrouded face. It comes robed in plethora with a cornucopia bigger by far than its predecessor's, the Ghost of Christmas Present, and that cornucopia is brim-tumbling-full of . . .

. . . Gadgets.

The very gadgets which are using the energy and eating the oil which will run out in our lifetimes and then all the gadgets will be lost for ever. And what will we do *then*?

Gears, Sturmey-Archer

Rapists lurk behind every bush. If not rapists, paedophiles[156]. If not rapists and paedophiles, robbers: people with sticks, youths with knives and hoodies, the dispossessed and disenfranchized, illegals[157], tramps.

Turn away from the bushes, innocent child! Move into the road! Better there, by far; your fate will be every bit as certain, but quicker; for, in the road, you are only at risk from drivers: drunk drivers, drivers distracted by smoking cigarettes, drivers eating chocolate bars, drivers arguing with their wives, drivers talking on their mobile phones, drivers arguing with their wives on their mobile phones. Not a driver gets into his car (they are men, these drivers; can't you tell, from how bad they are?) giving even the solitary tiniest damn about maiming or snuffing out lives, and if they, too, are killed or

---

156 Is there a cross-over point, like in hospital, when, once you are sixteen, you go into the adult ward – leading to the odd sight of hulking bearded fifteen-year-olds banged up with little children missing Mummy? And, if so, is it disputed? Is there a gradation of dishonour? How does it work? Do they take alternate bushes? And, above all (as a friend, a once-famous whore, once observed of a client who liked to put on a plastic mackintosh and have doughnuts thrown at him, 'How do they decide that that's what they like?'

157 Mexicans, if you're American. Asylum-seekers, if you're British. Benefit-scrounging, AIDS-ridden, *bogus* asylum-seekers if you're British and a reader of the *Daily Mail*, a newspaper which exists solely to makes its readers feel put-upon, affronted, angry, anxious and, of course, *fat.*

maimed in the process, so be it: that is the price of admission you pay to the Great Game.

True? Of course it's not true. It is no more than a subset of the general sense of lost personal security which afflicts our lives[158]. But all the same, it has had its effect.

Gone, now, is the accompaniment to so many childhoods: the scent of winter frost, the sharp tang of promise, always smelling of the full moon and a clear sky; autumn's melancholy leaf mould, soft and valetudinarian; the scent of spring, leaping and green[159]; of summer, dry as creosote, hard as dust. Gone, the scraped knees, the parched uphill throat, the icy sanctity of lemonade, the feral squish of soggy cheese-and-tomato sandwiches, the drag of gravel, the Doppler hoot of a passing Rover (a blur of trilby, spectacles and glowing Wills' Whiff behind the earnest windscreen), the shimmering mirage of hot asphalt[160], and, above all, the silent, leisurely tick of the Sturmey-Archer Three-Speed Gears which clicked in on third gear, the aural evidence that child and machine were working in harmony, that the ground was being covered, that all the world lay ahead but you'd still be home for tea.

Sturmey-Archer has gone now, overtaken by the malign fantasies collectively known as 'economics' or 'the real world'. In its

---

158 Although it is true that an awful lot of drivers – and these ones mostly *are* men – believe that the laws of physics are suspensible in their case, and that the inertia of a moving car is inversely proportional to its cost . . .

159 Isolated by perfumers as the characteristic odour of galbanum, the gum of *Ferula galbaniflua* and *F. rubricaulis* (*Umbelliferae*, natives of Iran and Afghanistan), and, more specifically, as the molecules 3(E), 5(Z)-undecatriene and 2-sec-butyl-3-methoxypyrazine. How curious that things which smell so beautiful should be named with all the clumsy galumphing practicality of sad girls at school dances; how much stranger that the scent of hope should grow in the Axis of Evil.

160 The world's largest asphalt lake – where the first asphalt used in America came from – was discovered on Trinidad by Columbus on his third voyage of 1498. And so the man credited with discovering America (but who refused to accept that he had done so) was also crucial in discovering the means to get around the place (but didn't realize it).

place is the inhuman rattle and clunk of the skeletal, creepy, Derailleur gear-train with its greasy trouser-legs, its sudden precipitous disengagements (hurling the unwary child, standing on the pedals for a rapid getaway, nuts-down onto the crossbar), its chain-shedding, its anatomical, brutalist nastiness.

The Sturmey-Archer stood in relation to the bicycle like the adult world to the child: secure, reliable, seemingly uncomplicated, its workings carefully concealed. Obviously it could not last; but nor could the excursions it made possible. Children now ride BMXs or mountain bikes around guarded courses, supervised and dressed for protection; the world has become too dangerous, so danger has to be synthesized in safety; and meanwhile, the works are showing, the choices are perplexing, the chain comes off.

Gloves

Loss and gloves are inextricably linked. If you have ever worn gloves, you have lost gloves. Never mind THE DOG; our gloves are the first to go. Given their evanescence, it is worth noting these points:

1. Driving gloves with string backs, to go with your car coat. These are COMMON.
2. No man ever successfully wooed a woman while wearing woolly gloves.
3. No LADY ever goes out anywhere without gloves nor has done since the twelfth century.
4. A present of gloves to a woman is an unequivocal sign of sexual intentions. If she accepts them, she accepts the giver, too.
5. The gloving room at Hampton Court Palace still smells of the perfumes used to scent the leather: ambergris, musk, civet.
6. The perfume industry at Grasse grew up around the scenting of gloves. Originally the town's main industries

were leather-tanning and glove-making; perfumed gloves caught on, Grasse supplied them, and the business of scent overtook the business of leather.

7. The oldest perfume in production is said to be *Peau d'Espagne* from Santa Maria Novella in Florence. It belongs to a family described as 'leather' scents, not because they smell of leather but because leather smells of them [161]. *Peau d'Espagne*, for example, smells primarily of birch, linalol from the Amazonian 'pau-rosa' plant (*Aniba rosaeodora*), and of lavandin, extracted from *Lavandula hortensis*, a 1900 hybrid cross between true and spike lavender.

8. The Comtesse d'Aumont created a spicy, mace scent to perfume her gloves. She was held to be an alchemist and burned as a witch.

9. Gloves were introduced into England after the Norman Conquest as a badge of rank. Throwing down a glove was an unequivocal challenge.

10. Queen Elizabeth I wore long, ornamented gloves which she took off and put on repeatedly, with studiedly elegant movements. She also wore them when playing the spinet.

11. Long ('opera') gloves were popularized by the Empress Joséphine. Although they may be the most erotically alluring garment ever invented, the Empress wore them not to increase her allure but because she thought her hands ugly.

12. As did Vivien Leigh.

13. Until the 1930s it was *de rigueur* for anyone with pretensions to class to be buried in gloves.

14. We still speak of kid gloves though they are almost impossible to find.

---

161 If it didn't smell of leather scents, leather would smell of leather, which is pretty rank and corpse-y.

15. We still speak of casting someone aside like a soiled glove even though we do not cast aside our own soiled gloves (if we have any).

16. It is not elegant to have your gloves looped up through your coat-sleeves on elastic. Better to lose them altogether.

God

'God? *Gone?*' you may cry in alarm. But it is true, at least partially. The greatest difficulty we face in understanding the past is the idea that religious faith of some sort was, intellectually at least, ineluctable. You had no option. Even apparent rationalists like Descartes or Newton got upset when they found their reasoning threatening to remove God from their picture of the world, because to remove God was to pull the ontological rug from beneath their own phenomenological feet. *There was simply no alternative.* Only recently – in the last blink of an eye, in terms of human history – have we had any way of dealing reasonably with a universe relieved of the awful presence of God.

Now, though, we do have a satisfactory alternative, and, armed with the ideas of natural selection through random mutation, of complexity as something which can emerge from simple systems arising by the operation of NORMAL probability, of the application of textual scholarship and historiography to 'sacred' texts, and of an understanding of the physical underpinnings, if not of the entire cosmos, at least of our place in it, God has become optional.

And an optional God is a weakened God, and a weakened God is no longer an omnipotent God. The spaces left which require God to fill them are now so small that we may see this once-tremendous and ineffable creation of ours (how obvious, how wonderful God was when we first shuffled, thinking, onto the ancestral savannah! How clearly He had made the world, and made it for us, because he *wanted* us, and wanted us to be *happy*!) reduced to the status of an alternately chummy and capricious ghost.

In a less developed world than ours, God's defenders would block their ears and minds, and hum loudly to drown out the noise of reason for fear that they might find it harsh and be driven to madness, and the greatest geopolitical power in history would stand with its religious finger in the rational dyke, suffering grief and monsters rather than rethink its first principles, while lesser powers would live in intellectual subjection and kill and die for their own tribal interpretations of the precise nature of the dethroned god.

Finally liberated from the Great Succubus, though, we can at last be free to celebrate ourselves, our diversity and creativity, and the magnificent impersonal random luck that brought us here: to create great art and drama and literature and music to enrich our own and only lives. Can't we? Can't we? Can't we? Can't we . . .?

Gods, The

Once, there were many gods and goddesses of varying functions and degrees of competence. There was Hermes and Tajika-no-mikoto and Ops and Mader-Akka and Ma'at and Nanook and Quetzalcoatl and Tekkeitserto and Anubis and Frigg and Aphrodite and Africa and Thor and Lennaxidaq and Apollo and Artemis and Selene and Ghidjja and Yhi and Odin and Jupiter and Isis and Marduk and Kibuka and Acuecucyoticihuati and Zeus and whatever you're having yourself, and they all existed in negotiation with mortals and each other and with mortality itself, and some were fond of a nip and others were shapeshifting knobhounds with the continence of weasels, and some liked their food raw and others liked the smoke of it burnt, and some liked the smoke of it burnt alive, and some lived on screams and some held butterflies between their lips as they kissed young warriors on the battlefield.

And then one day, some thousands of years ago, the greatest intellectual and disputatory people the world has ever known looked about itself and said, Hold on, this is very, very inefficient. What we require is *one* **GOD**, and He shall have a Capital Letter because He is so important – indeed, He is too important even for that, so He shall have one Capital Letter and one small letter and one no-letter-at-all and He shall be called **G*D** and into G*d shall be amalgamated all the little gods and they will stop their squabbling and they will *most certainly* stop coming to Earth and seducing our women and metamorphosing and generally behaving like nebbishes, and G*d has chosen us to tell everyone this extremely good news which benefits everybody providing they pull themselves together and don't fuck with us any more, ever.

But unfortunately they forgot to patent it. And . . . well, see **GOD**.

Golly, Mister

Golly had to go. Lamentably; but this is a vale of tears, and so, it turned out, was Enid Blyton's Toy Town.

Mister Golly's crime was being black. People thought it was rude, him being a caricature and called 'golliwog'. Wog! It's got 'wog' in it! That's *rude*. Worse than rude. Worse, even, than *offensive*[162]. What it is, is *inappropriate*: a smug, purse-lipped word which the professionally self-righteous can use as a cloak beneath which to don their neo-Stalinist robes.

Never mind that 'wog' was never used for black people. Never mind, either, that, if Mister Golly was a hurtful example for

162 Who are all these people so easily offended? Have they lost their *wits*?

black children, what sort of example did Noddy set for white children? Or, damn it, his *very* peculiar friend Big-Ears for men[163]? Golly had to go. And the excuse to get rid of him seemed to be that, as owner of the Golly Garage and Noddy's employer, Mister Golly quite properly lost his temper when Noddy kept honking the horns of the cars he was cleaning.

You can see why he had to go. A kind-hearted, successful businessman, a productive member of Toy Town society, who takes good care of his workforce but, all the same, insists on standards and discipline in the workplace – even if it means chewing out a *white boy*? We can't be having that. Wrong impression entirely.

So he was deported from the books, stripped of his business, and replaced, like a doctored photograph, with Mr Sparks, a splenetic, camp, porky and, above all, *white* man in a bully's bowler. Elsewhere, Mister Golly was replaced by Dinah Doll, 'a black, assertive, ethnic-minority female'. And all the other Gollies were obliterated, too; even tiny figures at train windows. And Golly Town was razed. Obliterated: Monkey Town built upon the ashes: *Damnatio Memoriae*.

Presently, even the jam makers Robertsons removed *their* Golly from the jam jars and no more will children save up labels for the little enamel badges: Sailor Golly, Pilot Golly, Nurse Golly, Astronaut Golly, Policeman Golly, all rather good role models, one might have thought.

Guilt? Stupidity? An inability to do JOINED-UP thinking? Or just *courtesy* gone mad? Who knows . . . but Golly had to go.

And he went.

---

163 Big-Ears got it, too. Offensive to people with big ears. (Perhaps that's why Tony Blair eschewed public life.) Now he is 'Whitebeard'. Are men with white beards up in arms? To hell with them. They don't count.

Grail, the Holy

The Holy Grail is the other Lost Thing. What's the *other* other Lost Thing? Oh, for **GOD**'s sake, see the **ARK OF THE COVENANT**.

Greek, Ancient

No culture has ever been as extravagantly praised, nor any language so fawned upon, as that of ancient Greece; or, more specifically, the Athenian city-state. **LATIN** was, for centuries, the *lingua franca* of the literate West, but it was Greek which contained the magical seed of distinction, and knowledge of Greek which, by some curious linguistical osmosis, imparted scholarship and, presently, marked the Gentleman[164].

It is one of the most expressive and aurally beautiful of all languages; but, from the nineteenth century (once the swooning Hellenophilia of the Romantics had been ground beneath the utilitarian feet of Progress) there were moves to dethrone it from its position as a prerequisite of entry to the great English universities. At the end of that century, a motion was placed before the Senate of Cambridge University to abolish compulsory Greek: it was a *cause célèbre*, with voters being whipped in from every backwood, shire and fastness in the country and beyond. The trains disgorged hundreds upon hundreds of voters, convinced that the abolition of Greek would be almost the abolition of the University, and the motion was defeated.

---

164 In an extraordinary and moving interpolation, Tony Marchant's adaptation of *Great Expectations* for the BBC had Pip recite, to the dying Magwitch, a passage from Homer, in ancient Greek. This was proof, to Magwitch, that he had at least succeeded in his one great ambition: to make Pip into a gentleman, and that, in his last moments, Magwitch could not understand what Pip said: thus was the implicit made explicit. But who would know that now?

142

The First World War was the last flourishing of the Greek ideal, and children of seventeen and eighteen marched off to die in the mud with Homer in their knapsacks. The guiding ikon of the gilded Pindaric youth, brave in arms as he was noble in peace, could not survive the impact of gas gangrene, of mud and machine guns, gas and trench foot. The jig was up for ancient Greek as the foundation of our civilization.

Shortly after the war ended, the motion was again placed before the Senate.

It passed almost without opposition.

Handkerchief, the Gentleman's

Not to be confused with the ladies' handkerchief (a pointlessly delicate little piece of frippery useful for nothing except dropping[165]),the handkerchief used to be an essential part of a man's attire. Men got them for Christmas, monogrammed; where they were carried was an infallible class marker (tucked in the sleeve for gentlemen, on the basis that tucked in the sleeve was the most improbable place to carry one, therefore unlikely to be guessed at by the proletariat); brightly coloured, they served to absorb the unwholesome detritus of the SNUFF-taker; worn on the head, they protected the Englishman against the fierce, beating sun of **CANFORD CLIFFS**; tucked in the armpit while dancing, they would later, according to the old **AMERICAN** custom, be presented to his partner, presumably to inspire her devotion with the odour of pheromones, if not of blatant **B.O.** The breast pocket 'display handkerchief' told you that the wearer Would Not Do[166]; if folded according to the

---

165 The perfect example of Lost Delicacy.
166 Particularly not the breast pocket of a **BRITISH WARM**.

Turnbull and Asser method[167], that the wearer was well off, if slightly caddish; if formed of a few starched peaks glued to a piece of cardboard, that he was simply COMMON; if scented with Guerlain's heavenly *Mouchoir de Monsieur*[168], that he would (a) have his hand up your wife's skirt within seconds and that (b) your wife would be rather glad.

Now the handkerchief has fallen out of favour and yet another harmless tool for prejudice, snobbery, and intricate little games has gone for good. You disagree? Ask yourself how *Othello* would have turned out if it had been a Kleenex.

Harmony, Close

From time to time, in strange parts of the world as well as in America, you will come across groups of men, mostly in middle age or elderly, almost invariably either short and fat or tall and thin, dressed identically in blazers of a colour that no sane man would ever wear unless he were (mistakenly) trying to impress a woman.

These men are close-harmony singers in a barber-shop quartet. Quartet, that is, if you can see four of them[169]. Sometimes there are more. Quintets. Sextets. Octuplets. Who knows?

The main thing, though, is that they sing in close harmony, which is, like all other forms of harmony, a dying art; not quite lost, but on the way, lost both to the lamentable decline in public taste and to the relentless introspection of contemporary artistic endeavour. Harmony, as the non-gender-differentiated human person in the

---

167 Hold the handkerchief – silk, of course – by the centre point. Draw it through the finger and thumb to form a peak, as if about to do a conjuring trick; push the peak back through the finger and thumb, forming a sort of mushroomy invagination; place with careful negligence in the breast pocket.

168 Lit. *Mister's Hanky*, which doesn't have quite the same elegance.

169 And not necessarily even then. To see four of them together might just mean you'd seen two-thirds of a barber-shop sextet, the other two having snuck off to buy presents for their wives,

street comprehends it[170], is, my dear, utterly *vieux jeu* as far as 'classical' composers go; and, in pop music, the triumph of rap, hip-hop, drum-and-bass, and all the other technological arts of musical recycling has meant that harmony (and melody, and variety of tempi, and subtlety of colouration, and modulation, and development, and everything else which makes music music apart from the relentless mechanized pulsing of a drum machine[171]) is entirely out of reach.

And it is in close harmony that they travel the world, their original purpose – to amuse themselves while they wait their turn in the barber's chair – having long since vanished thanks to men's mistaken urge to reduce their own faces to the texture of a woman's inner thigh. Soon they will be as much of a curiosity as Bulgarian microtonal folk-singers, itinerant hurdy-gurdy players, accordionists, polka groups and harmonium artists; and all we will have to fear is that they cease to confine themselves to their strange but probably gratifying international convocations and leak out onto the street, singing their larynges out (their hearts having long since turned to stone[172]) in return for money in the hat. A boater, of course.

Hats

A personal, as well as a social, loss, this. When I think of the hats I have lost, or lost track of . . .

---

170 That is, as the silky petticoats which make melody's lovely frock sit perfectly on the figure.

171 An experience, to the discerning ear, a bit like being poked repeatedly in the chest by a bore making the same easily grasped point over and over, while simultaneously being non-consensually sodomized from behind (where else?) by a parking-fine bailiff from Tredegar in a puffy anorak and thick-soled shoes.

172 As whose wouldn't, were the *ne plus ultra* of one's art 'Sweet Adeline', terrible enough sung in unison but apocalyptically grim with addition of any harmony at all, but especially close.

1. A grey fedora from Bates, high-crowned.
2. A straw-coloured velour fedora from Herbert Johnson.
3. A raspberry ditto.
4. A pale blue ditto.
5. A black Fischer velour fedora from Bates.
6. A featherweight racing trilby from Lock.
7. An elephant-grey snap-brim from Herbert Johnson, from the very block used to make Humphrey Bogart's hats.
8. A Stetson 'Gun Club' bound-brim, blown off into the mud outside the Groucho Club in London by Terry Jones.
9. A leather kangaroo-skin cap.
10. A fawn wide-brim fedora from Bates.
11. A white Borsalino 'Sicily' from New York.
12. A pearl grey Calvin Coolidge from Herbert Johnson.
13. A sand-coloured 'Drover' by Akubra, from Darwin.
14. A dun-coloured Akubra 'Birdsville', from the Innamincka Hotel, the only pub in the world with its own hat department.
15. A 'Planter'-style panama from Phoenix, Arizona.
16. A lamb's-fur *tschapka* from Krakow.
17. Many others.

Where did they go, these hats? Thrown away? Stolen? Lost? Lost track of? Vanished by the operation of time? Lost to the depredations of love? Disintegrated? Left behind deliberately or accidentally? In the fate of these hats can be found the entire tax-onomy of loss.

But my hat loss is only a microcosm of the world's. Only in the south and western United States and in Australia do you regularly encounter not only men in hats, but hat shops: not urban-poser hat shops, but hat shops which are there because hats are something you *need*.

Elsewhere (outside the military) you seldom see a hat, apart from the vile, proletarian, gum-chewing, shouting-in-the-street, bum-cleft, baggy-trousered, back-to-front, I-am-an-inarticulate-moron, why-don't-you-punch-my-lights-out-and-choke-me-on-the-cord-of-my-iPod baseball cap, which is such a negligible item, worn by such negligible 'people', that it is impossible to have strong feelings about it.

Real hats, though, have all but gone. When did you last see a homburg, without which no doctor fifty years ago would have been able to practise, his hat making good the inadequacies of his **MATERIA MEDICA**? When did you last see a trilby, outside the race-course? When a fedora, a bowler[173], a balmoral; a tam-o'-shanter, a Bombay Bowler, a pork-pie or a floppy-brimmed wideawake[174]? It simply doesn't happen; and to walk the streets with your head properly shod invites cries of 'It's George Melly/Indiana Jones/Doctor Who/Crocodile Duneffingdee' and raucous chants of 'where did you get that 'at, Where did you get that 'at?'

The sad desuetude of the lid or titfer is a cause for curiosity as well as regret. How can something so simple yet so stylish have simply gone away? Look at any crowd photograph of the 1930s or 1940s: a sea of hats. In the 1950s, they were fading a little, helped by sad variants from **DUNN & CO** in corduroy and unper-suasive tweed; by the 1960s, there was hardly a hat to be seen.

Now they are the preserve of old movies, or of idiosyncratic film heroes, it being impossible to imagine Bogart or Indiana without his hat[175]. And yet the hat is a sad loss. Never mind its

---

173 The best ones coming from Lock of St James's Street, but if you ask for one they won't sell it to you, because in Lock's, it's called a Coke hat, after William Coke (later Lord Leicester) who first commissioned one. And if you ask for either in America, you won't get one, because *there* it's called a Derby, after Lord Derby. Hatting would be a lot simpler without lords.

174 So called because its smoothly finished felt had no nap.

175 There is a whole website informing people how they can get themselves up to look just like Indiana Jones, ignoring the fact that people who are likely to be obsessed with looking *just precisely like Indy* are equally unlikely to look anything like him at all.

practicality in keeping off the rain or protecting the head from the sun; never mind, even, the sheer *style* a hat imparts to the wearer[176]; a whole lexicon of distinction has been lost. The hat was a great signalling device, indicating one's attitude to others by the decision to doff, touch, lift, or take off and hold in the hands. The screenwriter William Goldman, in *Adventures in the Screen Trade*, cites as an example of perfect economy a scene where a man is in an elevator with his wife. He is wearing his hat. The lift stops and an attractive woman gets in. The man raises his hat. This, says Goldman, tells us everything we need to know about the relationship.

Alas, Goldman is wrong. A man would remove his hat if he *met* his wife in the street, but if they began to walk along together, he would replace it. And an elevator is considered a room; a man would always raise his hat to a woman, even if he did not know her, under such conditions. (Had the mystery woman appeared in the corridor – a version of 'outdoors' in hat etiquette – he would have had no need to raise his lid.)

The rules are wonderfully complicated. American men tip their hats to strangers, but not friends, except in the West, where to tip your hat to any man is asking for a fight; it suggests you regard him as a woman. Quakers wear their hats in the meeting house, and Jews cover their heads when addressing **GOD** directly, in the synagogue or at Shabbos supper (devout Jews cover their heads at all times, since the whole of life is a continuing discourse with God[177]). Catholic women wear hats in church; the men remove theirs.

---

176 Though it is important to wear one's hat, not to be worn by it: a mistake beginners cannot help but make. The only answer is persistence. Eventually the tyro will find he is just wearing his hat, rather than, self-consciously, Wearing His *HAT*.

177 Not to mention with each other, as in the case of the great rabbis, who argued so much with God and each other that presently, lost in the virally replicating network of their own disagreements, the rabbis ceased to be mere men and became the sum, not of their thoughts, but of their dissensions. Like intellectual sharks, they had to keep arguing or die.

The uses of a hat are many and strange: water bucket, vomitory, campfire bellows, sleep mask, collecting box, and, above all, signalling device. The modern man, seeing a friend across the road, must risk death in crossing it, or forego the encounter. His hatted forebear would simply have removed his hat *and held it in his hand*, signalling to his friend that he intended to join him for a chat just as soon as the traffic permitted. In *Scouting for Boys*, Baden-Powell claimed to be able to tell whether a man would pay his debts by the angle at which he wore his hat; probably as good a predictor as any computer-generated credit rating. Above all, the hat encouraged the powers of discernment between friend, stranger and acquaintance; between the man and the gentleman, the LADY and the mere woman, between inferiors, equals, and superiors; the social divisiveness being levelled out by the use of the lost word, MISTER.

But all things must come full circle. Sooner or later, people will grow tired of compulsory slovenliness and formality will return; and with it, the hat. Let us just hope that there is still someone around who knows how to make them.

Head, Vanishing, The Emperor's

Having written the official history of the Emperor Justinian, Procopius decided to set the balance straight in his alternatively naive and barking *Secret History*. He attributes Justinian's besottedness with his empress, the former courtesan Theodora, to her casting an evil spell on him, so that he continued to desire her despite the fact that she was a promiscuous and insatiable exhibitionist – never considering that Justinian's devotion might not be 'despite' but 'because of'.

But that was relatively straightforward. More peculiar by far was his observation that 'Justinian's head would momentarily disappear' while the rest of his body continued pacing around the room. '[L]ater the head returned to the body . . . contrary to expectation, filling out again.'

We no longer have rulers like that, at least. Although . . . no. No. That's just a *silly* idea, and we'll have none of it.

Incomprehension, Absolute

The idea that our words, once written down, may die with us – or, at any rate, some time after us – is strangely foreign to us. Once a language has risen up, it can never sink down again into utter incomprehensibility; even the murkiest of tongues has yielded to scholarship, surely? Think of Egyptian hieroglyphics; think of the Mayan glyphs of Central America; think of Linear B, found in the Labyrinth of Minos, silent for millennia but finally decoded.

But think again. Think of the Sudanese Meoitic, the Etruscan; think of Linear A from the Aegean and the proto-Elamitic of Iran. Undeciphered, their words lost[178]. What did the people of Easter Island have to tell us in Rongorongo, or the writers of Zapotec and Isthmian scripts from Mexico? What might the Indus script of Pakistan reveal to us (we must pray it is not the WISDOM OF THE ANCIENTS)?

Language tells us more than it says it is telling us. Think of Henry Rawlinson climbing a mountain at Bisitun to read the cuneiform inscriptions of Darius the Great of Persia, the first time that Old Persian had been written down: the deciphering of cuneiform scripts revealing an ancient world of over half a million square miles, bound together by a web of cuneiform documents, not just diplomatic correspondence but accounts, legal contracts, astronomical observations, histories, theologies, medicine and magic. Nineveh may have sunk beneath the sands but as long as the words remain, it too will remain. But lose the language and everything is lost.

---

178 Though quite possibly very dull words, about goats and bride-prices. But all the same . . .

Invention

J.C. Boyle's automatic self-raising hat. G. Singer's self-ventilating rocking chair. Lillian Hoover's scrotum-supporting bowls. M. Goetze's dimple-producer. Julian Fogg's Patent Coffin. Thomas Burghart's Thief Trap, a comfy chair which automatically manacled your friendly local fat-bastard burglar when he paused for a nice sit-down[179]. The gas-powered pogo stick, the self-back-patter, the Nuclear War Camp Site, the Dog Protector, the birthday cake candle-blower-outer, the, **GOD** help us, 'Lap Dance Liner', a device for secretly wanking in lap-dance joints[180]. The laser-powered shaver. The mouth-shaped urinal. The 'protective device for storing and transporting a banana carefully'[181], which

> 'includes a container having a first cover member and a
> second cover member being hingedly[182] attached to the
> first cover member and being adapted to store a banana
> therein; and also includes pad members being securely
> disposed upon the first and second cover members for
> protecting and cushioning the banana . . .'

And this is not a joke. You can buy one from As Seen On TV in

---

179 See www.patentoftheweek.com and www.patent.freeserve.co.uk for a full range of naff patents.

180 The people involved with this enterprise need to be recorded: US Patent 6,406,462. Primary Examiner: Dennis Ruhl. Gene Scott of the Patent Law and Venture Group. Inventor: Wesley Johnson of Burbank, California. People will do anything for money – but the legalese! The jargon! The pompous citations! The disclaimers! The notices! And all so that repugnant herberts can toss off in reeking lap-dance joints without their wives noticing semen stains on their powder-blue nylon underpants or their polyblend trousers. It's enough to bring the law into disrepute (although the law needs no assistance in that area).

181 US Patent 6,612,440 of 2 September 2003. Primary Examiner: Mickey Yu. Assistant Examiner: Troy Arnold. *Two of them*. One so hopes that when their spouses said 'Hi, honey; what did you do today?' they told the truth.

182 'Hingedly'? *'Hingedly'?*

151

Toronto, or Market Kitchen in Vancouver. 'Are you fed up with bringing bananas to work or school only to find them bruised and squashed? Our unique, patented device allows for the safe transport and storage of individual bananas, letting you enjoy perfect bananas, anytime, anywhere,' says the website breathlessly, because there is, of course, a website, and you can buy one there, too[183].

And so the parade of state-protected lunacy goes on, with the Bouncing Christmas Tree, the Electro-Ejaculator Probe, the Pneumatic Shoe-Lacing Apparatus, the Bogus Wheel Clamp[184], the Chin Dildo, the Combination Cup and Spittoon, or even the wild insanity of the User-Operated Amusement Device For Kicking The User's Buttocks:

> An amusement apparatus including a user-operated and controlled apparatus for self-infliction of repetitive blows to the user's buttocks by a plurality of elongated arms bearing flexible extensions that rotate under the user's control. The apparatus includes a platform foldable at a mid-section, having first post and second upstanding posts detachably mounted thereon. The first post is provided with a crank positioned at a height thereon which requires the user to bend forward toward the first post while grasping the crank with both hands, to prominently

---

183 Which must annoy British Telecom. This astonishingly unpopular company would have stopped you doing so, or at least charged a licence fee, if it had succeeded in one of the most crassly opportunistic legal claims of all time: its attempt to patent the hyperlink.

184 Looks like the real thing but the 'ticket' on the windscreen contains an advertisement. How pleased your potential customers will be! But, like so many patents, this one – US 4,422,633 – has a despicable underpinning. 'This invention,' says the Abstract, 'relates generally to novelty devices which do not function in accordance with the function normally associated with their external appearance . . .', effectively giving the patent-holder the right to demand money from, or shut down, anyone who makes anything which masquerades as something it isn't.

present his buttocks toward the second post. The second post is provided with a plurality of rotating arms detachably mounted thereon, with a central axis of the rotating arms positioned at a height generally level with the user's buttocks. The elongated arms are propelled by the user's movement of the crank, which is operatively connected by a drive train to the central axis of the rotating arms. As the user rotates the crank, the user's buttocks are paddled by flexible shoes located on each outboard end of the elongated arms to provide amusement to the user and viewers of the paddling. The amusement apparatus is foldable into a self-contained package for storage or shipping[185].

But who was the greatest of them all? There is a faintly delicious symmetry about the career of Arthur Pedrick who, after a lifetime working as a UK Patent Examiner, retired, went happily mad, and spent the rest of his life applying for lunatic patents which his old employer, perhaps out of some sense of solidarity, astonishingly granted: the plan to pipe snow from the Antarctic to irrigate the Australian deserts; the horse-powered car, the 'television tower with revolving restaurant, airship-mooring mast and a transparent globe for transcendental meditation [with] tanks in the tower for the gravity supply of beer to the surrounding district'[186]; the system for ending the cold war with automatic nuclear bombs; and (among his selection of patents

---

185 Distinguished from previous, less sophisticated devices by keeping going, unlike, for example, 'U.S. Pat. No. 920,837, issued to De Moulin, [in which] a device is disclosed for lifting and spanking of the user for secret-society initiation ceremonies.' The world is an infinitely stranger place than most of us can dream of.

186 As the author of *Patently Absurd!* (www.patent.freeserve.co.uk) observes, 'Pedrick envisaged a world-wide system of such towers. If you were rich enough, you would be able to spend your entire life off the ground level, moving from one tower to another in airships fitted with sleeping accommodation.'

based upon his belief that physicists had got physics entirely wrong[187]) a patent for 'Using Electrostatic Levitation To Reduce The Resistance To The High-Speed Movement Of Ice- Or Oil-Filled Balls In Tubes With An Explanation Of The Enigma Of The Nucleus Of The "Splittable Atom".'

Close; very close. But the palm and the laurels must finally go to the even more barking Winifred G. Barton, who obtained Canadian Patent No. 2,010,312 for the 'Cosmic Cube':

> The 'Cosmic Cube' creates cubical wavefields by an entirely novel method of technology. Working across a time axis, it correctly identifies and cristalizes all components involved in any project. It is universally applicable and quantums the competitive edge of the user. It establishes a mathematically precise cause-effect solution to within .0007% accuracy by the use of 72 interrelated electro-magnetic circuits. These have 144 entree-exit windows which can allow a single or multiple user (individual, group, profession, corporation, village, town, city, province, nation etc.) to plot a precise course of action, and get a full cause-effect diagram, graph, printout, bilan spreadsheet, free of human error, before a project is started. In scale it runs from the simplest maths of 2+2=4 to E=mc3. [*sic*]

And just in case you haven't quite got it:

> In those days[188] Egypt was known as 'The Land of the Mr' which is the meridian triangle of the pyramid. (See Kepha-a-Ra, c. 147795 Winifred G. Barton, 1974.) In essence, 'Mr' means a right-angled triangle, with one

---

187 A belief apparently shared by Pedrick's cat, and collaborator, Ginger.
188 Which days? She doesn't say.

angle of 36° and another of 54° of a pyramid whose hypotenuse is the apothem . . . In Cube Geometry, the triangle is the basic building block, duplicating the Cosmos. This method of geodic survey was used for all planning in the ancient world. It was demonstrated by Chemist Dr. Marcel Vogel in a cristology [*sic*] thesis which won him a Nobele [*sic*] Prize, for the pyramidal 'Five-brain cluster'[189]. The Cube's 'Command Cristal' is built to these specifications. It resonates at V.P.S. 55x10^3.

Well, it would, wouldn't it? Stands to reason.

Jantzens

Imagine swimming trunks and bathing costumes made before swimming-trunk and bathing-costume technology arrived. Imagine them made from a sort of wool which absorbed ten times its weight in water, so that when the wearer rose from the sea, he (if male) would be debagged by gravity and she (if female) would be sporting a gangsta knee-crotch and the belly of a drop-sical Falstaff. And yet they were yearned for. They were *so* yearned for.

Joan, Aunt

Anyone born before 1960 will have known Aunt Joan, or a vari-ant of her. Neat, effective, cheerful, Aunt Joan's response to the

---

189 In case you were fearing for the sanity and reputation of the Nobel committee, it should be pointed out that no Marcel Vogel is on record as having won the Nobel Prize for anything.

slenderest of pleasures was: 'How lovely!' She lived alone in a little house on a fixed income and did wonders for charity. All her Christmas presents for the nieces and nephews and great-nieces and great-nephews were bought carefully, with thought and love, throughout the year; Aunt Joan never had to make the panic-dash on Christmas Eve, nor did she ever forget a birthday. She was tiny, courteous, well groomed, well loved and lived an orderly life, never causing pain or even upset; and at the heart of this little life was an incalculable loneliness.

Aunt Joan had a secret. It was always the same secret, for all the Aunt Joans: a young man, an understanding, plans, hopes – and a war from which the young man never returned. The end. You kept going, you did your best, you looked on the bright side and remembered that there were lots and lots of people much worse off than you were. How much of what Aunt Joan was, was because of what she had lost – or had had taken from her, Lost in Time of War?

Joined-up, Things Which Should Be But Aren't

It's not just writing. Governments, think-tanks, vainglorious 'con-sultants' and even more vainglorious corporations speak glibly of 'joined-up policy' and 'joined-up thinking' but the truth is that the first thing to go was joined-up writing. Look in any old minute-book and see how the hands change from elegant and almost invariably characterful to clumsy, ill-formed, disconnected and simian, as though a half-set clay Golem had been let loose on the page.

The change occurs in the late 1960s/early 1970s, and seems to coincide with the acceptance of the Biro in schools. Until then, children were taught to write, using first pencils, then dip pens. After then, basic roundhand letter-shapes were imparted, casually as it were, so as not to disturb the little ones' creativity; and then they were on their own.

But perhaps that was a mistake. Perhaps neither joined-up thinking nor joined-up policies can emerge until they are formulated in joined-up writing: not the infinitely correctable digital pokings of the word processor, but the preconsidered writing of pen-and-ink, in which a sentence must first be cast in the mind, then recast, and finally committed to the page, or else the whole folio must be rewritten. Joined-up writing disciplines the hand; the dip pen, requiring constant replenishment, forces pauses for reflection; the computer keyboard disconnects the hand from the brain, and its endless supply of electronic paper hinders the sense of navigation. When everything is electronic and eternally renewable, the gap between the rough draft and the fair copy is eroded; and perhaps it is within that gap that thoughts, as well as letters, are finally joined up.

Knife, Buck

While many of us may wonder just what the hell it *is* with AMERICA, there are few of us who would reach the conclusion that, gosh darn it, the American male has been emasculated. If anything, quite the reverse: the American male, on the world stage, is generally perceived as a support system for weaponry, assembled from testosterone and hamburger, and held together by polyester.

Not, however, according to prominent American knife person Don Rearic. Mr Rearic thinks that all America's troubles stem from the 'Emasculation of the American Male Child'[190], and the emasculation, contrary to the usual method, has been carried out, not by a knife, but by withholding one.

Withholding, specifically, the Buck 110 folding knife, allegedly

---

190 Can't say 'boy' in case them damn bleeding-heart pinko faggot pacifist scumbag anti-paedophilers come a-calling, prob'ly.

a rite of passage for all right-thinking, clean-living, critter-skinning, twig-whittling American boys. They aren't allowed to have them any more. Poor things might, you know, *cut* themselves. And to hell with them cutting themselves; the real problem is they might sue someone.

Rearic may, however, have a point. My first knife was a fearsome-looking miniature bowie, its handle stuffed with lethal tools and the blade tucked in a leather sheath. It was actually my second knife; my *first* first knife was given to me by Nanny Parkin for swimming a width. It was then removed by my **MOTHER** on the grounds that I would have someone's eye out with it. The second first knife was given to me secretly, again by Parkie, as a consolation prize for having my first first knife removed.[191]

Did I cut myself? Yes. Repeatedly. Did I learn how to handle myself in a tight spot? No. I learned to get into fights with great ease but not how to get out of them again. But did I learn how to handle a knife? Again, no. Why, only a week before writing this, I closed my new folding Spyderco Delica on the fleshy pad of my thumb.

But was I *emasculated*? No. So maybe there is something in the theory after all, more than just the faintly diverting picture of American boyhood being returned to a lost sort of **SCOUTING-FOR-BOYS**, Jimmy Stewart, frog-hunting, straw-chewing, prairie-rambling, sunburned innocence by the mere possession of four inches of razor-sharp steel (please state Plain, Serrated or Combo when ordering).

---

191 I have just remembered that Parkie also crept into my bedroom at 5 a.m. on my fourth birthday and muttering 'Don't tell your mother, dear,' handed me my birthday present: a pair of garden shears. Perhaps there was a subtext all along.

Kunzle Cakes

When Christian Kunzle made cakes at the House of Commons, could he have foreseen that, by the 1960s, forty thousand Showboat cakes – never mind the other sorts – would come off the production line every week? They were an odd sort of product: not so much a cake (small, chocolatey, filled with a butter-cream and decorated by hand with a squiggle) as a gesture of benevolent luxury. To be given a Kunzle cake was to be reassured that one mattered. And while, at one end of the chain, stood the great mysterious LEO, the world's first commercial computer, built by J Lyons, Kunzle's owner, at the other stood little Beryl Price, outside Lime Tree Cottage, Walcote, with her mother Minnie, in 1927[192].

Minnie left school at fourteen and went into service with:

> A lady in the village who wanted help in the house . . . I
> [was] paid seven shillings a week, starting at eight o'clock
> each morning until six o'clock on five days but finishing
> a little earlier on Wednesdays and Sundays. It was quite
> a large house and also there was a smaller house next
> door, eleven rooms in all plus the bathroom. I had to do
> all the cleaning and polishing and washing-up for the
> five people in the families but I did have good times when
> the lady had visitors for tea. She used to give me some of
> the goodies, including lovely Kunzle cakes.

Kunzle cakes have gone now, and Minnie has gone now. But the little gesture of luxury at the end of a chain of industrial technology, and of another chain of social inequalities, remains. And as epitaphs go, 'lovely Kunzle cakes' is not so bad.

---

192 You can see her still, at http://www.johnfinnemore.freeuk.com/ wberylprice.htm.

Lady, A

A lady doesn't. A lady is a sort of human female ELEVENTH COM-
MANDMENT, a generalized proscription of jewellery, scent, heels,
rouge, blue eye-shadow, noticeable hairdos, enthusiasms and
appetites. A lady does not dress up. A lady has orgasms only as a
point of good manners. A lady is fond of her children but would
not dream of letting it show. A lady does not make a fuss. A lady
is dying out. A lady is followed to her grave by self-controlled
friends and howling shopkeepers. A lady would have been mor-
tified at the spectacle. *Such* a fuss.

Latin

Have we lost Latin? The Roman Catholic church seems to think
so, and so do schools; once the prerequisite of scholarship and
statecraft, Latin has fallen away from use, and arguably the stul-
tifying early stages of *amo* and *mensa* and the ablative absolute
should not be mourned. Nor are the old arguments – that knowledge of Latin fits a person for logical thought; that the discipline
of learning this most rigorous of tongues[193] makes all other disciplines seem simple in comparison – blessed with any particular
validity.

And yet the language retains a strange beauty not approached
by any other. Perhaps it is that it reveals so many of the roots of
our own speech, English, which has replaced it as the *lingua
franca*; perhaps (more likely) it is that Latin is the language of
command, not only of others[194], but of itself. So structured are

---

193 Or, rather, pens; for Classical Latin was never a spoken language, as one of
    its greatest writers, Cicero, acknowledged when fretting that he was fine in
    speech but wrote (he feared) like a peasant.
194 Latin has no word for 'yes', acquiescence being, presumably, taken for
    granted.

the words themselves that their order in a sentence is almost a matter of caprice, and the subtlest of effects, of demoting or emphasizing or almost banishing a word while keeping the surface meaning of a phrase intact, can be achieved at the cost of endless recasting and eventual lunacy. The great satirist Juvenal reckoned that writing a couple of lines in a day was a good rate of production; and how Virgil – perhaps the greatest writer (in the sense of pure command over his language) of all time – managed it, remains beyond comprehension.

And now we are driving it away. It is elitist. It is dead. It is European. It is white. It is, above all, *male*. And so, by the tenets of the times, it must go.

But what we lose in elegance (and, too, in translation; for it is harder to translate, tightly compressed and endlessly unpackable as it is, than any other language) we perhaps gain in the death of obfuscation. A world in which the *homme moyen sensuel* can only read Horace in translation is also a world in which no lawyer will ever look down his expensive nose and murmur '*De minimis non curat lex*, old chap.' Such a world has its compensations.

Letter, Office, the Dead

To contemplate the Dead Letter Office is to gaze into the abyss; unlike Nietzsche's abyss, which gazes back, the Dead Letter Office whispers like dry leaves, sometimes plaintive, sometimes sibilant: declarations of love, everyday trivia, threats which will never find their target, bills for ever unpaid, invitations which will never now be received. Melville's Bartleby – the office copyist who refused every request with the simple statement 'I prefer not to' and ended up living in the office and, presently, dying in prison – once worked in the New York Dead Letter Office, and perhaps that was what turned his head.

It is, of course, pure NORMALITY that this place should be the fate of a certain proportion of our correspondence. But – like death itself – its inevitability doesn't make it any more acceptable, or any less eerie. Fortunately, though, the Dead Letter Office no longer exists. In 1881 it was renamed the Returned Letter Office to pacify a public which, in its fatuity, insisted upon associating the title with the "Land of the Dead". And now it is slowly fading away as more and more of our business is transacted on-line. Soon, it itself may be undiscoverable. The Dead Letter Office: **404**.

Little Room, The

Absent violent death[195], the Little Room is the modern locus of final loss. It's the Little Room our friends or family will be called into, for a word with the doctor. She will break the news gently and wait for our response. We will turn it over in our mind and say 'I feel that perhaps heroic measures are inappropriate and nature should be allowed to take its course,' or, if more at ease with the jargon, the brutal-sounding but kindly meant 'DNR': Do Not Resuscitate. And rippling out from the Little Room will propagate a sort of clinical Lethe, of interventions withheld, of drawn blinds, lights dimmed and only a matter of time.

But the Little Room can be treacherous with pitfalls. A doctor a few years ago was once confronted with the family of a man who had fallen from a cherry-picker, putting up the Christmas lights in a London street. The poor fellow was beyond hope. 'I am afraid,' said the doctor, 'the news is very grave. His brain has ceased to function. We have done all the tests and he is, in fact, brain-dead. I am very sorry. Now, I know this is the worst possible moment, but I have to raise this: have you given any thought to the question of organ transplantation?'

---

195 We *think* of al-Qa'eda but we'll *get* a seedy pile-up on the A417.

And with one accord they rose and said 'Yes; yes; he *must have one.*'

Laugh . . .?

Logistics

In early seventeenth-century Cambridge, it was Hobson's Choice. Tobias Hobson, the carter, rented horses and you took the one nearest the door; or you took none at all. Now, choice (or the illusion of choice) is everything, and Hobson's descendants cannot be hauliers; instead, they must seem to be different, and so they refer to their trade as 'logistics'. Except they all do; so they aren't different at all. We know they are hauliers. They know they are hauliers. All they have done is come up with 'mission statements' which convince nobody, and lose their dignity[196].

London Particular

Bad PR, the end of the London Particular: that yellowish, catlike fog, celebrated in T.S. Eliot's 'Love Song of J. Alfred Prufrock' and in every Sherlock Holmes film ever made, which gave London detective stories their distinctive quality of English *noir* – or, perhaps, *jaune* – and which so seeped under the threshold of the American consciousness that they named their spiffiest raincoat the *London Fog* and were then surprised when English people were bemused[197].

---

196 I am indebted to Wendy Christian for pointing out that the truth concealed in any given Mission Statement can be revealed by simply inverting its terms. She offers this example: 'This school is a cold and unwelcoming place, whose barely qualified staff pay scant regard to the needs or achievements of its pupils either inside or outside the classroom.'

197 As if British Indians were to wear, in homage to the Old Country, a particularly fine brand of sari called *Unreliable Plumbing System.*

The last true London Particular sat over London – and spread over much of England – for four days in 1962 and might be said to have marked the boundary between the Old Days and the Swinging Sixties[198]. London moved into its future uneasily, sliding on black ice, in a visibility varying from zero to fifty yards, with a scarf around its mouth, the windows closed and the fire banked down. It was the last gasp of the coal-burning, lung-eroding industrial age which created so much prosperity and so many CHRONICS. After that, the Clean Air Act finally took hold; the British coal industry was slowly wound down to oblivion; and Britain shambled forwards towards the bright sunlit uplands, blinking uneasily in the light. Now we look at the black-and-white photographs of the past and we forget that, at times of the London Particular at least, the past *was* black-and-white.

Long Handles, Mirrors on

The train ran from the Hook of Holland to Warsaw and on into Leningrad, but at the Berlin frontier between East and West, it pulled into a covered shed on a bridge, the windows frosted in case we saw them or, more likely, they saw us. Pale, pimply soldiers boarded the train and woke the sleepers. 'Papieren!' they shouted; the cry of the functionary in every repressive régime; 'Papers!' Harsh lights infiltrated the sleeping-car windows; outside, equally pale, equally pimply, but colder soldiers extended mirrors on long handles to look for defectors clinging to the bogies, in case anyone was misguided enough to want to leave the socialist paradise.

Then, one day, the mirrors must have slipped, and the jailers saw themselves, and, seized by the rage and fear of Caliban seeing his reflection in the glass, they turned and hid, and the Wall came

---

198 Although everyone knows – everyone who can remember, at least – that the 1960s actually happened in the early 1970s.

down. The mirrors have gone now; and with them, a whole genre of fiction: the Cold War espionage novel. This leaden-grey border could have been made for fiction: its cold, the hiss of train brakes, the clank of couplings; breath steaming in the freezing air; soldiers muffled in fur and wool; the chiaroscuro of cheap communist cigarettes; the sudden absence of advertisements because there was nothing to advertise: no beauty products, no patent medicines, no cars, no SHOES. Footsteps on silent streets; the snick of a rifle in a watchtower; the TEXTURE of repression in the days before surveillance was reduced to a matter of data on a screen.

But the mirrors on long handles: perhaps these have only been lost temporarily. They are still around, somewhere. Soon, perhaps, they will be exported to the new world leader in surveillance of its own citizens: AMERICA. Surely *they* will have a use for them, even as the rest of us have thrown them away along with torture, absolutism and religious bigotry.

Look-See, a Proper

You knew you had a PROPER DOCTOR when he suggested opening you up for a proper look-see. The manoeuvre was usually in vain, and was in reality a polite way of saying that the proper doctor hadn't much of a clue what was wrong but was pretty certain that you were going to die.

And so you'd go into hospital and the next day they'd have a proper look-see and you'd come round, bleary, vertiginous, disorientated and vomiting, from the proper old-fashioned anaesthetic, into a proper old-fashioned kidney dish[199] and there would be the surgeon, grave with news.

---

199 So called because it was kidney-shaped to fit under the chin, not because you put kidneys in it. You *could* put kidneys in it, but you wouldn't have much occasion to do so because the sort of thing which would involve taking kidneys *out* would be the sort of thing which a proper look-see would reveal as hopeless.

After he had gone, the CHRONICS would gather round your bed. 'They were,' you would say, 'baffled. I was,' you would say, 'riddled. There was,' you would say, 'nothing they could do. They just,' you would say, 'sewed me up again.'

And so you would reach man's estate (in the eyes of those most uncompromising of critics, the Chronics) just in time to die.

Now they can have a proper look-see without opening you up, thanks to MRI[200], computerized axial tomography, PCRs, laparoscopy, bronchoscopy, proctoscopy[201] and all the other -graphies and -scopies of modern science. So now you just die. You don't even get a scar, let alone any chronics to show it to.

LPs

Never mind the large area of laminated cardboard, so welcoming to cover art, or the sleeve notes on the back. Never mind the *smell* of a new LP, because a new LP had a smell, unlike the cool, detached, digitally affectless CD. Never mind the friability, the all-round fragility of the LP, the *tick* of scratches, the more leisurely way in which the needle could get stuck in the needle could get stuck in the needle could get stu*whuuup* in the groove, compared with the frenetic way a CD gets stuckuckuckuckuckuckuckuck . . . no; what passed with the passing of the LP was yet more TEXTURE: the special cleaning fluid, the special antistatic cloth, kept anti-

---

200 Which stands for Magnetic Resonance Imaging, except that it isn't. What it *really* is, is Nuclear Resonance Imaging. But it was generally felt that, if they called it that, patients would cavil. 'Nuclear?' they'd say, 'I'm not getting in no nuclear thing,' and there'd be nothing for it but a proper look-see. (Misunderstandings still arise. A young man recounted the other day that he had been alarmed and disappointed when he had just been slid out of the MRI scanner. When asked why he was looking so crestfallen, he explained to the radiologist that he had expected to be expelled forcibly from the thing, shot out like a human cannonball in the circus.)

201 The proctoscope being defined by all but proctologists as 'twelve inches of stainless steel with an arsehole at each end'.

statically damp in its special box, the little brush for cleaning the cartridge, the counterweighted antistatic roller with integral groove-dusting brush, the careful matching of stylus and cartridge, the mechanical springs and balances of the arm, the satisfying *klud* as the speed switched between 33 & 45r.p.m., the sheer industrial *machininess* of the process, as though putting a record on was almost as complex an art as performing the music or making the gramophone.

Now it's a platter in a slot and glowing numbers on a screen. Like all digital technology, CDs offer nothing but the experience itself. All ancillary value has been stripped away, and how sad to think that the people of the future will never hear the run-off as the stylus moves beyond the edge of the music into rhythmic white noise. When you heard it, and realized that you had been hearing it for maybe an hour or more, and that *she* had been hearing it for maybe an hour or more, yet neither of you had noticed and now neither of you could be troubled to get up and put a stop to it: why, the run-off was the soundtrack of bliss, once heard, never forgotten. The music of the spheres? Certainly: *hhhrrrSCHIK, hhhrrrSCHIK, hhhrrrSCHIK, hhhrrrSCHIK . . .*

Man, Hexamethonium

Picture him:

> He is a pink-complexioned person, except when he has stood in a queue for a long time, when he becomes pale and faint. His handshake is warm and dry. He is a placid and relaxed companion; for instance he may laugh but he cannot cry because the tears cannot come. Your rudest story will not make him blush, and the most unpleasant circumstances will fail to make him turn pale. His collars and socks stay very clean and sweet. He wears corsets and may, if you meet him out, be rather fidgety. He dislikes speaking much unless helped with

something to moisten his dry mouth and throat. He is long-sighted and easily blinded by bright light. The redness of his eyeballs may suggest irregular habits and in fact his head is rather weak. But he always behaves like a gentleman and never belches or hiccups. He tends to get cold and keeps well wrapped up. But his health is good; he does not have chilblains and those diseases of modern civilization, hypertension and peptic ulcer, pass him by. He gets thin because his appetite is modest; he never feels hunger pains and his stomach never rumbles. He gets rather constipated and his intake of liquid paraffin is high. As old age comes on he will suffer from retention of urine and impotence, but frequency, precipitancy and stranguary will not worry him. One is uncertain how he will end, but perhaps if he is not careful, by eating less and less and getting colder and colder, he will sink into a symptomless, hypoglycaemic coma and die, as was proposed for the universe, a sort of entropy death.

Thus 'Hexamethonium Man', described by the clinician Paton in 1954. Hexamethonium, once used in the treatment of, among other things, high blood pressure, has now disappeared from the MATERIA MEDICA, as has Paton's masterly, and curiously moving, style of clinical writing. PROPER DOCTORS could do that, but the skill died with them and now, faced with *The Lancet* or the *Journal of the American Medical Association*, it is best to get the lips freely moving before starting to read, otherwise they are liable to lock up at the same moment as the jaw drops and the brow furrows[202].

And yet . . . it doesn't seem so bad. 'A sort of entropy death.'

---

202 One wonders whether Botox injections would prevent doctors understanding their professional journals at all. The same applies for most scientific disciplines; but not, of course, for readers of management publications, which contain no extractable information in the first place.

It's what the universe has in store for us anyway, and there's nothing either we or **THE GODS** can do about it. One day the sun will go out; another day (if there can be days, once the sun has gone out) the whole universe will go out. And it won't be the Galilean who has triumphed, but the greater principle embodied in hexamethonium, whose Man is the exemplar for us all.

Margie

Margie's gone. She was the National Airlines air hostess. 'I'm Margie. Fly me.' The invitation was too good to miss[203], not least for Wall's, which, with its eye on the British **BREAKFAST** table, relaunched its famously pointless sausages: 'I'm meaty. Fry me.'

Masculinity, Models of, Inadequate

Sometimes it's hard to be a woman, as the blasted song reminds us; but it's always hard to be a man. Men have . . . *gone*. Nobody knows what a man is any more. **GRANDPA BEANS** knew, but there aren't any Grandpa Beanses any more; no place for them in the modern world, and all the alternatives are risible: the bottom-sniffing, drum-bashing sweat-lodger with his dodgy mythos; the Marlboro-smoking cowboy, shovelled to the sidelines by agribusiness and lung cancer; the deep-sea trawlerman, forbidden to deep-sea trawl; the statesman, reduced to a shifty liar, spinning for the boss; the wise old **PROPER DOCTOR**, now derided for his archaic paternalism; the squaddie, the politician's gull, a faker of photographs and a former of human pyramids; the lorry driver, now a **LOGISTICS** operative with haemorrhoids and hypertension; the engine driver, now a lorry driver who isn't

---

203 They didn't have feminism then, and flying was sexy and exciting.

even trusted with his own steering wheel; the pilot, now a 'systems manager[204]', bossed around by computers ... what is a man to do? Worse, what is a *boy* to do, to ensure that he becomes a man?

The answer is: pretend. Women may find this hard to believe, but most men in the contemporary post-industrial West simply do not really exist. Deep inside, there is no deep inside; they are just a shell of carefully calibrated mechanisms to protect them from other men and from their own vulnerability. Gay men have constructed models of an external masculinity, but they are too often minatory, based on submission to the male gaze; heterosexual men are never quite at ease in the world unless partially, at least, separated from it by some kind of ecstasy, whether it is the ecstasy of sport, of the pack-bonding games of business, of scholarship, or, most of all, the nearest men can get to completion and intimacy: perhaps men betrayed the world for too long; now, the world has betrayed them back, and they can only find peace by returning whence they came, briefly, and under sufferance, between the thighs of a woman.

The John Wayne days are long gone, when, as John Bernard Brooks in *The Shootist*, he could answer without hesitation what makes a man:

'I won't be wronged, I won't be insulted, and I won't be laid a hand on. I don't do these things to other people and I expect the same from them.'

Do we long for it? Yes. Do we stop to think what we have gained by the trade? No. All we know is that we have lost something which once we took for granted and knew instinctively.

The poet Rainer Maria Rilke spoke of a time when women would cease to be defined merely as the 'feminine' complement

---

204 And headed inevitably for the Cockpit of the Future which, it is said, will contain one man and one dog; the man is there to feed the dog; and the dog is there to bite the man if he tries to touch anything.

to masculinity, and looked ahead to a new sort of love between men and women:

> [which] will (at first much against the will of the out-stripped men) change the love-experience, which is now full of error, will alter it from the ground up, reshape it into a relation that is meant to be of one human being to another, no longer of man to woman. And this more human love (that will fulfil itself, infinitely considerate and gentle, and kind and clear in binding and releasing) will resemble that which we are preparing with struggle and toil, the love that consists in this, that two solitudes protect and border and salute each other . . .

And is that so great a loss?

Materia Medica

Those Victorian paintings of the Doctor, standing hopelessly consoling at the LAST AGONY. He had no option. He had no drugs. No antibiotics, no immunosuppressant, no antifungals, nothing for cancer, depression, schizophrenia or cardiac arrhythmias, no anti-inflammatories . . .

To see what he was up against, turn to the first edition of *Merck's Manual* in 1899: it ran to a mere 192 pages, much of which, even fifty years later, would seem horribly primitive.

Under *Classifications*: Turpentine for cancer. Arsenic for the liver. Alcohol as a 'motor excitant'. Aconite to quieten the heart, cascara and syrup of figs to move the bowels, carbolic acid as a deodorant, creosote and eucalytptus as a vermifuge.

Under *Indications*: Ulcers – formaldehyde. Typhoid – a bath[205].

---

205 'Agreeable to the patient and reduces [the temperature].'

Prostate – juniper oil. Meningitis – alcohol[206]. Migraine – Guarana. Gleet[207] – juniper oil. Catalepsy – chloroform[208]. Alcoholism – milk, opium[209], an orange[210]. Atrophy – arsenic; strychnine; electricity.

Not mentioned: an apple a day. But no wonder keeping the doctor away once seemed so important.

Maturity

Bogey? Bogey was a mature man. A man in a HAT. They all were. It was what you aspired to: maturity. Then suddenly it changed. If you had been born around the beginning of the Second World War, fate had a particularly nasty trick up its sleeve for you: just as you grew old enough to wear a hat without looking like a child dressing up, to order a convincing Martini, drive a convincing car, snap a convincing finger at a waiter, the rules changed. Suddenly your hard-won maturity was worthless. The paradigm had shifted; youth was all that counted.

The reasons were not hard to find. The opening up of mass markets after the Second World War meant that marketeers wanted, above all else, to find a gullible, insecure, easily led, discontented, foolish, tasteless, evanescent and, above all, ever-renewing target group to sell to. Maturity was no use to them; maturity looked at their hucksterism and snake oil and said: No, thank you; this is of no use to me. And so teenagers were invented and maturity vanished for good.

It is hard to find now. When the President of the United States of America resembles nothing so much as a petulant child got up

---

206 And a bath.
207 Look it up. This is a decent book.
208 Odd. You'd have thought the last thing a cataleptic would want or need would be an anaesthetic.
209 The cure as bad as the disease, you might think.
210 'Slowly sucked, a substitute for alcohol.' Better ban people from eating them in the car, then.

in his daddy's clothes; when the Prime Minister of Britain speaks to his electorate like a schoolboy doing show-and-tell to his little friends; when the range of popular music is largely one rhythm, one tempo, one key and one subject, and that subject petulance; when the great tradition of Western civilization has been infantilized beyond recognition with simpleton language, cartoon slogans, constant *ticking-off* notices, imbecile rhymes, giant porky adults in giant baby clothes wearing giant comfy kiddie-shoes and eating giant kiddie comfort-food: then we know that the very notion of maturity has vanished from our society.

What hope, therefore, do we have in the future for organized religion? For stuffiness? For bossy paternalism? For rigid social hierarchies? For repression? For all those other good things which maturity gave us, and which we must now do without? These are truly desperate times.

Meccano

Alan looks a nice enough sort of chap. Grey hair, T-shirt, neat house (with shed visible through the half-drawn blind). Fiftysomething. The faint look of a man who might fret about the water, abroad; maybe even carry a purifier.

But he's doing all right, is Alan. This is his new house, on his website; this is his Meccano room. Alan is a man of joys. In 1996 he achieved his lifelong dream by buying an almost unused 1950s red and green No. 9 and 9A from Geoff Wright. How many of us have achieved our lifelong dream?

It's Meccano he's talking about: the red drilled plates and green drilled strips and girders and tiny nuts and bolts, the magical screwdrivers, the plans, the gears, the *things you could make*[211].

---

211 And above all, the tiny but perfect 'K'-Type Oil Can, admired for its 'beautiful lines and perfect finish' by the then Prince of Wales.

Erector Set, the American competitor, never quite had the magic. Merkur, from Germany, never had the paint. But Meccano . . . '*Golly*, but it's fun to build Meccano models,' as the boy in the advertisement said, in the days when boys thought like that[212].

Meccano was from Liverpool, invented by a clerk called Frank Hornby and patented (originally under the snappy name 'Mechanics Made Easy') in 1901.

Then, Liverpool was a great seaport and industrial city, Europe's centre for the trans-Atlantic liners. We may picture Mr Hornby, excluded from the palpable virility of steam and coal, tar and hawsers, watching the cranes dip and pirouette on the dockside from his counting-house window. We can imagine him stopping for a drink, listening wistfully to the seamen's lies.

So what he could not have in real life, he made in miniature. A small-scale man's world, for small-scale men. Spend your pocket money on enough parts, badger your dad into buying you a big enough Meccano set, and you could make anything: aeroplanes, cars, pithead winding gear, quarrying equipment. The No. 10 set, in its multi-drawered wooden case, was as far as it went – 'For the boy who has everything' – but perhaps in some undiscovered Platonic overworld there was a No. 11: a Meccano set big enough to build anything. To build *everything*.

The No. 11 was, in truth, Real Life; and the twentieth century of the West was built by men who had been brought up on Meccano[213], and its home-building brother **BAYKO**, an arrangement of rods along which you slid pre-cast components to build seaside kiosks, suburban homes, roadside garages, lifeboat sta-

---

212 Probably an elided form of 'God love me' and nothing to do with **MISTER GOLLY** at all. But what the hell.

213 Much of Manhattan – think of the old elevated railway and those great steel bridges – is hypertrophied Meccano (or possibly Erector Set) made manifest, no question about it.

tions . . . all looking unnervingly the same. Drive along any 1950s street and narrow your eyes: Bayko, writ large.

Bayko is no more; Meccano, too (like everything else), moved from Liverpool in 1979. Though Meccano parts are still made in France and Buenos Aires, Meccano as an icon of boyhood ceased long ago. It's left to men like Alan now, building the models he dreamed of as a child, reading the 'Spanner Club' newsletter[214] and the proceedings of the International Society of Meccano Men.

For boys, though, the great world which Frank Hornby made small has itself grown smaller; and now children dream, not of cranes and beam engines, but of television stardom: the small made great, and time's revenge.

Meerschaum

Meerschaum is gone because the whale is going. They say it's still there: if you are the sort of fool who wants to poodle about with a stone, carved in the shape of a Pasha or a lion or a naked woman or an egg in an eagle's claw, hanging out of your mouth, disgorging smoke, you still can. But it won't be the same. Once, meerschaum was used for the finest tobacco pipes, tipped with

---

214 Not to be confused with the Spanner *Case*, in which a number of big blue incorruptible policemen spent hundreds of man-hours investigating a group of British men who got together, not to bolt little girders together with miniature tools, but to, *inter alia*, nail each others' full-sized tools to full-sized boards; and were told by a very disapproving judge that, whether they enjoyed it or not, it counted as assault and *would not do*. The case then went to the European Court of Human Rights, which in 1997 said it *definitely* would not do, except for a dissenting view from Judge Pettiti, who said that not only would it not do, they should have gone to prison. The mental picture conjured up by the activities of the Spanner defendants is unappealing, of course, while to imagine any judge at all, labouring away at his legitimate gratifications, is to experience an almost intolerable surge of raw lust. Whenever I meet one, I can barely contain myself, and I imagine you feel much the same.

amber, carved with delicacy, cured in a long and intricate process involving – O horror! – sperm oil, warm, fragrant and unctuous, fresh from the great head-cisterns of the sperm whale.

Now, the Turkish government hold a monopoly on high-quality meerschaum, won't sell it to anyone else, and use an inferior curing process which means that the bottom of your pipe may well get sodden and fall out (if the rather nasty plastic stem doesn't snap first). The stem is their fault. The curing process isn't. Sperm oil is . . . protected. Illegal. *Moby-Dick*? Now, it would be a novel about tofu.

And so the meerschaum's glory days are over[215]. The sea protects its own; for though meerschaum is nothing to do with the oceans in which the sperm whales swim, its name (derived from its whiteness and lightness) is. Meerschaum is Dutch for sea-foam.

Melancholy

(1) An excess of black bile, anatomized by Robert Burton, embraced by the swooning Romantics as evidence of their fine sensibilities, now fallen into disrepair, renamed as depression, wrongly attributed to a deficiency of serotonin and cured by infantilizing, self-indulgent 'therapy' and overpriced, addictive drugs pushed on harassed, gullible doctors by unscrupulous pharmaceutical companies which suppress their terrible side-effects in order to pursue their profits.

(2) A crippling disease of unknown aetiology which throughout human history has devoured hope, destroyed lives and, after a period of living death, sometimes relaxed its grip just long

---

215 Though there is, still, someone who makes them in the old way. Where he gets his meerschaum from is as much a mystery as where he gets his sperm oil from. Who is he? His name is . . . actually, no. If you want one that badly, you will find out for yourself.

enough for the sufferer to summon the energy for a merciful suicide; now, at last, frequently curable by a combination of therapy and antidepressants.

Which? You decide.

Mica

The stove had pride of place; not the cooking range, but the stove, maybe dark red, maybe black, with or without a back boiler. It had to be stoked; a coke hod stood beside it, and you could see what was going on inside by peering through the tiny liturgical window-panes glowing reddish-yellowish-brownish; a curious material, Mica. And you weren't to touch it or it would flake and crumble. There was biotite mica, which was black or dark brown, and there was Muscovite mica, which was pale or clear, but it all singed eventually. And behind it was the flame, the lovely heat which (like all heat in Those Days) was confined to a small space where your **MOTHER** stood, getting **CHILBLAINS**. The glow and the darkened translucency was vaguely like **CHURCH** and you used to think that mica was perhaps the glass through which you saw darkly; but now you have put away childish things and know it is nothing of the sort.

Microsoft

Microsoft is, sadly, far from lost [216]. But it is, in a precisely definable way, a loser, and what it loses is other people's lives.

Let us derive a conservative estimate of 200 million computers

---

216 One day it will be two vast and trunkless legs of stone, and we will wonder what its secret was, and how it got away with it for so long. Until then, it must simply be endured.

installed worldwide[217]. Let us take, also, the estimate of approximately five hours per computer lost each week to people's computer problems – crashes, viruses, incomprehension, upgrading and so forth[218]. This comes to over 114,000 person-years lost *each and every year* because of poor software design, and, given that Microsoft is by far the most successful supplier of operating systems and application software in the world, they must, surely, feel dreadfully saddened by this terrible loss of human time, maybe even, in their benevolent humility, blaming themselves for time equivalent to *one thousand, two hundred human lifetimes* wasted every year.

Not including the time wasted by Microsoft executives, worrying about it. This is a lot of irreplaceable time. Perhaps we should sue someone; but we just do not have the time[219].

Minerva, the Shield of

The Emperor Vitellius reigned for less than a year, in AD 69, but ate as much in that year as most men do in a lifetime. We shall not see his like again; nor shall we see his menus again, particularly the one in which he excelled even himself in gluttony. Here is Suetonius on the Shield of Minerva:

> This Platter he filled with an *Oglio* consisting of the Livers of Thornbacks, the Brains of Pheasants and Peacocks, the Tongues of *Phoenicopters*, and the Milky Guts of Mullets; for which the Bowels of the Ocean were Ransackt, from the *Carpathian* Sea to the Streights of *Spain* . . .

---

217 DG figures, 1999.
218 Shneiderman, *Leonardo's Laptop*, 25.
219 Or rather, perhaps *you* should. I don't use the stuff. This book was researched and written without the use of any Microsoft software at all. Such a pleasure; you can't imagine.

'A Man,' Suetonius continues, 'of an unsatiable and bottomless appetite . . . unseasonable and sordid withal.' He should have been living at this hour. Would he care to Go Large? Of course he would.

Mister

Consider the happy Frenchman. However he stands in his relation to his fellow man during the day, come the evening, when the shutters are closed[220], all is equality. And why? Because they can call each other 'Monsieur', a simple formality which smooths the differences between fishmonger and *notaire*, between *rentier* and artisan. English has no such word. 'Mister' alone is either a petition or an incipient threat. Combined with the surname, it indicates the functionary or the petty, burping enforcer. ('Mr Smith?' 'Yes?' 'Mister John Aloysius Podicarp Smith?' 'Ah.') Either way it will not do, any more than OLD CHAP will do. And until the English find an equivalent, their society will be riven with class and snobbery. 'Sir' would do; it always used to do, and the Americans can still operate it successfully; but the English seem somehow to have lost the knack.

Modern, Pride in Being

Perhaps we have just seen too much. Perhaps progress was once all very well, but just went on too long. But now it is hard to think of being modern as something to be proud of. The liberals are self-consciously, ironically postmodern. And the conservatives

---

220 As opposed to after lunch when the shutters were closed for the rather different reason that they were with their mistresses; which, too, nicely adjusted the relations with their fellow men.

want a return to Victorian values. Yet the most Victorian of all values was pride in being modern. Is this full circle, or a Möbius strip? Perhaps we have just seen too much . . .

Moleskine

The egregiously hypersensitive author Bruce Chatwin couldn't, my dear, write a *word*, do you see, unless he had these absolutely *exquisite* French notebooks, *cahiers Moleskine*, which he got from this *perfect* little stationer's in the rue de l'Ancienne Comédie in Paris. And then – it's too too marvellously ritualistic – he would *number the pages* and *write his name and address* on the *flyleaf* together with a promise of a *reward* for its return. Isn't that just too too darling? And one day he went in to buy up, my dear, *hundreds* of Moleskines and, guess what, they'd stopped making them. 'Désolé, m'sieu,' said the perfect little stationer. 'Le vrai Moleskine n'existe plus.'

And that was that for Chatwin, really. He lingered on for a while but the heart had gone out of him and presently he died.

An Italian company brought back the Moleskine in the 1990s and now not an over-sensitive backpacker leaves the shores of **AMERICA** but has its Moleskine in its rucksack; hence a whole generation of travellers who will leave no trace. You see them, poor things, wailing on the Internet: people who, by the cleverest and most specious bit of marketing around, now feel themselves intimidated by their Moleskine notebooks. What can they write (and what can they write it *with*, unless it's a Mont Blanc *Meisterstück* pen just like Bruce used?) that will *deserve* the Moleskine and its heritage of, not just Chatwin, but (so the manufacturers say) Matisse, van Gogh, Hemingway . . .

Let us get this straight.

1: The Moleskine of Chatwin is lost.

2: The new Moleskine is a different thing, its authenticity fatally compromised by its insistence on its authenticity.

3: The original Moleskine was not a carefully marketed designer brand. 'Moleskine' was just a generic waterproof cover.

4: And anyway, it was *just a fucking notebook*. Ça va?

Money

Not the money you lost chasing women or the money you wasted on your pension scheme, nor the money that the government wastes on your behalf on collecting figures which will be equally lost, nor, indeed, the fact that nobody knows where money comes from, or where it goes, or what it even *is*[221] . . . no; this is the money that your bank loses.

Pay in a cheque. The money is taken from the drawer's account instantly, within milliseconds. It will be in your account after three 'working' days. What is happening to it? Are little men in frock coats and battered bowler hats trotting around the City of London with slips of paper and ledgers and bags of coins? Are there vans, with money in, each in its envelope?

Pay in CASH. Pay cash into your account via a hole in the wall. On the other side of the hole, they take it out and count it. When does it appear in your account? After three 'working' days.

Pay money to your credit card. Pay money to your gas bill. Pay money to the truly, truly disgusting phone company. When does it leave your account? NOW! When does it get into theirs? Three, five, *seven* working days. With bank holidays and week-ends, that can be up to ten days when your money is . . . nowhere.

Where is it?

Gone.

They have lent it out, at interest, and never mind weekends or bank holidays; do you think the banks' computers are turned off

---

221 I know this to be true because I asked a banker.

then? Do you think their dodgy borrowers have to pay it all back because it's Sunday? Of course not. It's out there.

It's just lost to *you*.

Moon, World War II Bomber Found On

In consideration of the notion that nothing can be lost until it has been first found (and that beyond the purely lost lies the utterly unknown[222]) we should pay our respects to the *Daily Sport*, which dispensed with the idea that the 'news' should be 'true'[223]. This innovation allowed it to come up with perhaps the most engaging pair of front pages in the history of journalism. In the first, it took a picture of the moon and superimposed a Second World War bomber on it, under the headline: 'WW2 Bomber Found On Moon'. Shortly afterwards, it simply published the picture of the moon, headlined 'WW2 Bomber Found On Moon Vanishes'.

It was, perhaps, a strange rehabilitation of the moon, for so many millennia the site of our hopes, our fears and our romantic fixation. The moon was the locus of love, the harbinger of madness, the home of the Lizard Men with aerials in their heads, the mainspring of the celestial clock, younger sib of the Sun. Artemis and Diana, the Aztecs' Coyolxauhqu and the Mayans'

---

222 Which leads us into the dodgy regions of phony mythology, exemplified by the hypnotically barking H.P. Lovecraft and his *Cthulhu mythos*, the idea being that, Long Before Us, there was another 'civilization' now vanished without trace. Lovecraft expressed himself in such thumping, tortuous prose of, nevertheless, such remarkable predictability that it is hard to distinguish the real thing from the results of the Random Lovecraft Generator to be found at http://briac.net/lovecraft.html. The Utterly Vanished Previous Civilization hypothesis is so appealing that one would love to know whether it's really feasible for a society to vanish without archaeological trace, and if so, how long it would take. Unfortunately I have not been able to find the answer to either question so, for the time being, I would suggest you don't think about it and, if necessary, sleep with the light on.

223 A bit like the *Daily Mail* or *Fox News*, but more honest.

IxChel – Madam Rainbow – Soma, Yarikh, Sin and Khons . . . it was a deprived culture that did not have its moon GODS and myths. It was the private astronomy of endless generations of young lovers who, like Van Morrison's,

> . . . Sat on our own star
> And dreamed of the way that we were
> And the way that we wanted to be . . .[224]

and who can doubt that their own star was always the moon? And despite his later, more prosaic insistence on the immutability of naming –

> Richly cloath'd Apes, are call'd Apes, and as soone
> Ecclips'd as bright we call the Moone the Moone.[225]

– John Donne, as the younger, more libertine Jack, demands of his latest girl:

> O more than Moone,
> Draw not up seas to drown me in thy spheare,
> Weepe me not dead, in thine armes, but forbeare
> To teach the sea, what it may doe too soone . . .[226]

The moon illuminated the grottos of the romantic imagination, the ruins of the Gothic, the doings of the vampire; it curtailed the spadework of the body-snatchers (who must wait for a moonless night) and illuminated the homeward journeys of the Lunar Men of Birmingham, those eighteenth-century philosophical manufacturers who precipitated our modern

---

224 'The Way That Young Lovers Do'. *Astral Weeks*, 1968.
225 Elegie XVI: 'On His Mistris'.
226 A Valediction: 'Of Weeping'.

world. Only in its absence could the headless horsemen like the Dullahan of Ireland go about his headless business; only when it was full could the werewolf – despite his entreaties to friends and family – transform himself and burst forth to do his worst.

But that's all over now. Donne was right: now, the Moone is . . . the Moone. We know too much. Goddesses, werewolves, headless horsemen, lovers, Madam Rainbow: all were superseded by that first clumsy footprint and that first clumsy soundbite back in 1969[227]. Now the moon is whirling rock, all mystery gone; as soon as it had a man on it, it could no longer have a Man *in* it.

But for one glorious moment, there was the possibility that we had been wrong, that, as MacNeice wrote, *World is crazier and more of it than we think*, that there were possibilities of coexistence beyond our imagining once again, that we inhabited a cosmos in which there really could be a World War II bomber, Found on Moon.

And then it was gone again.

Mother

Mothers used to know best. Mothers were Authority. The old business of Wait Until Your FATHER Gets Home fooled nobody: here comes father, knackered after a day wrestling with his MASCULINITY, hoping for some peace, but suddenly cast in the role of headsman, executing summary justice on someone a third of his size without either of them quite knowing why, except that

---

227 Appropriate that the first sentence uttered by a human being on an extraterrestrial body should have been rendered meaningless by human error. 'That's one small step for man, one giant leap for mankind,' said Neil Armstrong. What a difference an 'a' makes. But, there, he was excited.

Mother said so. Mother was safe. Mother was always there. Mother was, if not literally, then spiritually, coated in a light dusting of FLOUR and though things could go wrong, nothing could go wrong.

Now Mothers are their children's friends and share in the sorrows and joys while pursuing independent lives of their own as fulfilled, self-actuating human beings. Sometimes they are on their own, and the *pietà* of our times is a lone mother and her child hand in hand; sometimes those mothers will weep or be distraught or simply not know what to do. Motherhood has always been fraught: like the orgy or the garden, it is always elsewhere, always better before or later. We prescribe paradigms of motherhood in order to first worship, then attack them, but it is *always* the Mother's fault.

But Mother remains Mother. Presently, if we are lucky, we will reach an accommodation; and, later, she will die. And no matter how mad or soppy or grim or capricious she may have been, it is a loss of a different category to other losses. There is the body from which we came, reduced to dust. And from then on, our own course is set. We are headed for the DEAD ZONE and we might as well make the best of it. It frees as it destroys: the mother of all losses.

Moustaches, Walrus

They no longer exist. You simply do not see them. MR PASTRY had one, and PROPER DOCTORS like ELSTON GREY-TURNER, and Grieg had one and so did Kipling, and LATIN masters – lots of SCHOOLMASTERS had them, actually, often yellow-stained with wholesome nourishing pipe smoke – but now you simply do not see them. They no longer exist. Could it be that moustaches are subject to the depredations of fashion? Or that we are so sunk in the cult of youth that the sole purpose of a moustache now – other than establishing that its owner is either a cross

Northerner in a small way of business, or a QUEER (as opposed to a POOF) – is to be *definitely not white*. We have reversed evolution, run against the Ways of the Wild, where the white fur of the silverback gorilla says: 'I have reached MATURITY; soon, perhaps, I will croak, but until then, *noli me tangere*.' Civilization has moved us beyond such bestial *Schweinerei*, and now a white moustache announces: 'I am past it, knackered and all washed up; an old git; kick me in my withered balls, steal my wallet; cry *Wuuuuuuuuuurrrrrrrr* with the exuberance of youth, and shamble off to spend it on McDonald's corpseburgers, alcopops and Beyoncé CDs, for you are the inheritors of the earth and the generation of the lost.'

Muggletonian, The Last

All those sects: the Lollards and the Familists, the Anabaptists and the Seekers, the Socinians, Ranters, Diggers, Quakers and . . . and the Muggletonians.

This is how it comes about: take two London tailors, John Reeve and Lodowick Muggleton. Put them through the Civil War and the roaring furnace of debate and dissension which followed. Suspend – for seven years, at least, between 1650 and 1657 – compulsory Sunday attendance at church. Mix in an unusual sexual levity and a lower-class tradition of promiscuity, and stir well. Result: in February 1651/2[228], Reeve – previously a Ranter[229] – has a vision. God appoints him the 'last messenger for a great work unto this bloody unbelieving world' and thoughtfully provided Muggleton to be his 'mouth'. They were,

---

228 Not a mistake. There was a crossover period at the time between the old and new ways of reckoning the new year. Have we lost that confusion? No; we have merely moved it somewhere else. This book, for example, is being published in the financial year 2004/5 . . .

229 His brother *remained* a Ranter, and died a drunkard, which goes to show.

said Reeve, the 'Two Last Witnesses' of the Book of Revelation, who 'shall prophesy one thousand two hundred and three score days clothed in sackcloth'.

One can see how it caught on, particularly if one considers the theology: the eternal indestructibility of matter, no ghosts or spirits, the death of the soul with the body (until the Last Trump), liberty of conscience, political activism to hasten the millennium, wide tolerance and the supremacy of conscience over ortho-doxy, the obligation to curse reprobates (which saw Reeve and Muggleton thrown into pokey under the Blasphemy Act in 1653) and, in due course, a GOD who no longer intervened in the world and thus was unmoved by prayer or suffering. Milton was said to have been a Muggletonian, but probably wasn't. So was William Blake, who probably wasn't either (though his mother may have been, and his visionary socialist mysticism fitted well with Muggletonian beliefs).

But there was, within the Two Last Witnesses' vision, a flaw: a refusal to proselytizing. The notion of an evangelical Muggletonian was as alien as the notion of an evangelical Jew, with the difference that the Jews had been told off for proselyt-izing by the Romans[230] whereas the Muggletonians derived it from their notions of an indifferent God. The result was inevitable; despite temporary resurgences in the mid-eighteenth century (under the influence of Swedenborg) and in the late 1820s, the overall trajectory was relentlessly downwards: 248 of the faithful attended Muggleton's funeral in 1697, there were just over 100 in 1803, forty-six met in Clerkenwell in 1850, seventeen came to the monthly meeting in 1906, only eight turned up in 1927, and, in 1979, Mr Philip Noakes, of Matfield near Tunbridge Wells, deposited the archives of the sect in safe

---

230 And had gone into a monumental sulk as a result, announcing that, right, fine, if that's the way they wanted it then *nobody* could be Jewish unless their mother was Jewish first.

keeping and ceased to exist, body and soul, pending the Last Trump.

So died the Last Muggletonian; but it is tempting to wonder how the world would now be if all religious sects followed their example, and wrote each other letters instead of evangelizing and going to church.

Nature

We bemoan the loss of Nature, but what do we mean? Are we thinking of something different from the Romantics, who managed, in the flower of their egomania, to insert themselves into their landscapes, not as consumers, but as *causes*, so that Nature reflected *their* moods in the full madness of the Pathetic Fallacy?

Or are we thinking of some **GOLDEN AGE** again, when we think we lived in a sort of harmony with Nature which would come as a frightful shock to any pre-industrial peasant who spent his life at war with Nature and its bugs and stones and blights and mud, its frosts and roots and worms and miasmas, the cold of Nature and the heat of Nature and the rain and the diarrhoea and the sickness and the toothache?

Let us not even speak of the dung, or the early rising.

In this imaginary Nature, the birds are always tweeting and the institutions of mankind are always far away; the weather is tolerable, and there are no bailiffs or tax collectors, no ugly neighbours or roaring cars, no junk TV, no retching leer of grease-spattered burger, no hook-faced chancers or bling-bling chavs, no Endemol TV or *Fox News*, no debt, no horror, no choking fumes. Everything in this Nature is lovely; and we are always the lucky ones.

It could not, in short, be more artificial. It is *virtual* nature, a computer-screen dream definable by what it lacks. The 'natural' landscape we base it on is as much a part of the built environment as the busiest city street, the work of ages and of human hands. And our longing for it is nothing but *saudade*: that Portuguese word which defines a profound yearning to recover something we never actually had.

It's unnatural.

Noddy

A bit like humankind, really, Noddy has lived under threat of the End Time since his inception in 1950. Shortly afterwards, librarians started banning him for not being literary enough. Then they banned him for being too middle-class. By the 1980s, he was being banned everywhere (though allegedly available under the counter at Harrods) for being not just middle-class but sexist, racist and white.

It has to be said that, despite his 300 million book sales, Noddy was a very strange role model indeed; considerably odder than the reviled and finally obliterated MISTER GOLLY. He apparently had a job (as a garage hand) but his attendance was sporadic. He was locked in a perpetual state of pre-pubertal irresponsibility, emotionally labile, fearful, borderline schizotypical. Nor can his sublimated homoerotic friendship with Big Ears – a considerably older, gnomic character who lived in a mushroom with only the most primitive of amenities, and on more than one occasion lured Noddy into his bed – be considered wholesome. He repeatedly exploited Noddy's (unexplained) ownership of a car, and encouraged him to act as unpaid chauffeur for ill-conceived expeditions such as the poorly planned trip to the 'seaside' which, due to lack of a formal risk-assessment, ended with the tent (which they were sharing in a close proximity which must be considered wholly inappropriate) being blown away in a storm which could have been foreseen with even the most minimal of meteorological information.

Noddy lived in a permanently renegotiated, liminal and ambiguous relationship with Toy Town society. He was also the focus of much of the trouble in the area, though apparently enjoyed a special dispensation with PC Plod, the local constable, for reasons which were never clear.

In the end, adjustments were made to the Noddy narrative – for example, the excision of the more lurid bedroom scenes between him and Big Ears – but subtextually things continued much as before. Once, Noddy was (mistakenly) accepted as the symbol of childhood innocence before the realities of the world supervened. Now he has become the bad boy of children's reading, acting out those primal fantasies which have been lost from our everyday lives.

Normality

And surely we are not suggesting that *normality* has been lost? How can *normality* be lost? Normality is, surely, *that which is*, somehow . . . averaged out.

Yes. But what has been lost is the *normality* of normality. Ever since the great French statistician Laplace – driven by the requirement of astronomers to find the precise centre of heavenly bodies from their imprecise and inevitably error-prone observation – produced his alarmingly precise predictions of the workings of the Paris **DEAD LETTER OFFICE**, normality has been a more complex, and more diverse, phenomenon than we could have imagined.

Normality, as Laplace and other statisticians showed, contains within itself those things which might at first appear outrageous, but which are, in reality, merely at the far ends of the famous 'bell curve'. No longer can the deviation from the mean be dismissed as pure aberration: a shift in understanding which should, inch by inch, and **GOD** willing, lead to greater tolerance.

But the consequences are far broader than having to admit that it would be abnormal not to have abnormally tall or short or black or white or clever or thick people. Coincidence, too, is demolished by Laplace's new normality, and much of the ignorant wonder of the world is thereby lost.

Isaac Asimov spelled it out in a celebrated essay, 'Pompey and Circumstance'. It would, he observed, be wildly improbable if wildly improbable things did *not* happen. Given the number of things that *can* happen, it would be equally wildly improbable if there were not wildly improbable coincidences.

Yet when coincidences happen to people, they tell you about them excitedly, before saying 'And what do you make of *that*, then?', the implication being that the dour, joyless rationalist must instantly awaken, shrug off the musty integuments of his intellectual tomb, and greet the world as the inexplicably mystical thing it really is. So, poor C.G. Jung with his 'Synchronicity', which laboriously attempted to explain coincidence as evidence of the Interconnectedness of All Things[231].

The answer to the question 'What do you make of *that*, then?' is, unfortunately, 'Nothing'. A coincidence is like aerial turbulence: when the aeroplane starts rocking and bumping, we are afraid because it feels like the beginning of something much worse. Similarly, when coincidences happen, we instinctively feel that we are in the presence of the Universe revealing its true, infinitely mysterious workings. Neither is true. Turbulence and coincidence are not harbingers, but the things themselves. They just . . . *are*.

Asimov makes his point with the Roman senator and warrior,

---

231 The motto of Douglas Adams's fictional detective, Dirk Gently. And speaking as the model for Dirk Gently, I feel entitled to say, *fair enough, but steady on*. On the other hand, Jung also believed that, when he couldn't find his tobacco pouch, it had been 'magicked away' and constructed elaborate explanations in his mind for how this could be so, just as he did for the workings of the Chinese oracular book *I Ching*, when it would have been simpler to say that, in the first case, he'd forgotten where he'd put it, and, in the second, that it works because everything in it is carefully ambiguous. However, one of the lessons of history is that psychoanalysis and Occam's Razor are uneasy bedfellows at the best of times.

Pompey the Great. Until he was forty-two, everything Pompey did went right. After he was forty-two, everything he did went wrong, to the extent that he ended up beheaded on an Egyptian beach by Cleopatra's young brother. And when he was forty-two?

When he was 42^{232}, Pompey penetrated, illegitimately, into the Jewish Holy of Holies at the Temple at Jerusalem: utterly forbidden for a Gentile, and a cause of amazement because he came out, apparently unpunished by **GOD**. But look what his life was like before! And look what happened *after*! And, whatever you do, *make nothing whatsoever of it*.

Laplace's work helped pinpoint with greater accuracy the centres of planets and stars. He gave us some elegant statistics and some entertaining observations about dead letters and marriage rates.

But more than that, he gave rationalists the answer to mystics. The rationalist (mystics believe) wishes to explain everything. But the mystics believe wrongly. The rationalist merely believes that the only decent way of explaining *that which can be explained* is by reason. Not everything needs to be explained, nor can be explained, because some things are wildly abnormal.

Which is, of course, perfectly normal, and only to be expected.

Which, in its turn, is what we seem to have lost sight of. Or maybe it's just that snake oil and the **WISDOM OF THE ANCIENTS** are comfier.

Opera, Drowned in a Storm

In December 1696, the opera company of Pierre Gautier de Marseilles, a composer, organist and opera director, finished a

---

232 And, yes, I know about 42. I wasn't going to mention it because *it's just a bloody coincidence*.

192

tour of southern France, having performed Lully's *Alceste* in Marseilles, Aix-en-Provence, Avignon and Montpellier. Having already been in prison for debt once, and having had to sell up all his company's properties, Gautier had an eye for cost-cutting, and decided to ship all the equipment, instruments, scores, scenery and costumes back to Marseilles by sea. A storm got up, and the ship, its cargo, Gautier, his brother, and many of the company were never seen again. Opera, that most fugitive of the arts, there reached the heights – or the depths – of its evanescence.

Opportunities, Lost, for Doing Something about Rock & Roll

'It's much too late to do anything about rock & roll now,' said Jerry Garcia. So it is.

Pampaglini, Zelinda

A modest life, Signora Pampaglini's, and, like most modest lives – like most lives, period – more or less unrecorded: when they are over, they are gone[233]. And so we know little about her marriage to Filippo, nor about their life in Perugia; nor, indeed, how they felt when their son Ruggero was born on 20 July 1864. We can assume Zelinda was pleased; we can assume they hoped that their infant might grow up to be a distinguished man. And so he

---

233 Here we might reflect for a moment on the contemporary article of faith that a life not spent in the spotlight of celebrity is a life not fully lived. Might not celebrity and its absurd pursuit be instead a desperate deficiency, a foolish struggle against the inevitability of personal oblivion? Contrast the ambition of so many adolescents to be 'famous' – what at? what as? – with the origin of the word in the Latin *fama*: what people who know you say about you, not how much is said by people you have never met.

did. He went to Perugia University, then to Bologna and finally to Florence, where he graduated in medicine and surgery in 1889.

Before he graduated, though, he achieved every medical student's dream: Ruggero Oddi made a discovery. What he discovered was a ring of muscle fibres by the papilla of Vater, where the common bile duct leads into the duodenum; and for almost 140 years that discovery bore his name. The Sphincter of Oddi: the name has a certain affable charm ensuring that, long after his death, Oddi's name was not only remembered but firmly lodged in the mind of every medic[234].

No longer. Oddi's Sphincter is no longer his, but the sphincter of the hepatopancreatic ampulla, dehumanized in the names of accuracy, modernity[235] and a queer diffuse urge to obliterate the names of Dead White European Males (and see also *Damnatio Memoriae*): a fate he shares with Bartholin, Lieberkühn, Graaf, Wernicke, and Langerhans and, of course, Vater[236] and all the many other lost eponyms – not forgetting, of course, Achilles himself[237].

Pan

Becalmed off the Ionian island of Paxos while sailing from Greece to Italy in the reign of the Emperor Tiberius (AD 14–37, and a thoroughly bad hat), a ship's pilot called Tammuz was hailed by name three times from the shore. He answered; and the unseen voice replied: 'Tell them the Great God Pan is dead.'

---

234 And should it spasm, affability vanishes on the instant, replaced by – literal – biliousness. It's hell.
235 By the body charged with updating the naming of body parts, itself defiantly still called the committee of the *Nomina Anatomica Basiliensis*, though for how long one cannot say.
236 Glands, crypts, follicles, areas and islets respectively.
237 A double loss: his reflex (now plantar) and his tendon (now calcaneal).

Tammuz did so as he presently sailed on, and weeping arose from the shores. But not from the early Christians; they were thrilled. This, they believed, marked the end of the pagan era.

But they were wrong. Ambient music everywhere now chiffs and huffs the breathy horrors of the synthesized pan pipes[238] into our innocent ears, so that we may long for Pan to come back and put a stop to it.

Paris, the Lost Smell of

Drains, BOYARDS MAÏS, steak, anthracite, garlic, perfume, **B.O.** but a peculiarly sexy B.O., not like the English sort which was merely rank; *French* B.O. came primarily from the women (the men smelt of alcohol and black tobacco) and was a musky, civety allure. Now Paris smells like everywhere else, and everywhere else smells of everywhere else too: this is the New Europe. This is what standardization has done. And to think that, just sixty years ago, Europe smelt so different: of blood and rubble and burning flesh.

Park Drive, Five

Five . . . Park . . . Drive.

This is a personal account, and the pauses are important. *Very* important. Five Park Drive? Nothing. A passing whim, a gratification as quick, thoughtless and reflexive as scratching your nose. Nothing. But Five . . . Park . . . Drive? Now *there* is a pleasure, there is a transgression, there is a daring, forbidden luxury, a

---

238 Or 'syrinx', after the nymph of that name whom Pan too was after; the earth-goddess Gaia changed her into a clump of reeds to escape his attentions. So far, so standard. But then Pan plucked the reeds and thereafter blew into them constantly. Many live women can tell similar stories.

dry run for later wrongs. You know you shouldn't. You know it's wrong. But, by all that's sleazy, you're going to do it anyway.

Five . . . Park . . . Drive. The Smirnoff of cigarettes. Vodka drinkers have nowhere to hide. Can't say they're doing it because they like the taste or the bouquet; it's clear they are doing it because they want alcohol. So it is with Park Drive. See someone smoking a Sobranie Black Russian, you think: oho, trying to give an intimation of his exotic tastes. See someone smoking a subtle, oval Passing Cloud, you think: here is one who prizes elegance above vulgar display. See someone smoking a Cohiba Siglo III and you think: punch his lights out.

But see someone smoking a Park Drive (do they still even *make* Park Drive?) and you think: there is someone who needs a fag. It is the choice of the fretful smoker: outside the office in the rain, standing on a sad reef of soggy dog-ends, the breakwater of the lost and damned. It is the prisoner's cigarette, the squaddie's tab, the snout of the moody, perfectly designed to be cupped in the palm behind the truck, up against the fence, in the bogs, round the corner. Three drags and a reeling head.

Park Drive. If you could bottle the smell it would be the smell of the bookie's shop, the B&B, the drop-in centre, the means-test waiting room. If they were French, Park Drive would be those crumbling yellow **BOYARDS MAÏS**. No: crumbling yellow Boyards Maïs which someone else had already partly smoked.

But *then* . . . Park Drive were the symbol of manhood. Cheap, too: all symbols of manhood were cheap when you were twelve, and in case Park Drive were not cheap *enough*, they made them in fives. Five . . . Park . . . Drive.

They weren't called that in the shop, though. In the shop, they were called, in a mutter, 'Fiepardrye' and the shopkeeper said 'What, sonny?' and you said 'Fiepardrye, peas' and he said 'And who might they be for?' and you said 'My Dad' and he looked at you hard and you went red and then he sold them to you. Five . . . Park . . . Drive.

We went halves, Litman and I. You had to watch the outlay on half a crown a week. Then we went to the pictures. We settled in our seats and lit up a Fiepardrye each, and the film started, and we were very very quiet because we felt sick, but it wore off after a bit and by the last reel (film came on reels in those days, little ones, and sometimes it broke, and sometimes the reels would be shown in the wrong order, because we didn't have digital in the 1960s, poor us) we felt like another one but prudence – manly foresight – kicked in, so we shared one on the way out, and went our separate ways: him to be sick in the Market Square toilets (**V.D.** notices and odd incomplete graffiti starting off 'I cannot satisfy my Wife so one Day my Uncle c'), I to be sick in Griffin and Spalding's (grumpily shopping husbands rattling the handle and muttering 'For God's sake').

We reassembled at the bus stop and hatched a plan. We would wrap the remaining two Fiepardrye in a plastic bag and bury them under a stone in the clay-pit near his house. Which we did. So there they were, safe.

They're right about nicotine's addictive powers. It can't have been more than ten months later that we felt the craving come upon us, so we stole his mother's potting trowel ('Where are you going with that trowel?' 'Nowhere') and headed for the clay-pit.

In the intervening months, some smug bastard had erected an entire neat, clean housing estate there; our stone had gone; over two Fiepardrye *belonging to us*, some ambitious executive was sitting, comfortably housed. We thought: how can this be?

The lesson is: the fulfilment of your dreams is built on the loss of others'.

Parsons

In these interesting times, when a colleague complained to me that he had recently been propositioned by the Vicar's husband, pray of your charity for the soul of Percy Dearmer, editor of *Songs of Praise* and author of perhaps the single most enchanting work of churchmanship in history, *The Parson's Handbook*. We barely have Vicars any more, so eager do they seem to be Just Ordinary People; but an actual Parson is a far rarer bird, fast approaching extinction.

Among those rare birds, Dearmer was the glorious peacock. His attitude to religion seems almost entirely a matter of ceremonial; his majestic book displays an extraordinary obsession with shelves and orphreys, the former for putting useful things away on, the latter for decorating chasubles, and strictly to be controlled. Vestries are another preoccupation of Parson Dearmer: 'It is difficult,' he writes plaintively, 'to put up with a single vestry of an eighteenth-century church' and proposes to make the ASSUMPTION that any well-provided-for parson will have at least three at his disposal. On all matters of decoration and ritual, he is stern. 'The parson should set his face against the use . . . of white flowers only on a white day,' he declares. One would like to see one of the current pipsqueaks try such a thing. Later, *inter alia,* he announces that 'there is no room for high dorsels in a church of Gothic architecture' and denounces 'the attempts sometimes made by tailors to reconstruct ancient shapes of the hood out of their own fancies. The idea that buttons should be used is especially unfounded[239]', before going on to declare that 'branch candlesticks and similar frivolities are unlawful' and warning Bishops against 'overlay[ing] the rite with excessive preaching'.

Even with the problems currently facing **GOD**, it is not beyond imagination that the return of the proper parson – Percy Dearmer at their head, like a liturgical King Arthur – would lead to an increase in churchgoing; and, while it might not usher in a new age of universal peace and love, it would certainly knock *Queer Eye for the Straight Guy* off the ratings.

---

239 Supported by a footnote questioning 'whether anyone, except the university authorities, has a right to alter the shape of a university hood'.

As so often – probably as usual, but who's counting? – New Business Terminology is an act of verbal misdirection, a sleight-of-mouth designed to make the poor punter swallow a lie. Sometimes the lie comes from nowhere; in the days of PROPER BANKS people had personal account managers and woe betide them; now they have 'Personal Account Managers' whose job is merely to read out, over the phone, what it says on the computer screen, but have no authority to do anything about anything.

Similarly, there was a time when, if you wanted a HAM SANDWICH on a train, you went to the buffet and the steward would sell you one. This will no longer do, and instead you must go to the 'Customer Service Host' at the 'Refresca Café/Bar[240]'.

All those terms are horrible, and most contain a lie, but the most horrible is 'customer'. Once, the person on the train was a passenger. The word made it quite clear what the deal was: the deal was *passage*; you paid your money and you expected to be taken somewhere.

That clear idea has now been excised. Under the orthodoxy of the free market – a narrow misconception imposed, like all orthodoxies, by those who misguidedly believe in it on those who equally misguidedly haven't thought about it – the only model and motivation for any human activity is the exchange of money[241], and at the ostensible pinnacle of that model stands,

---

240 Which is neither a café nor a bar, and as for the false branding of 'Refresca', it's sheerest balls. Branding exists to direct our choice, as in Starbucks. Hell's teeth, isn't there anywhere else? I'd rather be disfigured than go to Starbucks. When there is no choice – you cannot, on a train, say 'To hell with the Refresca Café/Bar; let's go to the *other* café/bar' – the process is a wearisome and all too familiar exercise in low-rent aggrandizement and infantilization.

241 Though even in that most obsessively free-market economy, the United States, daylight can be seen through the cracks, not least in the euphemism for salary-and-fringe-benefits: 'Compensation'. Compensation for *what*, exactly? (Though given the damage the American corporation likes to inflict on its employees, 'Reparation' might be an even better term.)

triumphant, satisfied and mired in debt, the Customer. Customer Relations are everything. The Customer must be appealed to, consulted, focus-grouped, cosseted, cared for, placed at the apex of everything you do, and treated as the most important part of the entire organization . . . and if you can fake all *that*, you've got it made.

Because faking is what it is. There is not a business[242] on the planet that does not secretly[243] despise its customers; it's just that sometimes it comes out into the open.

Which is what it did when the railways changed from talking about 'passengers' to talking about 'customers'. With passengers, it's a two-way exchange: they pay, and in turn they expect to be taken somewhere. Customers? Customers are there to fulfil the duty of the modern citizen. And that duty is simple.

The duty is: to pay, and to take what they're given. Everything else is just lies and marketing.

Pastry, Mr

Mr Pastry – Richard Hearne – was a comedian who first appeared on the Baird television system in 1936. His TV career lasted over thirty years with a variety of material that would last a MODERN performer, under the modern demands of the modern market, about a fortnight. Famous for his flapping coat-tails and white moustache, Mr Pastry's most celebrated turns were *The Handyman* – you can imagine, and you'd not be wrong – and *The Lancers*, a piece of balletic slapstick in which he danced through

---

242 And I use the term broadly. Have you any idea how much actors despise the audience? Of course they do: they're up there, performing (even though it's rather COMMON to perform), while we're down there watching. Of *course* they despise us.

243 Or not so secretly, in the case of banks, telephone companies and anyone with a customer-service CALL CENTRE.

an imaginary ballroom with an imaginary series of partners, completely out of step. If you want to picture him more clearly, think of a less dignified version of a PROPER DOCTOR like, for example, ELSTON GREY-TURNER. If, on the other hand, you want to picture Elston Grey-Turner, think of a more dignified version of Mr Pastry. It frankly hardly matters, since they are both dead and gone, and, for good or ill, we'll not see their like again.

Patchouli

Synecdoche is a rhetorical term in which the container and the thing contained are used interchangeably, as in 'Pass the milk' when we really mean 'Pass the bottle in which the milk is contained'.

Patchouli is a sort of olfactory synecdoche, the scent of the 1960s, heavy, sweet/sharp, cloying, woody and all-pervasive. It was popular because it was said to act as a sort of containment device for the smell of hashish. And it may well have done. It was just of no significance, because the moment you smelt patchouli, you knew there was dope being smoked.

It doesn't matter now. Who the hell cares? And so patchouli has fallen from favour.

Plato's Retreat

Artificial suntans. Grizzled chest-hair. THE GREAT SMELL OF BRUT. Sunglasses worn indoors. Medallions. Nibbles. The *Playboy* philosophy. Sweaty Naugahyde. Unspeakable carpet. Body fluids. 'The Lifestyle.' Men who looked like Richard Dreyfuss. Men who looked like Ron Jeremy. Women who looked like Madonna. Women who wanted to look like Madonna. Men who looked like Madonna. The glamorous, glamorous focus of 1970s and 1980s hedonism. Plato's Retreat. And it was started by a former McDonald's manager who moved from selling meat in buns to selling meat and buns. Plato's Retreat was closed down for good on New Year's Eve 1984.

McDonald's is still going. Virtue is its own reward.

Poofs

This is not about renaming, the odd belief that if you change the name of something its old meaning will not leak through. This is about poofs. We don't have them any more, with their ways and their furniture and their lovely friends and their floppy hats and little squeals of alarm and their serenely savage camp and everything else about poofs which so added to the general gaiety of nations. Poofs have inexplicably gone out of fashion. Where have they gone? Have they become QUEERS instead, to be *au courant*, my dear? No. No queer would ever want to be *au courant*. That was what poofs did. And how we miss them.

Power Company, Hydraulic, the London

Beneath the glamour of the theatre, strong currents run. None stronger than those which raised the Safety-Curtain, before the audience's reassured eyes, once each performance by law. The currents, in this case, were of water: water pressurized and pumped beneath the streets by the London Hydraulic Power Company, begun as the Steam Wharf and Warehouse Company in 1871. It wasn't just theatre safety-curtains, of course; the hydraulic power (clean, quiet, safe[244] and immune to damp) drove railway turntables, dock gates, pumps, and it raised the iconic bascules of London's Tower Bridge and the giant organ in the Leicester Square Odeon.

---

244 Except when pipes burst, sending great fountains 100 feet into the air.

Most of all, though, it operated lifts. And in a piece of brilliant chicanery as intricate as any derring-do enacted on the (hydraulically revolving) stage at the Coliseum, it was lifts which were its downfall. An enterprising lift-manufacturer bought them out: not to exploit the power, but to close it down. And why? So that the new owners could go to all the existing hydraulic lift operators, tell them the jig was up and the chips were down, and advise them that they would soon be needing new lifts, which could, of course, be supplied by . . . Exactly.

A strange and marvellous thought, ghostly and Gothic as so much Victorian technology now seems: millions of gallons of pressurized water pulsing beneath the streets of London. Even more extraordinary that the stream finally dried up for good as late as 1977.

Prester John, the Lost Kingdom of

The letter was fake, of course.

But there had been rumours: rumours of a Christian kingdom, somewhere in the East, beyond the far frontiers of the Islamic empire. Some – like Bishop John of India, who spent most of 1122 dining out on the story at the court of Pope Calixtus II – said it had been founded by St Thomas, who had travelled to India after the crucifixion, preaching and converting as he went. Others, like Hugo of Antioch, went further, telling of John the Priest-King of the Orient, a Christian whose army had defeated the Medes and the Persians[245], got as far as the Tigris, waited years for it to freeze over, finally realized it wasn't going to, and pushed off back to the Orient.

Some years later, in 1165, a letter surfaced from someone

---

245 Impossible, really, to imagine one without the other.

calling himself Prester John – 'Presbyter Johannes' – addressed to the Emperor Manuel Comnenus, in which the writer described his colossal domains, running from India to the lands of the sunrise, filled with fantastical animals, man-eating birds, seven-horned bulls and men with three eyes in the backs of their heads. The author was probably a Crusader, a monk or a European trader living in the East. The original has been lost, but reconstructions raise odd questions: the bellicose (and grandiose) tone of the thing, its peculiarly literary register, its lack of any date or place. What was it all about? Was it designed to embarrass the Emperors and the Pope with 'Prester John's' assertions that, despite it all, he remained a simple priest ruling over an egalitarian commonwealth? Or was it intended to encourage the Crusaders with the tantalizing prospect of a mighty Christian ally on the far side of the Muslim world?

In any case, it was a fake, and presently recognized as a fake; but whatever the motive, eleven years later, Pope Alexander III replied, courteously and respectfully but firmly stating that he, and he alone, was leader of the Christian world and that he was sending his personal physician, Magister Philippus, to offer guidance to Prester John. Why the Pope should reply to a fake letter which wasn't even addressed to him is a matter of speculation, as is the fate of poor Magister Philippus, who marched off obediently in the direction of Asia and was never heard of again[246].

Fake or not, the legend of Prester John took hold and maintained its grip for four centuries. In 1245, Pope Innocent IV sent the 62-year-old Franciscan John de Piano Carpini off to Asia with instructions to keep an eye out for the mysterious Christian monarch; Carpini came back with stern words[247] from Genghis Khan's grandson but only mentioned Prester John once, commenting that he was black. A few years later, William of

---

246 Evan S. Connell, *El Dorado*.
247 Including the word 'annihilation', than which there is none sterner.

Ruysbroek went on a similar expedition and came back with tall tales about Nestorian Christianity but little if anything of relevance to Prester John. Not even Marco Polo could scotch the fantasy, despite apparently nailing it with his tales of Uang Khan – 'King John' – who seemed to have existed once but was long, long dead in battle.

And so it continued. That great old liar, Sir John Mandeville, wrote at length on Prester John in the mid-fourteenth century: the magic Plinian magnets that pulled the irons from marauding ships, the parrots that spoke as men, the 'Gravelly Sea, that is all gravel and sand [. . .] it ebbeth and floweth in great waves as other seas do, and it is never still ne in peace, in no manner of season', of its precious stones and Prester John's anti-lechery bed, the faerie-fruit trees of the desert that 'after mid-day, they decrease and enter again into the earth, so that at the going down of the sun they appear no more. And so they do, every day. And that is a great marvel,' and the wild men with horns, and those that fear virginity, and the women who weep when their children are born and dance for joy when they die, and the 'cock-odrills . . . these serpents slay men, and they eat them weeping', and the 'many camles; that is a little beast as a goat, that is wild, and he liveth by the air and eateth nought, ne drinketh nought, at no time', and the 120-foot snakes, and the spotted multi-coloured pigs . . .

Then, in the fourteenth century, Prester John – now at least 200 years old – moved mysteriously to Africa, perhaps to Ethiopia. The late fifteenth century Portuguese explorers Affonso de Paiva and Pedro da Covilhao were sent to find him by King João – concerned, as always, to find out what the Muslims were up to and how they could be beaten – but although they made innumerable geographical discoveries, Prester John remained out of reach. He was a human wife-swapping party: always somewhere else, or last month, or next week, or just around the corner . . . and so eager was the West to believe in him that when, in 1520, another band of Portuguese explorers actually *did* reach the Christian king of Ethiopia, Lebna Dengel, and found him presiding over a poverty-stricken, dreadlocked land of mud huts and hardship, they nevertheless decided that here, at last, was the real Prester John.

Nor was it. But the non-existent chimera of Prester John, the Great Ally, the Ruler of the Land of Milk and Honey, the King at the far Side of the World . . . how much exploration did he drive? How much speculation and hope, this great un-person? And what is his position in an imaginary taxonomy of loss? Is it necessary for something to have once existed in order to be lost . . . or is the drive to find it enough? And what are *we* looking for, that might never have been there to be found?

Property, Lost, the Absurdity of

In England it's the Lost Property Office. In France, it's the Bureau des Objets Trouvés. Make of it what you will.

Psychopath, the Cleckley

They all gone, the psychopaths. And yet they've hardly been with us any time at all; *sub specie aeternitatis*, hardly the blink of an eye. The term itself didn't exist until the late nineteenth century, and it wasn't until 1941 that the American psychiatrist Hervey Cleckley produced the perfect description, in a piece of extended clinical observation as eerily beautiful and precise as **HEXAMETHONIUM MAN** himself. 'Only very slowly [. . .] does the conviction come upon us,' he writes,

> [that] we are dealing here not with a complete man at
> all but with something that suggests a subtly constructed
> reflex machine which can mimic the human personality
> perfectly.

> So perfect is this reproduction of a whole and normal
> man that no one who examines him in a clinical setting
> can point out in scientific or objective terms why, or
> how, he is not real.

The Cleckley Psychopath is a terrible affront to our MODERN sense of humanity and madness; while the ANCIENTS believed that madness was provoked by Demons or the MOON, and that the personality could be overriden or, more horribly, simply stolen, we post-Freudians have luxuriated in our understanding that, even in the maddest of the mad, the human being is in there somewhere, recoverable by drugs, love, talking or luck.

Cleckley, in *The Mask of Sanity*, introduces an infinitely nastier idea: that the psychopath has not lost his personality, but that there was no *person* there to start with. The Cleckley Psychopath is truly a *dybbuk*, a zombie, a *vrykolokas*, a robot.

Nobody home.

And now they are all gone. Not *actually* gone, but . . . unmentioned. Unmentionable. In a denial of Cleckley's distressing theory, we now call psychopaths 'people suffering from antisocial personality disorder', to reassure ourselves that there *is* a person there, somehow changed: a more soothing thought than the notion that, for example, a car is actually a horse suffering from horseness disorder.

But there are still psychopaths; it's just that they aren't people, although they *are* persons. The new psychopaths are corporations. The 2004 Canadian documentary film *The Corporation* suggests that companies, which, since the nineteenth century, have been 'persons under the law', betray all the traits of the classical psychopath. They are self-interested, manipulative, always the best, brook no competition, accept no responsibility, suffer no conscience, feel no remorse, present (via PR people, spin, advertising and marketing) phony, superficial versions of themselves to the world, dissimulate sympathy and all in all are perfect Cleckley mimics of real persons. This will come as no surprise to anyone who has encountered a corporation – that is to say, all of us – but will explain, perhaps, why we feel a vague but profound unease when we deal with them. We may think we yearn for the days when business had a human face; but the *face* of business has never been more human. It is the eyes that are oddly dead, the soul that is lost.

Pudeur

There is, in the minds of the English, a mythical Scotland: a strange mixture of somewhere-in-the-Highlands and the Morningside district of Edinburgh, where men still wear celluloid collars and women still wear tweed coats and skirts, where tea is poured from a silver pot and stockings are still made of lisle, where strange things with strange names ('Will you take another claghaddeách with your skully-dhù, dear?') are eaten at BREAKFAST [248] and Things which are Best Not Spoken Of are not spoken of.

These are the Things of the Body, and in this imaginary Scotland[249] their very existence is an affront to *decency*, let alone the naming of them.

The rest of us know, in our heart of hearts, that we have gone too far. When politicians propose an end to teenage pregnancy by not telling the little sods anything about sex, they know they are talking nonsense; what they want is for teenagers not to have sex, and for the rest of us not to have to talk about it.

And in truth, the rediscovery of lost pudeur might not be a

---

248 All of which, of course, turn out to be made of oatmeal, herring and whisky, in various proportions.

249 The Scots, in reality, being Europe's randiest nation, at it like knives, and who can blame them, what with the endless summer nights when the sun doesn't set till midnight, and the equally endless winter nights when it doesn't rise at all, and the best place is in bed; it doesn't matter with whom, because you can't see them anyway.

bad thing. Shame – also vanishing, led from the top[250] – is a powerful social glue. But it is also a taboo. The mooning yobs, the girls shrieking about blow-jobs, the drunks pissing in doorways, the spin-doctors flogging their ludicrous bullshit, stupid fat people suing hamburger joints for making them fat, hamburger joints for selling the filth in the first place, secretaries of state telling lie after lie, CALL CENTRE managers denying everything and doing nothing, Internet spammers peddling their junk, all the dodgy and the naff and the chancers and the yobs and thugs and smoothies and rats . . . *have they no shame?*

They have not. It's gone. We've lost it. Perhaps we should reinvent it. We could start with Things of the Body. The Unspoken. *Pas devant les enfants.* The locked bedroom door, the tweeds, the teapot, the delicious claghaddeách and the crunchy skully-dhù.

And, above all, what happens when a lady and a gentleman love each other *very very much*, and they decide that . . .

No. No. Maybe when you're older.

Pyecraft

Pyecraft is a lesson to us all[251]. *He sits not a dozen yards away . . . Poor old Pyecraft! Great, uneasy jelly of substance! The fattest clubman in London.*

He eats, does Pyecraft. The invention of H. G. Wells, he eats and eats, and takes no exercise, and gets fatter and fatter and blames it on everything except himself.

---

250 When did a businessman with his hand in the till, or a politician caught out in a lie or the bushes, last resign, for shame and honour?
251 Though of course the most significant thing about lessons to us all is that none of us ever learns them.

. . . He began to talk about his fatness and his fatness; all
he did for his fatness and all he was going to do for his
fatness; what people had advised him to do for his fatness and what he had heard of people doing for fatness
similar to his. 'A priori,' he said, 'one would think a
question of nutrition could be answered by dietary and
a question of assimilation by drugs.' It was stifling. It was
dumpling talk. It made me feel swelled to hear him.

Wells's narrator, Formalyn, has a Hindu great-grandmother (this
was in the days when Hindus were strange, inexplicable, mystical
people possessed of the WISDOM OF THE ANCIENTS, you understand) and Pyecraft eventually prevails on Formalyn to give him
the secret recipe for Loss of Weight.

It works. It works all too well. Pyecraft ends up weightless,
floating against his library ceiling, or bleating from beneath a
heavy mahogany table where 'he wallowed about like a captive
balloon'. But Formalyn has no sympathy:

'You committed the sin of euphuism. You called it not
Fat, which is just and inglorious, but Weight. You—'

But it is too late. The job is done. And in an age when the easiest ways to make a lot of literary money are to write cookbooks
or diet books; when City office workers punish themselves in the
gym[252] (though no woman over the age of twenty-five likes
worked-out men) and women deny themselves food (though most
men would prefer a woman who enjoyed the pleasures of the
table, as an indicator of the future pleasures of the bed), we are
clearly as confused and self-deluding as poor Pyecraft.

Doctors encourage us to work out our 'body/mass index'.

---

252 Which used to be something you got out of at school; now it is something
you pay to get *into*.

The manly belly is now an object of scorn. Magazines, *on their front covers*, promise readers the secret of a flat stomach. Images of anorexia assault us from every side. The pleasures of the flesh, in some strange re-invention of mediaeval Christianity, are predicated upon the denial of the flesh.

And Rosemary Conley became a millionaire from telling women how to scrawn their hips and thighs; and Dr Atkins from teaching people that spuds are poison, and it's all right to have reeking breath if only you're thin[253].

It is a strange insanity, and a murderous one for anorexics. We pursue lost weight as avidly as lost treasure. At night we are encouraged to cuddle up to washboards and sticks: not the ineluctable muscles of the manual worker or the taut form of the dancer, but artificially sculpted meagreness, the antithesis of sensuality. Instead of exulting in the wonderful diversity of humanity, we have prescribed the One True Shape, and we swallow our own prescription as eagerly as poor Pyecraft swallowed his catastrophic potion.

But one question remains as valid as when Formalyn asked it of the fattest bore in clubland:

> ' "What in Heaven's name, Pyecraft," I asked, "do you think you'll look like when you get thin?" '

Think of it. Just think of it. And then for **GOD**'s sake have that second éclair.

Queers

A queer (excuse me) sort of loss, this, and not to be confused with **POOFS**, nor indeed with that particular sort of **SCHOOLMASTER**

---

253 But he's dead. He's dead! He's dead, he's dead, he's DEAD! And so is the jogging bastard, Fixx. Dead! Both of them! Not gone before, but *dead!*

who was merely That Way Inclined and lived with **MOTHER**[254].
Once, queers were a slightly shifty, marginally predatory sub-
group of homosexual – the cottaging, Hampstead Heath-y sort –
who tagged along when everyone became Gay. For a while, we
all knew where we stood, despite Sir Ian McKellen's linguistic
concerns. 'Gay,' he declared one evening, 'came into fashion
because everyone got a bit fed up with being called "bent" and so
forth by the straights. Absolutely fair enough. But you see, if you
look up "straight" in the dictionary, it says "not bent", so really
we're back to square one.'

Perhaps it was this which led to the more radical gays to repos-
sess the old insult, 'queer'. But now that the intellectually
rigorous, clear-headed, straight-talking gay isn't gay, but queer,
where have all the queers gone? Perhaps they're now gay.
Perhaps they're something else altogether. The only thing we
can be sure of is that they're not poofs.

Radio, Car, Removable

A fine irony, barrelling along on a beautiful day with Joni
Mitchell on the radio singing *Don't it always seem to go That you don't
know what you've got 'til it's gone; They paved Paradise, put up a parking
lot . . .*

Which would be all very well[255], except they didn't. They
promised to – that's where the parking charges were supposed to
go, that's where the fines were supposed to go – but they didn't.
Get to the other end and it's on-street parking if you're lucky;

---

254 I remember a maths master at school said to be That Way Inclined. Pure
    speculation, but later confirmed by my old headmaster. 'Of course he was,'
    he said, 'No question. That's why he was such a superb teacher.'
255 Within the constraints of pop songs, which exist to slip truisms beneath our
    guard by repeating them insistently under cover of music; which makes it
    rather like politics, except with politics you don't get the tune.

and, what's more, you know all too damn well what you've got or how could you tell that it's gone?

By the broken glass, if it was a car radio; by the wires sprouting out of the derelict empty hole; by Joni Mitchell, abruptly silenced. Eventually we got sick of it, and technology came to the rescue with the removable car radio[256], the only drawback being that you had to remember to remove it.

And so the composer Michael Berkeley removed his radio and his mobile phone, did the necessary juggling with the keys and bits and pieces, let himself into his house, came back for the few bits and pieces he'd left by the kerb, and found that the artists' portfolio containing the notes, sketches and piano reductions for his opera *Jane Eyre* had gone.

The brain tries to help in such circumstances, coming up, if possible, with a plausible story. The first terrible, lurching despair is followed by an equally terrible, lurching hope[257]. Usually the best it can come up with is: 'It hasn't happened, it's not real, close your eyes then look again and it'll all be all right.' But on this occasion there was an alternative reality to hand. Berkeley had been working on the score at his house in Wales; and so his brain simply informed him that that's where it still was. He hadn't packed it all up carefully! He hadn't put it in the car to bring back to London! He hadn't left it by the side of the car for thirty seconds! And no opportunistical ratbag slime-sucking thief had come and stolen it, no sir!

Yes sir.

---

256 Removable by the owner, that is. Thieves never had any trouble with the old sort, to the extent that, at one stage, cars in New York would have signs in the windows saying 'No Radio'. Which in turn led to the rather dilapidated Chevrolet (in that very particular colour which can only be described as 'old car') down in the Garment District, before it became fashionable, sporting a carefully hand-lettered sign reading 'RADIO, AND PROUD OF IT'.

257 Brian Stimpson, the hapless headmaster in Michael Frayn's *Clockwise*, summed up much of the human condition when he said: 'It's not the despair, Laura. I can stand the despair. It's the *hope* . . .'

So after the initial hideous shock, and rejecting the temptation to simply not do it at all, he squared his shoulders and executed the Carlyle Manoeuvre and started again, finding in the process a curious sense of liberation, and coming up in the end with a tighter, more disciplined work[258].

Technology once again came pre-emptively to the rescue. Not in the sense that Berkeley switched over to working on his PowerBook, using the Sibelius program and backing up his work, thus benefiting from the computer's great gift to us all: the power of ubiquity, so that the same thing may be in many places at once.

No; the real technological change was simply this: he instinctively went for the root causes of the trouble, and *bought a fixed car radio*. A retrograde step? No. And perhaps the car radio is a modern sin-eater or scapegoat; perhaps, like mugging-money, its real function is to be stolen, to take the bullet, to stand between us and greater harm. Not so much a hostage to fortune as a down payment on our luck. *Don't it always seem to go . . .*

Yes. It does. And that's the point of it.

Rhinoceros, the Nasal Membrane of the

It has been said that, if we knew the whole picture, it would kill us. Our brains and our senses exist, not to funnel, but to filter the world, so that we only perceive that bit of it that we need and can handle.

---

258 And one which of course got even more public attention than it would otherwise have attracted, not just from opera critics and music journalists, but from leader-writers, mediums, DJs and even the Queen, not normally known for her interest in contemporary music. Thanks to the thief, a whole swathe of society became aware that opera isn't just a business monopolized by dead guys. Such is the magical power of resurrection, of things clawed back from the edge of oblivion.

Most of 'reality', by that token, is lost to us; and some might say that in itself should be enough to disabuse us of our ideas of intellectual superiority. We are not playing with a full deck, and never have been.

More than that, though, our whole construction of the world, which we suppose to be based on rational empiricism, is arguably just one model among many, and based as much upon anatomical happenstance as on any response to even partial 'reality'.

Take, for example, the simple rhinoceros. Unravel his olfactory apparatus – his nasal membrane, for simplicity's sake – and you will find, it is said, that its surface area (the important dimension, on which it depends for trapping and analysing molecules) is larger than our entire brain's. Size, particularly in neurology, is by no means everything; it's the density of interconnections that counts. But all the same, the rhino's nasal membrane is something to be reckoned with.

One of the things the rhino reckons with it is, of course, time. We – literally – *see* time pass. The rhino does not. The famous ending of *Rosencrantz and Guildenstern are Dead*:

Now you see me, now you—

would be entirely lost on the rhino. He would have no mechanism for processing a sudden disappearance. Nobody could materialize in his world; nobody could vanish. Instead, he inhabits a universe of gradual cross-fades as other creatures fade into or out of his olfactory world. The slice of 'present' between past and future, which we, privileging vision[259] over all other senses, experience as razor-thin, almost imperceptible, is, for the rhino, a thick, juicy slab of time which he can chew over at his leisure. And what he can tell would make even the architects of the US

---

259 Which changes, of course, at the speed of light, even though we cannot process it that fast.

Patriot Act – even The Home Secretary himself – happy: who you are, what you've been eating, your sexual history, your state of health, where you've been, who you've been there with . . . all these are accessible to his majestic nose.

What, though, is the rhino doing in a glossary of loss, apart from the fact that we are doing our best to extinguish him for good?

What he is doing is this: he is here to raise the question of continual loss. Does he, as we do, experience the world as a system in which things are brought to us, then taken away again? Or is his a more benign world, a gentler, more gradual fading in and out of experience? And, if so, which of us is right?

Ronco

The Veg-O-Matic, the Buttoneer, the Outside Inside Window Washer, the Mince-O-Matic, the Spiral Slicer, the Rhinestone and Stud Setter, the Miracle Broom, the Inside-the-Shell Egg-Scrambler, the Chop-O-Matic, the Beauty-Rite Plastic Plant Maker ('Now you can make realistic plants that never need watering'), the Food Glamorizer ('Turns any meal into a feast fit for a king!'), the Record-O-Vac-O-Matic (just add Ronco anti-static cleaning fluid and your **LPs** are good as new), the Sit-On-Trash Compactor (looks like an ordinary kitchen stool but your weight will effortlessly compact the trash inside[260]), the Retract-O-Net Compact Fishing Net[261] . . . did you have one of these great Ronco gadgets that you always wondered how you ever managed without?

And if so . . . where is it now?

---

260 Obesity isn't all bad, do you see?
261 Which turns into an oar . . .

Sandwich, Ham, the Railway

A masterpiece of air-dried lamination technology known and reviled the world over, the British railway sandwich – one translucent wafer of sodden ham glued between two layers of dessicated curling 'bread' by a thin layer of margarine – has vanished entirely. Instead, PASSENGERS now have humous-and-chargrilled-red-pepper-on-softbake-seeded-bread, and if that weren't bad enough, they have it at the Refresca Café/Bar.

Schoolmasters

Schoolmasters used to be like PROPER DOCTORS or PARSONS and, in many cases, not unlike MR PASTRY. You knew where you stood: in the shadow of THE CANE. Now they wear bright clothes and want to be your friend and, like PARIS, they have lost their proper smell of chalk and pipe-smoke and no longer creak when they walk or sleep hanging upside-down from the staff-room rafters.

Septum, the Nasal

For countless millennia, the humble nasal septum was the must-have facial accessory. It kept the two halves of the nose pleasingly separate, and, once technology had advanced sufficiently, gave us something to pick in traffic jams[262].

The only way to divest yourself of the septum was to contract the pox, and by the time your conk had caved in you had also lost

---

262 A simple experiment – try it yourself at home – will reveal that at least eighty per cent of non-elective nasal detritus (as opposed to SNUFF or cocaine) is to be found on the septum rather than in the lateral crannies.

your marbles and were stumbling about with burned-out tabes from **V.D.** to boot.

Then came cocaine.

Now, soap stars and moddoos, Ci'y boys and paunchy super-annuated record producers wander the world with the wind whistling through their single gigantic nostril. Presently, perhaps, the lost septum will become, like a suntan, a status symbol, an indicator of wealth, leisure, alpha status, and stupidity. Until then, it just looks horrid. (But so, probably, when it first started, did walking upright.)

Seventies, The

Has there ever been a more intrusive decade than the 1970s? A great, sweaty, grinning, brainless decade; a decade in an open-to-the-navel, floral-patterned, round-collared, jersey-knit shirt with a chest wig and a medallion; a multicoloured, platform-booted, *Denim*[263]-reeking decade, poised clumsily between the politicized idealism of the, like, 1960s man, and the raw, padded-shoulder greed of the 1980s.

Eventually, as decades do, the 1970s passed. But it left its spoor in a trail of musk, glitter and bondage trousers; it cast a long and lurid shadow; and its icons and brand names hang just below the level of our collective consciousness. To recite them is to awaken a primitive sort of horror, like intoning the names of half-forgotten, monstrous demons from the Age before Humankind. Cleanse your spirit. Apply a little **PATCHOULI** oil. Say *Ommmmm*. Gird your soul. Fold your hands. Devoutly intone the Hundredfold Litany of the 1970s.

---

263 'For the man who doesn't have to try . . . too hard.' Didn't get laid, either, but, hell, this was the 1970s.

1. 10cc[264]
2. Appliqué[265]
3. Aqua Manda[266]
4. Ayatollah Khomeini
5. Bay City Rollers
6. Bean Bags[267]
7. British Leyland
8. **BRUT**
9. Cambodia
10. Cheesecloth shirts
11. Chopper bikes
12. *The Clangers*[268]
13. Coal shortages
14. Columbo[269]
15. The Common Market
16. Corduroy shoes
17. Cyprus
18. Decimalization[270]
19. Digital watches[271]
20. Ding-dong! Avon calling!
21. Disco Fever
22. Drought
23. **DUNGEONS & DRAGONS**

---

264 'I'm not in love': the theme song of the pre-Aids one-night-stander for a decade.
265 Applied to everything made of denim. And everything *was* made of denim.
266 Unisex perfume for hopeful bisexuals.
267 Once you got her down on one, she was helpless. This was not yet politically incorrect in the Seventies.
268 Knitted proto-environmentalists from space who communicated with strange, sad, hooting sounds, just like the real thing.
269 Uhh . . . one more thing. Writers Richard Levinson and William Link allegedly modelled Columbo on Petrovitch, the detective in Dostoevsky's *Crime and Punishment*.
270 How much did that cost in the old money?
271 The highest aspiration of mankind.

24. Earth shoes[272]
25. Eight-track cartridges
26. Evel Knievel
27. *The Fall and Rise of Reginald Perrin*
28. *Fawlty Towers*
29. *The Female Eunuch*
30. *Floppy disks*
31. Football hooligans
32. *The Godfather*
33. *The Goodies*
34. Hai Karate
35. Hamlet Cigars
36. Harold Wilson
37. *The Hitchhikers' Guide to the Galaxy*
38. Inflation
39. The IRA
40. *The Joy of Sex*[273]
41. K-Tel
42. Kohl
43. Lebanon
44. Liebfraumilch
45. Loons[274]
46. Lurex
47. Mannix
48. Mateus Rosé[275]

---

272 For that, like, stoned-looking walk.
273 The beard! The beard!
274 'Hey – let's make trousers with bottoms wider than your feet and no waistband! Then people will trip up on their own trousers, which will then fall down!'
275 Uri Geller allegedly transformed some, in the presence of a Greek Orthodox Archbishop, into what the prelate identified as Manischwitz. Whether or not that is an improvement is debatable. But how does an Archbishop know what kosher wine tastes like?

49. Maxi-coats[276]
50. Medallions
51. Mood rings[277]
52. Moon Buggies
53. Mrs Thatcher Milk Snatcher
54. *The New Avengers*
55. North Sea oil[278]
56. Oil spills
57. Pan's People
58. Panne velvet
59. Patchwork jeans
60. Pet Rocks
61. Petrol shortages
62. **PLATO'S RETREAT**
63. Players' No. 10
64. Pocket calculators
65. Pong
66. Power cuts
67. Punk
68. *Randall & Hopkirk: Deceased*
69. Rats[279]
70. Red Barrel[280]
71. Restrictive Practices
72. Rhodesia
73. **RONCO**
74. Rubbish in the streets
75. Skinheads
76. Skylab

---

276 With – oh God, oh God, thank you, God – miniskirts underneath. Or – yes! yes! – hotpants.
277 E.g. 'credulous', 'stoned', 'vacuous', 'cynical', etc.
278 Not gone quite, but going fast.
279 Gnawing on the dead bodies etc. in the streets during the strikes.
280 Not beer as such.

77. Space Hoppers
78. Spandex[281]
79. St Bruno
80. *Star Wars*
81. Stockhausen
82. Studio 54
83. Supertramp
84. *The Sweeney*
85. T Rex
86. Tartan[282]
87. Ted Heath
88. Test Tube Babies
89. Three Mile Island
90. The Three-day Week
91. Tiger Balm[283]
92. Tiswas
93. Tricky Dicky
94. Unemployment
95. Unions
96. Vietnam
97. Watergate
98. *Wheeltappers & Shunters Social Club*
99. Women's Lib
100. YMCA[284]

Here endeth the Litany. Though some of its artefacts remain, the 1970s are lost for ever. Which proves that not all that's lost is a loss.

---

281 See Maxi-coats.
282 Sewn onto jeans in recognition of the Bay City Rollers, *vide supra*.
283 Expensive version of Vick's Vapo-Rub; oriental, so must have been imbued with the WISDOM OF THE ANCIENTS.
284 If you know the hand movements, it will soon be time to die.

Shoes, Just

Shoes. Loafers (penny or tassels or snaffles, black or brown or oxblood or suede (ginger suede or brown suede (or sometimes black suede)) or brogues (or half-brogues) in black or tan (dark or light) or oxblood (or suede), not to mention boots (walking (hill, fell, mountain (three-season or four-season (Gore-Tex®))) or hiking or stomping or beetle-crushing or even elastic-sided (oiled leather, Nu-Buck™, kangaroo leather, calf))) . . .

Was there – there must have been – a time when you could think to yourself 'Shoes' and go to a shoemaker and say 'Shoes' and the shoemaker would say 'Fair enough, come back in a fortnight', and there your shoes would be, ready, like it or lump it, take it or leave it? Just . . . shoes? Was there?

There was. There was, and not so long ago, on the far side of the Iron Curtain. Winter, but warm spells, so constant cold and slush and your other shoes – no, let's be frank, your only shoes – leaking, so you go into a shoe shop in Novy Targ and there on the shelves are some shoes. Not many, but some. And you say to the woman 'Do you have any shoes?' and she says 'What size are you?' and you say '42' and she says 'These', and hands you a pair of shoes which look as though they have been made from liver, string and tyres by dyspraxic Russian dissidents conscripted at gunpoint into Novosibirsk Cobbling And Pork By-Products Factory No. 171.

As they probably had.

But it didn't matter. They were shoes. They were approximately your size. So you bought them. They cost approximately one dollar[285]. And as you were leaving the shop, an old man shuffled in. His shoes were visibly in tatters, and you watched through the steamed-up glass as he spoke to the woman. She shook her

---

285 A lot in Poland at the time of Solidarnosc; you could have bought a house in the Tatra mountains – a sort of Switzerland, but without the Swiss – for $800.

head. He pointed at his shoes. She shook her head again. He laboriously drew a roll of soggy, rumpled zlotys from a wash-leather[286] bag. She shook her head a third time and pointed through the window at you. The old man's shoulders slumped even further, and he sat down on a flimsy chair, disappointment leaving him incapable of standing. So what did you do?

You scuttled off, carrying the last pair of serviceable size 42s in Novy Targ[287].

But it was strangely comforting, the absolute absence of choice. If there was something you wanted, whatever it was, there was only one variety, which you could either get or you couldn't. Soap, lavatory paper, biros, envelopes, potatoes, shirts . . . the only consumer choice was (a) Yes, we've got some or (b) No, out of stock.

Now we marvel at the paucity of our forebears' possessions. One coat. Ten books. One pen. A table. Two beds. To our inflated appetites, to our unconstrained belief that nothing is unattainable, it seems a life bordering on intolerable poverty. We live surrounded by things, not only a profusion of things but each one of those things having been chosen from a dizzying mêlée of competing things, and by this we measure our prosperity. Before the fact, too, we think these things are a measure of our happiness: if only we had this wristwatch, if only we had that car, if only we had these designer radiators[288], we would be happy.

We are not, of course; and the failure of the equation {prosperity = choice = happiness} is once which perplexes politicians and will go on perplexing them.

---

286 Whatever that may be.
287 At least, that's what I did, and have regretted it for over twenty years. And if I go to hell, that is one of the two – so far – reasons I'll go there.
288 And how did the other, non-designer radiators come into existence? Chance? A happy accident in the foundry ('Oh, look, Geoff: a *radiator* has come out. This is our lucky day . . .')?

Not so long ago – until, perhaps, about halfway through the last century – choice was limited. Anyone born before 1960 grew up with roughly the same toys, the same sweets, the same clothes. We played with our **BAYKO** and yearned for a Magic Robot, or vice versa; our little swimming trunks were yellow and ruched or blue, knitted and hideous; our meals were the same, plain dull British food[289]; we read the same stories, wore the same shoes, woke at night when our parents returned from the same sort of evening out, smelling of the same perfume and the same cigars. Our copies of the *Radio Times* lived in the same folders underneath the same televisions, and when there suddenly erupted a new variety of thing, we all enjoyed (or endured) it, whether it was unbreakable Melamine cups in luridly chemical colours with tea-stained cream insides, or slippery, toenail-catching, sweat-provoking horrors from Brentford Nylons.

Compared to our ancestors, people then were indescribably materially well-endowed. But compared to now, the choice was minimal. Were people happier?

It seems so. Choice perplexes us. It puts the burden on us, so instead of shrugging and making the best of it, we traduce ourselves for our failure to make the right choice. A European, a Japanese or an American wanting to buy a camera faces an appalling task of discernment, in an area in which he or she is probably no expert (the difference being that he thinks he is), being thrown to the mercy of salespeople who are working to an unknown agenda, and one may be sure that, whatever they eventually come out with, there will be plenty of evidence to suggest that they made the wrong choice[290].

---

289 Has the phrase 'British food' ever prompted salivation in anyone?
290 In the heyday of the People's Republic of China, there was one camera. The Seagull. It wasn't particularly good but nor was it particularly bad. Its great strength was that you didn't have to choose it. All you had to decide was: *Do I want a camera?*

Whole websites have sprung up to let us kid ourselves we have made the best choice. We can spend hours, evenings, days reading the on-line reviews of thousands of complete strangers: reviews of, yes, cameras, but also reviews of deodorants, stockings, penknives, tobacco, *komboloi* worry-beads, CD-labelling kits, glass-cleaners, loudspeakers, loudspeaker cables, wallets, luggage, diaries, everything. Even our doctors now try to 'empower' us by offering us 'choice' in a 'mutualistic' model of 'patient-centred health care'. The burden of choice, the near-certainty of making a bad decision (because nothing is ever perfect), the endless responsibility for everything is never lifted for a moment; and our yearning for less of it may be partly sentimental but it is yearning all the same.

Even in our private lives, choice is endless. Even in bed (or on the floor? In leather, in PVC, in chains, in the fridge?) we have to make decisions and invent the rules as we go along. And all that invention is . . . tiring. American psychologist Barry Schwartz calls this 'the paradox of choice' and in the end his advice is simple: we should lower our expectations.

Difficult, when a multi-billion advertising industry exists solely to raise them. And perhaps it is too late. But think about it. Not Church's or Trickers or John Lobb, Nike or Puma or Adidas; not Manolos or Prada, not kitten-heel or stiletto, but *shoes*.

Just shoes.

Shop, Left in the

Timothy spelt it out unequivocally: *We brought nothing into this world, and it is certain we can carry nothing out.* And in between, we go shopping. Perhaps we'd be more circumspect if we had to take it all with us. 'I'm sorry. There's nothing more we can do. You'd better pack.'

But it's all an illusion anyway. Shopping is more about what we leave behind than what we carry away. Not just SHOES ('No, chuck them. They're dead.') but everything: in THE SHOPS we shed our old skins, our fat bellies, our short legs, our headaches and dry lips. We change our owlish bespectacled selves for new, contact-lensed, sexier ones; we do not buy a new suit because we need a new suit, but because we need a new *us*. The expensive bottle of perfume is not bought for its SILLAGE – *muguet de bois*, rose, orris root, ambergris – but the new life which follows in its wake. We go shopping to lose the old, anxious world (whether those anxieties were our own, or created by the manufacturers[291] anxious for our CASH) and replace it with a new one in which we are, if not perfect, at least perfectible.

Sometimes the thrill of the new leads us to abandon more than we would like. In 1905, Maurice Ravel was working on his *Introduction and Allegro for Harp, Strings, Flute and Clarinet* when some friends invited him on a boating trip along the rivers of Europe. Certainly not (said Ravel), I am working. But only hours before they were due to leave, Ravel changed his mind.

You can't just go on a river trip as you are. Essential to buy new clothes. So off Ravel rushed, manuscript under his arm, and back he rushed, shirts under his arm. And manuscript in the shop.

Not for long. The shopkeeper was an amateur musician and had taken the manuscript home. When Ravel called to reclaim his creation, the *chemisier*, it is said, put up a fierce argument. Hard to imagine what his grounds can have been. Ravel eventually got his manuscript back (and missed, literally, the boat). But how one would have liked to overhear the intervening conversation, now lost (unlike the music) for ever.

Shops, The

Not, of course, to be confused with *shops*. *The* shops were different. They were nearby, and people would pop out to them. Not a

---

291 The principle of all successful non-essential marketing is the same, epitomized in **B.O.**

particularly good choice in The Shops. A grocer, a greengrocer, a newsagent selling shag tobacco and dirty magazines, perhaps a fish and chip shop open on cold evenings, stirring the blood with its mysteriously, inexplicably exciting smell of batter and vinegar[292], a butcher who couldn't get things because there was no demand for them. Sometimes there was a bicycle-and-radio-repair shop selling valves and solder and pumps and John Bull puncture outfits. But if you wanted anything else, you went into Town.

Supermarkets killed The Shops. Now, at best, you get The Shop. The singular is crucial. Asian people, often newly kicked out of newly dictatorial African economies where they had been doctors, physicists, professors, engineers, discovered on reaching Britain that they were regarded by their native inferiors as wogs. So they looked at The Shops (which couldn't get it, no call for it, we're closed, this isn't Harrods you know, No Tick, we've run out, we're closed, sorry) and thought: we can do better.

So they did. The Shops slowly bit the dust, prey to the supermarkets. But The Shop, in its tens of thousands, prospered as people realized, at 10.30p.m. on a Sunday, that they really, really *had* to have some paracetamol, a packet of fish fingers, a jar of Lime Pickle, ten **PARK DRIVE**, a swatch of elastic, a reporter's notebook, two doughnuts, a copy of *The Economist*, a box of Tampax, some cat food, a litre of bleach, a bag of pretzels, some leftover Christmas decorations, a pink fluffy toy dog, three samosas and a packet of disposable plates.

And now, two generations on, their children are doctors, physicists and engineers again. And the owners of The Shops, joyless and disobliging? Why, they aren't even shopkeepers any more.

---

292 Or 'non-brewed condiment': basically a solution of acetic acid for those whose religious scruples or brushes with gin had given them a doctrinal rigidity against all alcohol. It made the food taste terrible, of feet and photographic stop-bath, but terrible-tasting food was how food was *meant* to be, and if **GOD** agreed, then so much the better.

Sign, Elston Grey-Turner's

Another lost eponym used by **PROPER DOCTORS** to denote discolouration of the flank indicating pancreatitis. A useful way of making the patient feel important while not scaring him ('Mmhmm . . . Grey-Turner's sign, **OLD CHAP**. Better get you in for a **PROPER LOOK-SEE**,') as well as a means of distinguishing Dr Grey-Turner from **MR PASTRY**. 'I say,' you'd say, 'I did so enjoy learning about your Sign when I was a medical student, before I gave it all up and forgot everything they taught me, especially that improbable nonsense about the so-called clitoris, ha ha ha,' and if he looks back at you blankly over the white **WALRUS MOUSTACHE**, you know it's Mr P[292A]. Except, of course, that they are both dead now.

Sillage

Sillage is the perfumers' term for the trail of scent which follows the wearer (and, hopefully, draws admirers to follow in their turn). Scent is by its very nature evanescent – designed to be lost – yet the sillage exists over time as well as in space. Even we, with our tiny olfactory bulb, can sense someone's presence when they are no longer there; sometimes, if their *sillage* is powerful or unique enough, we can detect how long ago they were in the room[293]. Think how it would be if we had the nose of the **RHINOCEROS**.

292A If on the other hand he looks back at you over the ditto and says, 'For God's sake, you fool, that wasn't my sign, it was my father's', you know it's Elston Grey-Turner anyway. The argument is a bit circular but since they're *all* dead, the chances of putting it to the test are remote.

293 The two most striking examples I encountered were Aramis (Dr Michael Tanner, the distinguished philosopher and opera critic of *The Spectator*) and feet (a man called Gerry who was a porter at a hospital where I worked in my gap year.) In both cases their *sillage* was so persistent and *sui generis* that one knew to within a couple of minutes when they had been present; the difference was that in Dr Tanner's case, one was sorry to have arrived too late; in Gerry's case, relieved.

Perfumery is an art of incredible complexity and subtlety, and the only one whose creations we perceive directly, without the modulation of thought. It is, as one perfumer said, 'A memory game', and anyone who has had the presence of a lost love momentarily restored by finding a long-abandoned scarf or a scented handkerchief will know that the memories perfume – created or natural – can provoke are almost three-dimensionally vivid.

Yet perfumes, too, are lost. It is only by visiting King Juan Carlos of Spain, or my rooms, or the Aladdin's Refrigerator of the perfumer Roja Dove that you will ever again smell Guerlain's *Eau d'Hégémonienne*[294]. *Crêpe de Chine* has gone for ever; *Vent Vert*, the 'fresh wind' that marked the end of the Second World War and the triumph of the self-determining woman, still exists but is not what it was. Daddy's favourite, Old Spice, bears no relation to what it once was; *Cabochard* persists in name only, a thin, marketing-man's, accountancy-driven, mean-spirited travesty of the original; Coty's *Chypre*, which gave its name to a whole genre, is no longer made; nor, too, is Jacques Guerlain's gloriously named *Voilà Pourquoi J'Aimais Rosine* (a double-edged present to give to someone not named Rosine) or the equally glorious but perhaps nowadays more ambiguously named *Jardin de Mon Curé*.

Lost, perhaps, in some cases, because the market changed (though who would trust a marketeer's version of anything?); lost, in others, through the evolution of ethical sensibilities; lost, in most, because accountants with the shrivelled souls of Internet chat-room lurkers thought there would be a cheaper way. But lost all the same.

---

294 And you'll have to hurry; I can't speak for the other two, but I only have a couple of drops left.

Snuff

Princes and Princes Special, Macouba and Morlaix, Seville, Santo Domingo and French Carotte; Garden Mint, Golden Cardinal, Orange Cardinal and Tonquin; Crumbs of Comfort, George IV, Finisterre; Astaroth, Brunswick, Beau Nash and Café Royal. A tap on the box, a pinch between the fingers, sniff, sneeze and blow the nose. Once a mark of discernment and elegance; now entirely risible. What are we doing now – discerning and elegant as we are – that our descendants will laugh at, and wonder why? And how can we tell? And why should we stop? It's their problem, not ours.

Span, Spick and

Little magazines. Little magazines with ladies in. Little magazines with *naked* ladies in, bosoms jouncing. Little magazines you'd try to steal from the Dirty Bookshop by slipping them innocently into a copy of *Eagle* or *Musical Opinion*. Little magazines, *Spick*, there was, and *Span*, and there was *Beautiful Britons*, art magazines they were, art being engaged, like sex itself, in a constant war against death and oblivion. And there would be the bosoms, and there would be the STOCKING-top[295] and in between ... a strange, egg-like smoothness, a marmorial nothing, obliterated by the airbrush in case anyone should See Something[296]. The Mystery of the

---

295 Women may think that, sexually, they have the upper hand, but they will *never* know the heart-thumping, spine-chilling, mouth-drying, tongue-cleaving transcendence of that first glimpse of stocking-top, nor the male equivalent of it. Why not? Because (a) there isn't a male equivalent – posing pouches, anyone? – and (b) even if there were, women *simply wouldn't care enough.*

296 In an adolescent fit of autodidacticism, we would then *draw in*, shakily and sketchily, the missing parts, so anxious to see them represented on the page that we were prepared not only to put them in ourselves, but to put them in *without any idea of what they looked like.*

Vanished Pudenda is now long-solved, the solution available on every newsagent's shelf. But which is the greater loss? Ignorance? Or terrible, lurching, mind-boggling *hope*?

Spitting, No

'No Spitting', the signs used to say. They were everywhere: in cinemas, on buses, in railway waiting rooms, anywhere where the public could assemble long enough to hawk up a phlegmy bolus and discharge it – hhhhhhhhhrack-*ptui!* – in a glistening splat.

The signs have gone now. Have we learned to behave ourselves? Have we become less brutish? No. Clearly not. Our streets have not yet achieved the scented delicacy of a Victorian parlour; so why is there no *No Spitting*?

Were this America, one might assume it was because of the decline of chewing tobacco. Once upon a time, every saloon had its brass spittoons and a male rite of passage (as important as slicing the ball of your thumb on your **BUCK KNIFE** was the first time you chewed your wad of plug into pulpy submission and hit the pot with a brown stream of juice and a brazen clang as definitively masculine as testosterone itself.

However, this was not America but England, and the cause was more sinister. British lungs, always damp-weakened, were further ruined by the great **LONDON PARTICULARS** and bronchitis was endemic. Yet while the majority of the population could expectorate without causing anything worse than the salutory dismay of the genteel classes (itself a damn good reason to spit your lungs out, if need be), a substantial majority carried pestilence in their phlegm.

Consumption.

Tuberculosis.

Even in the 1950s, the two great pathological bogeymen were initials: **V.D.** and TB. V.D. made you go blind and lame and your nose dropped off and you walked with the high-stepping cotton-wool gait of *tabes dorsalis*, but TB killed you dead. *Dead* dead. You got pale and thin and then you lay in hospital with a sputum-cup, coughing, and then you died.

But doctors had already got on top of it; TB was becoming a folk memory, the No Spitting signs a *memento mori* for a dead disease. Presently the smogs stopped, and doctors (and central heating and proper housing) got on top of the bronchitis too and by the time the No Spitting signs had all been removed (or painted over with other, equally threatening signs about what would happen to you if you didn't pay your fare, or warning you that you were being watched on camera by unseen forces, too far away to be of use) we didn't need to spit anyway.

Now TB is coming back, among the junkies, the winos, the migrants and the urban poor. Who will tell *them*: No Spitting?

Stockings . . .

. . . *by Kayser Bondor* (it used to say in the old theatre programmes, along with *Cigarettes by Abdullah*). Why mention who made the actresses' stockings? Was it because until not long before, actresses had been considered next only to prostitutes, their underwear a matter for public consumption[297]? Was it to inflame the men in the audience, who, bored to distraction by the play, could comfort themselves by speculating on the Paradise Strip between stocking-top and knicker-leg?

So far, so understandable. And understandable, too, that the Paradise Strip should have possessed its magical allure; to see – or even to touch – it indicated that a man was near his goal of

---

297 Not much has changed; now we know little about who made their stockings, but a lot – too much, probably – about whether, and to what extent, they remove their pubic hair.

disrobing and intimate abandon. Stockings were what women wore under their clothes; to encounter stockings meant you were getting under their clothes; and all was well.

What is odd, though, is that, even once stockings *stopped* being what women wore under their clothes, they retained their iconic power while tights, or, heaven help us, Pop Sox, never acquired any at all. Stockings have now become the badge-of-office of the woman who is ready and willing, even for men who have never encountered them in their natural habitat but only donned as a sexual trope, a uniform, a 10-denier ticket to ride.

And so they have become . . . different. The difference is subtle: the difference between a promise and a guarantee. But something has been lost, and we are the poorer for it.

Stories, School

It is a fundamental tenet of manipulative psychology that the easiest way to create a dependence is to involve someone in a routine − any routine − and then suddenly, without warning, break it. So it was with school stories, the staples of childhood pulp literature throughout the twentieth century. Gothic public schools with arcane rituals; the horrors of fagging and the joys of sports; improbably peculiar SCHOOLMASTERS who today would be hauled off to prison, chipped, tagged, wired up to lie detectors, connected to GPS trackers and eventually set 'free' to be lynched by tabloid readers who had mistaken them for paediatricians[298]: midnight feasts, crushes, pashes, hero-worship, rude awakenings, capricious injustice, the lash of fate, income disparities, bullying, snobbery, and, above all, *no parents in sight* . . . this was the diet, and it nourished (or seemed to nourish) children from all backgrounds, whether

---

298 Or *Daily Mail* readers who had mistaken them for asylum-seekers.

they attended Gothic public schools or the local Bash Street Comprehensive.

And then, suddenly, the tap was turned off. Children's writing had to be relevant to 'kids'' own lives, and allowing Those Less Fortunate to see even the most fantastical glimpse of a never-never Greyfriars was a devastating abuse of their personhood.

But the routine had been established through some strange inter-generational collective unconscious. In the absence of school stories, the hunger grew until someone, finally, found a magical way round the unspoken ban.

Enter J.K. Rowling.

For what is Harry Potter but another schoolboy, in another school story: perhaps at a school more explicitly magical than most, but nevertheless a school. And now we are back where we always wanted to be: in a Manichean world, free from invasive parents, where good and evil are clear, where loyalties are pre-defined, and the outside world is held at bay . . . for the time being.

Texture

One of the great losses of the Information Age is texture. Consider the pre-computer desk: a litter of papers, large and small, handwritten, printed and typed, coarse and fine; letters in varying hands, envelopes of various sizes bearing stamps from all over the world. Here are books, annotated and bookmarked; here is a typewriter with its ribbon and its heavy steel frame. Here are photographs and drawings, coins and banknotes, documents bearing seals and counter-signatures, pristine originals and faded carbon copies, correction fluid marking the palimpsest of human error, dog-ears distinguishing what has been well-thumbed from what has been largely ignored. Papers lie in piles, navigable vertically according to what has been most recently consulted; some are turned sideways-on to mark the stack. Boxes of note cards are neatly indexed; bundles of them, held with rubber bands, less neat but closer to hand; notes and memoranda are thumbtacked to the bulletin-board.

Now consider today's equivalent. All is stored on the network and accessed via mouse-clicks on a clean glowing screen. Everything is the same: an image seen through glass. We touch nothing, mark nothing, smell nothing. In the new world of I.T., it is not just the desktop that is a metaphor: *everything* is a metaphor, where nothing yellows with age and everything is clean and new. We are become creatures of sight alone, our whole attention focused on a hundred and fifty square inches of expensive glass.

We have lost something in the process. Not just texture. Something more. The computer makes everything retrievable; but it doesn't retrieve everything. Only the surface. Scratch that surface and – look! – more surface. The rest is lost.

Throat, Cigarette Smoke that was Kind to your

There once was a time when smoking didn't give you bronchitis, lung cancer or emphysema. Craven-A cigarettes, in those days, would 'not affect your throat' and doctors recommended them. Those were the days, too, when the Esso sign meant happy motoring, when Guinness gave you strength, when Horlicks guarded against night starvation and Arlene Dahl[299] loved to see her man smoke a Cigarillo: 'stylish manly shape and cigarette convenience'.

All advertising has changed beyond recognition, but cigarette advertising most of all. It's gone. Banned. But in its heyday . . . in its heyday, 'A responsible consulting organization reports a study by a competent medical specialist and staff on the effects of smoking Chesterfields . . . "*It is my opinion that the ears, nose, throat*

---

299 An actress, of course.

and accessory organs of all participating subjects examined by me were not adversely affected in the six-month period by smoking the cigarettes provided." ' Pall Malls? 'Guard Against Throat-Scratch.' Chesterfields? 'A Well-Known Industrial Research Organization Reports: "Chesterfield is the only cigarette in which members of our panel found no unpleasant after-taste."' Camels? 'Gene Nelson, screen and stage star, says: "I've tried 'em all. It's Camels for me."'

In those enlightened, happy days, was smoking incompatible with the healthy life? No! The bronzed, muscular lifeguard who 'alone rules the happy chaos of a million beach-goers every summer' did 'a job that takes skill . . . and patience. And like men everywhere, he makes the going easier by enjoying the *cigar* that's one in a million – mild, yes . . . *tastefully* mild – Dutch Masters.' Chesterfield were 'perfectly packed' with 'Accu-Ray', Winston were 'sure making friends in a hurry', 'Your voice of wisdom says SMOKE KENT!', while the question 'Is WAR PRESSURE making you SMOKE TOO MUCH?' was easily answered. 'Why cut down on the relief and enjoyment of extra smoking now, when you feel you need it most? Even chain-smokers find that new Julep Cigarettes banish unpleasant over-smoking symptoms. Unlike ordinary cigarettes, Juleps sparkle up your mouth, refresh your throat, keep your breath clean, inviting. With Juleps, you end over-smoking jolts, you enjoy every puff, and you smoke all you want. If smoking is one of your big pleasures, smoke Juleps!

'1. No "stale-tasting" mouth: The miracle mint in Juleps freshens the mouth at every puff. Even if you're a chain-smoker, your mouth feels clean, refreshed at end of day.

'2. No raw "burned-out" throat: Miracle mint stays in the smoke of Juleps, caresses your throat. No harsh, "burned-out" feeling, even if you smoke 20–40–60 Juleps a day.

'3. No heavy "tobacco-breath": Unpleasant tobacco-breath is a common form of halitosis. But . . . the hint of mint in Juleps lingers, leaves your breath pleasant and inviting.'

Now they just kill you, and everyone around you. And this is *progress?*

Tide, the, Forsaken or Overwhelmed by

There is a peculiar relentless horror to the slow receding of the tide; those who visit Bruges in Belgium to see a perfectly preserved mediaeval city may prefer not to contemplate the impotence with which its inhabitants watched the river slowly silt up and the trade which once made their city rich cease altogether when the ships could no longer reach the quaysides. Locked in political hostilities, the burghers could not agree what to do; and so they did nothing, and the city fell slowly asleep beneath a rank, muddy sort of aspic.

So, too, Lympne, once the Romans' *Portus Lemanis*, their only harbour on the southern Kent coast. Presently the tide forsook it and the river ceased to flow; the harbour choked with silt, and they made a new one at what is now West Hythe; it too died as the sea receded; the Romans moved eastwards yet again, only to meet a similar fate.

But the waters run two ways, and can engulf as well as recede. Dunwich, in the thirteenth century, was the sixth greatest town in England. Its first church had been founded by St Felix around AD 630, and in its heyday it had, according to John Stow (writing in 1573) 'before any decay came to it, 70 pryse churches, howses of religion, hospitals, & chapelles, & other such lyke'. Then the sea came. A spit had narrowed the port, then blocked it entirely; the cliffs had been crumbling for centuries; and on New Year's Day 1287, storms hurled the seas at the friable cliffs and swept away 'houses, shops, churches, orchards, livestock and people'. The seas struck again in 1328, and then in the early sixteenth century, and Dunwich was reduced to a mere nothing. Legends grew of a city beneath the waves where the churches still stood

238

and where on certain nights their bells could be heard tolling before once again being engulfed[300]. Whatever the tales surrounding Dunwich – including the legend of the THREE CROWNS[301] – Daniel Defoe's observation seems entirely reasonable:

> But for a Private Town, a Sea-Port, and a Town of
> Commerce, to Decay, as it were of itself, this I must
> confess, seems owing to nothing but the Fate of Things,
> by which we see that Towns, Kings, Countries, Families
> & Persons all have their Elevations, their Medium, their
> Declination, and even their Destruction in the Womb of
> Time, and the Course of Nature.

Tonic, My

There was Brodum's Nervous Cordial (5s. 5d. for the smallest bottle) and Abercrombie's Genital Nervine Solution (7s. 6d.) Senate's Balm of Mecca was 7s. a packet, Perry's Cordial Balm of Syriacum and Balm of Gilead from Solomon were half a guinea. Stimulants. *Tonics*. Tonics were what people had, and most of them were cocaine or opium or alcohol or cannabis or all four. You'd have to have cancer now to get that sort of thing, but up until the 1920s they were common, and many of them persisted until the 1970s; not as strong in the hard stuff, but standing them to settle, followed by careful filtering, would generally do the trick.

---

300 An effect eerily reconstructed – this time for the cathedral bells at Ys – in Debussy's *La Cathédrale Engloutie*.

301 Not to mention the inevitable aggregation of tales of Romans, Angles, saints, barons, burghers, politicians, priests, lepers, fishermen, lords of the manor, pirates, and smugglers . . .

Now it's all illegal, and Great Aunt Betty would find herself in jug; then, it put a spring in what remained of her step and lined the pockets of the local pharmacist rather than the local drugs gang. Have we learned so little from the Volstead Act, which introduced Prohibition into the USA and so allowed the bootlegging Mob to take a position in the governance of that country which arguably still casts its shadow today? People have always needed their Tonic, and arguably a spoonful from a legitimate bottle ('Oh, I feel quite myself again!') has the edge, both over the depredations of the drug trade and the more foolish offerings of the snake oil men. Perhaps what we have lost is not the old Tonics, but our memory, and our wits.

Twang, th'Eastwood

We're about fifteen minutes into the movie. The situation has been set up, the hero and his motivation established, the dilemma explained. Now comes the First Encounter With The Evil Mastermind . . .

INT. THE DESERTED WAREHOUSE – NIGHT
The docks are silent. The wind wuthers round the cranes. A sudden rustling SOUND whips our HERO around. But it is merely a RAT, scuttling into the shadows.

Then, slowly, the door CREAKS open. A beam of SILVERY LIGHT, rippled with the reflections off the water. SILHOU-ETTED against the light stands A FIGURE in a floor-length overcoat and a wide-brimmed hat, holding what appears to be a large SEAL.

A beat.

Our HERO takes a pace forward, squinting into the light.

HERO
You . . . You. So you're . . . THE CLAW!

A FIGURE
Arrrr. So oi be, zurr [302].

The SEAL barks.

THE SEAL
Aaook! Aaook!

CUT TO:

. . . Immediate loss of credibility. No West Countryman could ever be a villain. Machiavellian scheming is ruled out by the way he pronounces his words. We hear a Gloucestershire or Devon or Somerset accent and we hear affability, innocence, perhaps slightly soft in the head, leavened with a pinch of apple-cheeked rural guile. But The Claw? Impossible. If one wanted to set up as a confidence trickster, the first acquisition should be a West Country accent.

But surely we are all egalitarian now? Surely we no longer judge each other on our accents [303]? Alas, no. Bred into our bone is an urge to spy out difference, and accent is one of the surest ways of telling that someone is not the same as you are. Sometimes we live in denial; Australians will tell you (insistently, in support of their founding myth of egalitarianism, despite the truth that Australia was founded on one of the most divisive of

----

302 If American, substitute rural Minnesota: 'Uh, yaah. I guess. Yaah.'
303 As George Bernard Shaw wrote in the introduction to *Pygmalion* (1912): 'The English have no respect for their language, and will not teach their children to speak it. They spell it so abominably that no man can teach himself what it sounds like. It is impossible for an Englishman to open his mouth without making some other Englishman hate or despise him. German and Spanish are accessible to foreigners: English is not accessible even to Englishmen.'

distinctions, between the settlers of Victoria and the convicts of New South Wales) that they have no accents: all men beneath the Southern Cross speak the One True Australian (and woe awaits the one who tries to diverge). To the visitor, though, this is sheerest nonsense. Australian, like any other language, changes and mutates with place, whether geographical or social. From the broad blast of Daaiiirwin (like a badly tuned motorbike exhaust) to the clogged strangulations of the Melbourne sophisticate, from the flat sinus chug of Adelaide to the dusty rasp of the Kalgoorlie goldfields, the Australian announces his origins as certainly as if he had been bar-coded when he learned to speak.

It is the same everywhere. The twanging Provençal identifies the mumbling of the Pas de Calais (and makes of it what he will). Californians wonder why Minnesotans sing in Swedish, and Minnesotans wonder why the Californians are all stoned; and both wonder why New Yorkers are so cross, and New Yorkers can't understand why the people of Chacaga make do with just the one vowel.

The English are the most famously accent-conscious. Do what you will – go to three different posh schools, have a duchess for a mother, get yourself educated at Cambridge, move to London – an expert will still be able to place you within a five-mile radius ('the northern side of Cricklade, I'd say') after a couple of sentences. Southerners still think Mancunians sound aggressive, Scotsmen disapproving, Liverpudlians thick, and the Welsh, Welsh.

But it is changing. Just as languages are dying away at one a fortnight, so accents are smoothing, eliding, moving slowly towards the norm. The rate of disappearance changes; for a while, last century, it looked as though everything would flatten out into the clenched suavity of Received Pronunciation; that is, what the Man on the BBC spoke. Then, with the 1960s, regional accents made a comeback. Currently it is rare to hear RP English on the television at all; instead, viewers are treated to either an odd, all-purpose Northern, or a glottal Estuarine.

The process is as old as speech. Language shifts, dialects fall away, pronunciations move according to rules as seemingly inherent as gravity or the continental drift. Once, peers in the House of Lords spoke with the accents of their domains. Then, for a while, they all spoke Lordish. Now, once again, they speak with a range of voices.

Yet mobility and television conspire to erode diversity. Once I was involved in a production of D.H. Lawrence's play, *A Collier's Friday Night.* Brought up in Nottingham[304], I had always thought Nottingham's great man of letters had a tin ear. His dialogue, carefully transcribed onto the page, just did not sit with the voices I heard every day. Now, with the fine actors of the Nottingham Playhouse making their best efforts with his clunking dialect, the problem could wait no longer.

So off I drove to Lawrence's home, the mining village of Eastwood, a few miles outside the city. I stopped a young woman and asked her where the oldest people she knew lived, then went and knocked on their door.

I explained my mission to the tiny, wizened ex-miner – he must have been well into his nineties – who opened the door.

'Ah,' he said, 'Tha wants t'hear t'oald Aistwood twangg, dost tha?'

He and I and his wife talked for three hours, and every word could have come straight from one of Lawrence's pages. He didn't have a tin ear at all; it was just that the accent had almost vanished. His was the last generation that spoke it, and as they died so it was lost, not to the influence of television (which came later) but, more likely, to the easy delights of the RIPLEY BANG-BANG.

---

304 Home to surely the nastiest of all English accents, an affronted, disgruntled,
     curled-lipped snarl that manages to sound simultaneously bellicose and
     simpering.

University, the Idea of the

The University is a Paradise, Rivers of Knowledge are there, Arts and Sciences flow from thence. Counsell Tables are Horti conclusi, (as it is said in the Canticles) Gardens that are walled in, and they are Fontes signati, Wells that are sealed up; bottomless depths of unsearchable Counsels there.
(John Donne, *LXXX Sermons*, xvii)

Not any more; and the idea that there may be a ravishing beauty in simply knowing – or, better still, finding out – that Dr Donne's *horti conclusi* and *fontes signati* are from the Song of Songs[305] is about as acceptable now as pederasty.

Dorothy L. Sayers quoted Donne at the beginning of her novel *Gaudy Night*, a novel which, though on the surface a Peter Wimsey detective story, was really a meditation on the idea of the University and the status of women in it (and there were still, in 1936, plenty who would have preferred them to adopt the **ANCIENT GREEK** posture of being invisible), on chastity and on passion, both intellectual and emotional. Then, a lifetime ago, it was still possible to think of the University as a *Paradise*, to speak of *Arts and Sciences* in the same breath, to mention the notion of *Knowledge*; now almost heretical, with its implications of right and wrong, true and false.

Universities now are no Paradise, but a mundane right. Scholars must publish or die, when they are not engaged in the endless bureaucracy of meaningless 'targets' invented by obedient knaves for the placating of ambitious fools. Universities must now 'serve the community'; undergraduates must hock their futures to pay for their education; our governments, sunk in demotic pandering, either do not believe, or dare not say, that thinking and knowing are what distinguish us from the animals, and that thinking and knowing are absolute goods in themselves.

---

305 'A garden inclosed is my sister, my spouse; a spring shut up, a fountain sealed.' (4.12)

Instead, we have degrees in Sport Studies and Leisure Management and Hospitality, foolish makeweight glosses as unconvincing as the cheery, cheesy, 'motivational' drivel ('I'm Lovin' It') doled out by fast-food executives to their underpaid staff, or the curse of Descriptor Bloat which makes a dustman into a Recycling Operative, as though the one has more human dignity than the other, as though the job itself does not leak through.

But relief is at hand. Soon, in Scotland, there will be no more universities at all. Instead, there will be Specified Tertiary Education Providers. 'Specified' and 'Providers' says it all, and just to ram home the point, there's a jaunty acronym: *Steps*. Steps, do you see: like a toddler. We're all children now. Thank God (and he did) that Donne is dead and gone.

V.D.

The warnings were in every public lavatory. Watch out! There's V.D.! Go to the V.D. Clinic! *Now!* The fear spread. Certain toilets at school were designated the V.D. Bogs and nobody would go in them. 'You've got V.D.' was a vicious insult, second only to calling someone a 'git', which, it was believed, meant that their mother was a prozzy. We would have killed for the chance to *get* V.D., but died if we'd got it, even though a shot of penicillin ('This huge syringe. Like for horses. *In your knob!*') would cure it[306]. But it wouldn't *really* cure it. You would carry the mark around for the rest of your life, and everyone would know, and point at you behind your back.

Better, though, than what replaced it.

---

306 I was informed, when contemplating it as a career, that ship's doctoring was pretty straightforward and only involved one diagnostic question: 'Does it hurt like hell when you pee?' If they said 'No', you gave them the athlete's foot ointment because that was the only other thing sailors ever got.

Voice, Anne's

John is twelve years older than his wife Anne, just turned eighty, and you'd think you could be fairly sure, in his case, that you'd not be left alone. She went into hospital for an operation. It seemed to go right, but in fact went wrong. Another operation made things worse. Tomorrow[307] there will be a conference after which they will turn off her life-support. In the LITTLE ROOM he was stoical, English, matter-of-fact at the imminent loss of his partner of half a century. Then he said: 'There is one thing I regret.' An old friend with him said, 'What?' 'Nothing,' he said. 'No,' she said, 'tell me. What is it?'

He started to speak. Couldn't. Began to sob.

'I never recorded her voice,' he said.

And so what was once unthinkable has become a lost opportunity, a reason to make mourning more painful. Until a handful of years ago, the sound of the voices of the dead was the mark of lunacy or divine inspiration (although some six thousand years ago, according to American psychologist Julian Jaynes[308], the hallucinated voices of the dead were what we heard in our mind's ear instead of the endless chattering of our own, personal, conscious narrative[309].

---

307 Tomorrow in writing-time for me; in reading-time for you; in John's time, a tomorrow indefinitely prolonged. How, given our foreknowledge and our imaginations, do we ever manage to do anything?

308 Author of *The Origin of Consciousness in the Breakdown of the Bicameral Mind*, described, accurately, by the late Douglas Adams as 'Perhaps the greatest book I've ever read which I wish was true but know is wrong from beginning to end.' Adams entertained ideas of making it into a film, starring Sigourney Weaver as the Origin of Consciousness, and the current Governor of California (how Adams would have loved to have been alive for that) as the Bicameral Mind. (There is, incidentally, a Jaynesian equivalent of gaydar which enables people who've read the book to detect the fact in each other within ten minutes of meeting.)

309 Most perfectly expressed by Snoopy in *Peanuts*: 'Here's the famous World War One fighter ace climbing into his cockpit . . .'

Even long after Edison, long after the Dictaphone, the tape-recording *hobbyist*, the cassette recorder, the integrated circuit digital voice memo, we still have no auditory equivalent of the snapshot. We can say 'smile' but we cannot say 'speak'; we can perform the cheesy pose for the camera, but to talk, off the cuff, for the unblinking ear of the microphone, is beyond us, and so we don't ask[310]. Look at any home video: the only time people speak is when they are unaware they're being recorded. Unless it's for the answerphone, and how many people have been ambushed by the dead when they return from the bedside vigil, the cold kiss, the formalities, to slump, emptied out, in the FAVOURITE ARMCHAIR. The phone rings but they can't face answering it, not yet, not just yet. The answerphone kicks in, recorded before everything . . . 'Hello. I'm sorry I can't take your call . . .' Not now; not ever.

But, otherwise, the voices pass away unregarded, only to return to us in that sleep where lost reconciliations haunt us and we wake with the tears wet on our cheeks. Yet the voice, the sound of the voice, is still the marker of true intimacy. 'I dreamt I saw you' is a neutral observation; 'I dreamt I heard your voice again' speaks of a terrible clarity of loss; like the voice itself, it gives too much away; not just the sound, not just the words, but the *pneuma*, the breath, the soul. Once we came to terms with it; now, because we have the means of lessening the loss, the burden can be hard to bear.

---

310 Even professional broadcasters clam up when asked to speak without an agenda. 'Can you give us a few words for level?' is a phrase which can reduce even the most glibly articulate to a tomb-like silence. So studio managers more often say 'Tell me what you had for breakfast.' The result must be, on tapes and DAT cartridges and SCSI disks around the world, a huge archive of Breakfasts of the Celebrated which is surely begging to be snapped up for a book.

Wad, Joan the

In 1931, B.C. of Tredegar wrote: 'Two weeks ago I bought a "Joan the Wad" and to-day I have won £233 10s. Please send two more.'

'One lady' was pleased, too. 'My sister suffered very badly for years,' she wrote to 183 Joan's Cottage, Lanivet, Bodmin, 'but since I gave her a "Joan the Wad" to keep near her she is much easier[311].' But 'One lady' is less trusting, more cynical than B.C. of Tredegar. Hardened, presumably, by all those years of her sister being difficult, One Lady goes straight for the tricky question: 'Do you think this is due to Joan or the Water from the Lucky Well?'

Older readers will require no explanation; the very mention of Joan the Wad will carry them back in time to a more innocent age, before computers and atheism and nastiness and the Advertising Standards Authority, when the back pages of long-dead magazines like *Tit-Bits* and *Reveille* were filled with advertisements for lucky trinkets, thrice-blessed mascots and odd forms of postal augury.

Joan the Wad was the undisputed queen. Masquerading as an ancient Cornish good-luck charm – 'Queen of the Lucky Cornish Piskies' – this strangely gnarled and squatting hobgoblin, allegedly dipped in 'lucky water', was actually the core of a business dreamed up by Doreen Nettlinhame of Polperro (still going strong in her eighties the last time we looked). Readers of the low-rent magazines, the sort of people probably down on their luck, or, at least, Micawberishly optimistic, were lured in by the offer of 'a history of the Cornish Piskey folk and the marvellous miracles[312] they accomplish' for a mere one-shilling

---

311 Suffered from what? And much easier what, too? In her mind? To be near? To fool?

312 As though there were another sort of miracle, not marvellous at all.

248

stamp[313]. Joan the Wad worked as Healer, as Luck Bringer ('coincidence if you like, within a week I got a much better job, and my wife had some money left her . . . we swear by "Queen Joan"'), as Matchmaker ('it was not until she had visited Cornwall and taken Joan back with her that she met the boy of her dreams, and as they got better acquainted she discovered he also has "Joan the Wad"'), as Prizewinner ('For two years,' writes A Young Man, breathlessly, 'I entered competitions without luck, but since getting "Joan the Wad" I have frequently been successful although I have not won a big prize but I know that—, who won £2,000 in a competition, has one because I gave it to him. When he won his £2,000 he gave my £100 for myself, so you see I have cause to bless "Queen Joan"'), as Speculator ('I had some shares that for several years I couldn't give away,' writes A Man. 'They were 1/- shares, and of a sudden they went up in the market to 7/9. I happened to be staring at "Joan the Wad" . . . I thought I saw her wink approvingly. I sold out, reinvested the money at greater profit, and have prospered ever since.')

As the advertisement used to say: 'Ask yourself if you have ever heard before of anything so stupendous. You have not.'

The days of *Reveille* and *Tit-Bits* and Joan the Wad in the back are long gone and we know now – of course we do – that such claims, where not actually made up, are fine examples of the old LATIN fallacy *post hoc ergo propter hoc*: the attractive (and instinctive) assumption that if B follows A, then A caused B. It has got us into more trouble than almost any other assumption – in a particularly convoluted way, it even got us GOD – but we have come on at last, and no longer would we find One Lady wondering whether the heuristic goodness lies in Joan or the Lucky Water.

Would we?

---

313 Say roughly £2 at today's prices.

Yet educated people read, in their quality Sunday papers, the repugnant effusions of Snake-Oil salesmen who are capable of replying, for example, to a woman writing in with what could be the early symptoms of a brain tumour that she is suffering from 'damp on the spleen'. *There is no such thing as damp on the spleen.* What purpose can it serve to join in the fiction that there is?

Perhaps in some way we are hard-wired for credulity. Perhaps credulity is necessary for us to function, and without it we would either have to go into desperate negotiations every time we wanted to do something, or simply grind to a halt. MONEY, for example, requires credulousness, as does homeopathy.

And homeopathy has more in common with Joan the Wad than you might at first think. *Is* it Joan, or *is* it the Lucky Water? Homeopathy would say it's the Lucky Water. Almost literally, in fact. Homeopathic remedies are produced by diluting the solution of the 'active' ingredient until, on statistical probability, there is almost no chance of even a single molecule of whatever it was remaining. *But the water has been changed, by a force we do not understand.* Quackery has always been filled with *forces we do not understand*, of course, and the homeopathic theory is even sillier than most because it is claiming a local disturbance of the rules of the universe[314].

But instead of saying 'Right, this is obviously bollocks, come up with a sensible explanation or abandon your claims', our credulity gene kicks in and we erect the special Magic Barrier around the central idea, the same one that stops us questioning other people's gods, or telling people with obviously nonsensical food 'intolerances' that they should shape up and show a HEALTHY APPETITE.

---

314 It's not like ANGELS, for example. Angel-believers simply state that the rules of the Universe are not what we think they are. Homeopaths say, no, the rules of the Universe are absolutely spot-on, dead right, tickety-boo and well done, chaps . . . except in the case of homeopathy, where they are different. This is special pleading, and should be regarded with profound scepticism.

And once we do that, the jig's up and it's only a hop, skip and a jump to Crystal Homeopathy, which combines the principles of homeopathic medicine with the healing power of crystals. First announced on the Crystal Chamber website in 2003, crystal homeopathy, according to *New Scientist*, uses crystals which, 'while they were forming in caves over thousands of years, have picked up minute, homeopathic quantities of substances that will benefit you through their influence on your aura', adding, reasonably enough, 'Does this sound like complete garbage to you?'

It certainly sounded like garbage to one 'Gareth Thomas', who wrote a long posting on the self-explanatory www.ukpagan.com site denouncing the whole thing as 'transparent balderdash'.

Retribution was swift as outraged UK pagans rushed to defend it, quoting theoretical physics, insisting on the validity of their beliefs and denouncing 'Thomas' as a cynic.

What they didn't know was that 'Gareth Thomas' had made the entire crystal-homeopathy nonsense up – Crystal Chamber website, caves, substances, auras and all – as a test of credulity. Which his critics failed. Point proven; but he has said that he has one regret: that he resisted the temptation to claim that the crystal had been 'mined by elves'.

Or, better still, by Joan the Wad.

Warm, the British

Basil in his British Warm. Short. Thick. Double-breasted. Like Basil. Basil knows why it is called that. From the quartermaster's listing: *Overcoat, British, warm, officers of field rank, for the use of.* Centre vent, peak lapels, breast pocket, HANDKERCHIEF absolutely *not* for the use of. Up the sleeve, a gentleman. Basil uses the word 'gentleman' a lot. Thinks it, still more. Not a mealy-mouthed word for a 'man'. 'Man', 'gentleman', two very different things. Fish, fowl. Chalk, cheese. Important. Just the ticket. Won't do.

Basil had a good war, though not as such. The big show was over by the time he went into the, went into the, the, actually, LOGISTICS, keep things ticking over, army marches on its stomach but who fills that stomach, tell him that? Hmm? May seem boring compared with the gung-ho lot, but, truth to tell, never a dull moment.

Married? Not as such. Was a girl, one point. Pretty little thing. Uncle was a general. Aldershot. Poet chap – Betjeman, odd name, Dutch? – got it to a tee, Miss someone-or-other:

> By roads not adopted, by woodlanded ways
> She drove to the club in the late summer haze
> Into nine-o'-clock Camberley, heavy with bells
> And mushroomy, pine-woody, evergreen smells . . .

Joan Hunter-Dunn, that's the one. All gone now. All lost as though it had never been, Camberley just another blasted suburb, didn't come to anything in the end and in any case Basil was never much of a ladies' man. Happier with the boys. Old Hoggy. Best friend a chap could have. Inseparable, Basil and Old Hoggy. Then Hoggy married, overseas posting, lost touch, the way of things.

Bursar now. On the scrap heap at fifty-five, army. The way of things. Something else to do. Pension, fair enough, no wife, family, a man needs, a man has to, it wouldn't do, sit around, can't . . . Nice college, bit like the regiment, retiring soon, all changed. The old dons all dead, nobody comes to High Table any more, formal hall a special occasion now, not like it was. Interviewing the new chaps: young, spruce, MBAs, careerists. He won't be sorry to go. Last of a breed. Dying out.

Like the British Warm. Don't see them now. Don't think of Basil wearing his coat. More that his coat represents *him*. A pro-

252

tective shell in which Basil can grow and be animated like an Elizabethan homunculus in its bottle. Don't see *them*, now either. *O tempora, o mores*. The only LATIN Basil remembers. He knew it would come in handy.

Warning, the Four-Minute

There can be nobody brought up during the Cold War who did not have nightmares about the four-minute warning. That was what we were going to get. Four minutes to say goodbye. Four minutes to experience a terror which, although we had rehearsed it countless times in our minds, remained, we knew, unimaginable: we would try to imagine it, consciously or, in our dreams (the missiles roaring overhead like fiery Gargantuas, or looking down a country lane and seeing the flash rise above the horizon) but we knew instinctively that the reality would be far worse.

The Cold War – the consequences of insane macho strutting, of American and Soviet mutual terror – stole millions of lives, not just directly, but indirectly by the inflicting of perpetual fear. We did not know then that the *Tsar Bomba*, the biggest nuclear bomb in history, had been hobbled, so as to produce just fifty per cent of its 100-megaton yield and only three per cent of its potential fallout. We didn't know that its original name was *Ivan* and that it became known as the *Tsar Bomba* in a reference to the *Tsar Kolokol* and the *Tsar Pushka*: the giant bell and cannon at the Kremlin, both impressive on display but useless for anything in practice.

We didn't know that the military had no possible use for the thing, or that Khrushchev ordered it as a political display. All we knew was that one bomb, one *Tsar Bomba*, could level all of greater Los Angeles, cause, at the least, terrible third-degree burns across the width of West Germany. We didn't know that the only thing capable of carrying it was the prop-driven Tu-95, an old, slow aircraft; that the *Tsar Bomba* was of no use in Europe and designed to

253

frighten the Americans; that even if the Tu-95 had been able to get to the United States it would have been so slow and so easy to spot that it would have been a sitting duck for eight hours between the early-warning line and any feasible target.

All we knew was that they dropped it over Novaya Zemlya in the Arctic Sea at 11.32a.m. on 30 October 1961 and we then knew how the world would end. At the Trinity test on 16 July 1945, Robert Oppenheimer – the wealthy, brilliant Jewish, New York Communist intellectual who was, if anyone was, the father of America's A-bomb – had heard, in his mind's ear, Krishna's words from the *Baghavad-Gita*: 'I am become death: the destroyer of worlds.' If Trinity was death, the destroyer of worlds, then the *Tsar Bomba*, over five and a half thousand times more powerful, was become the destroyer of *words*. In the face of such a thing, language lost all power.

The shadow of the four-minute warning, of the prospect of the utter blotting-out of life on earth, of nuclear winter[315], imposed a background of fear and darkness on millions of lives and (as Jonathan Schell wrote in 1982, at the lowest depth of the Cold War, when 'MAD' – Mutually Assured Destruction – seemed likely to be with us for ever) broke the contract between the present and its posterity.

Seven years later, the Berlin Wall came down and the hegemony of the old men in the Kremlin was lost . . . for ever?

Terrorism is terrorism and to call it, as idle journalists, egged on by demotical politicians, do, 'terror' is to diminish the true terror of living under the shadow of the end of the world. But the price was worth paying. We are alive. Had it not been for the military men escalating the level of potential, mutual destruction, their political masters might have been tempted to take a

---

315 Now largely discredited as a likely or even possible consequence of even global nuclear annihilation; the Earth is far more robust than we are, it seems.

risk which would have brought the same carnage, but more slowly[316].

The *Tsar Bomba* is gone. The Berlin Wall is gone. The Soviet Union is gone. But the certainty that our civilization will always continue: that's lost, and may never return.

Was, I Think it

Everybody in our clever postmodern[317] world knows better than to take a text – any text – at face value. There once was a time when the canny reader could read between the lines. Now we assume that the author is *writing* between the lines[318]. But if I say one thing while meaning another, and what you read is what I mean, not what I say, where does that leave us?

Hopelessly confused, pissed off and unnecessarily complicating things, is where. Dear **GOD**, it's not even new. The ancient historians did it all the time, and some of them – Lucian, for example – even admitted it[319].

But there are some figures of speech which are not to be taken at face value, but which *are* to be taken precisely at their between-

---

316 Can we imagine what a George W. Bush might have done without the *Tsar Bomba* to scare him?

317 You think this is just showing off? You want me to define 'postmodern'? No: *you* define postmodern. After all, your definition is as good as mine, if not better. Damn. I just defined 'postmodernism'. Or did I?

318 The only immune postmodern text would be the one which the author wrote *without actually reading it.* And there is no shortage of those, as anyone who has ever read a proposal for a reality-TV show, a self-help manual, a business how-to book, or a Coalition Forces press release will attest.

319 If we can believe what he said, which was, in effect, that we couldn't believe what he said. Or, rather, that we *could* believe what he said, provided we defined 'believe' carefully enough. Again, a Coalition Forces press release provides a good test, as does the definition of truth offered by the editor of the *Daily Sport* in defence of, for example, his 'World War II Bomber Found On **MOON**' story.

the-lines value. Take, for example, the hoary old 'I think it was X who said . . .' followed by a plausible but obscure quote. What that meant was 'I have just looked through my *Oxford Dictionary of Quotations* and found this quote from Pindar, whom I have never read but who is generally thought to be the marker of a pretty spiffy sort of mind. Since I would like you to think that I have a pretty spiffy mind, I wish to give you the impression that I am intimately familiar with the works, not only of Pindar, but of absolutely bloody *everybody*, so while I am happy to expose to you an inch or so of my massive, throbbing intellectual armamentarium, I do so with the entirely false *caveat* that, having been plucked from my capacious intellect, it may be falsely labelled.'

'I think it was X who said . . .' plays Mutt to the Jeff of 'Who was it who said . . .?' which is, if anything, an even bigger bluff. What *that* means is: 'I have found this quotation in the *Oxford Dictionary of Quotations* but in order to put you even further off the scent, I have suppressed its authorship because I want you to imagine that I am writing this in a simple log cabin by candlelight on a simple 1.3MHz PowerBook running Mellel 1.7.5 under OS X 1.3, while under a simple wolfskin blanket on a simple rustic cot, a simple naked wriggling redhead waits simply *desperate* for my intellectual, writerly attentions.'

But it will no longer do; 'I think it was . . .' has lost its power to persuade, thanks to the Internet. The gag no longer functions; the cogs are showing, and the hidden wires are visible round the back. That hoary old stunt, ignorance posing as knowledge, is done for. Now we read it and think 'Well, why not look it up, then, you fool? Five seconds on Google is all it takes.'

Waters, Many, Can Quench What They Like

Many waters cannot quench love, nor can the seas drown it; once again we turn to the Song of Solomon in which, if we are fanciful, we can catch an echo of Noah's Flood, which swept away all the Earth but not **GOD**'s love for his creation; nor, by extension, human love.

The proposition is, of course, nonsense. Just a few waters can quench love; six inches in a bucket will do it. But more to the point, the many waters of the next flood – and there will be one – will quench everything in their path. We know it's coming. We know that we're helping it on its way with our burning of fossil fuels. We know that we ought to do something about it. We know that we won't. We know that we are, as a species, quite likely to cop it badly as the polar ice caps melt and the many waters rise. We speak about saving the planet when we should speak of saving ourselves; but if we spoke of the latter, we'd have to do something; the planet . . . the planet's *big*. The planet's always been *good to us*. Things have always turned out all right in the past, or we wouldn't be here to say things like 'Things have always turned out all right in the past'.

And so we'll go under, one day. That's how it is. First of all you lose your sense of proportion, then you lose your wits, then finally you lose everything. And it won't matter any more.

Weakling, the Seven-Stone

There you are, on the beach, like the milquetoast in Robert Burns's 'Address to a Haggis':

> Poor devil! see him owre his trash,
> As feckless as a wither'd rash,
> His spindle shank a guid whip-lash,
> His nieve a nit:
> Thro bloody flood or field to dash,
> O how unfit!

You *know* you don't look quite the thing in your saggy **JANTZENS**; you *know* you've got an Adam's apple and a caved-in chest and

257

your nieve[320] is definitely a nit[321]; but the sun is shining, nobody is asking you to dash through a flood or field, whether bloody or not, and you're chatting to a pretty girl . . . when along comes the Bully and, merciful heavens, *kicks sand in your face*. Doesn't matter whether we are talking Bondi Beach or **CANFORD CLIFFS**; the humiliation is absolute.

But help used to be at hand, with Charles Atlas. 'I used to be a 7-stone weakling,' his ads declared[322], and so he did. He also used to be Angelo Siciliano, an immigrant from Calabria, until he discovered . . . *Dynamic Tension!!!!!* from watching lions in the zoo. Siciliano built himself up, became Atlas the model and strongman, and made a fortune by selling body-building courses to what would now be fashionably scrawny geeks with the absolutely *perfect* Body/Mass Index.

You don't see Charles Atlas any more, nor sand in people's faces. It's broken bottles now, and the expensive gym with personal trainers, Nautilus machines and defibrillators on standby. But although he may have gone, the model remains: the male beauty of the ancient Greeks, of which the god Atlas was merely one exemplar. **THE GODS** may have gone, but their pecs live on for ever.

Weasel, Pop Goes the

> Half a pound of tuppeny rice
> Half a pound of treacle
> Mix it up and make it nice
> Pop! goes the weasel . . .

---

320 Fist.
321 No bigger than a nut.
322 Or 97-pound weakling in the United States.

258

And what the *hell*, we ask (as we do of most nursery rhymes) is *that* all about? Carry on . . .

> Up and down the City-Road
> In and out the Eagle
> That's the way the money goes
> Pop! goes the weasel.

Nursery rhymes all too often drifted from the adult world of satire, lament and admonition into the nursery, where their meaning was lost, and getting it back can be difficult. *Ring a ring of roses* was once thought to refer to the plague: the 'ring of roses' being the initial rash of buboes – inflamed, infected lymph nodes in groin and armpit – which heralded the arrival of the disease. Then the sneezing ('A-tishoo! A-tishoo!') and the general collapse ('We all fall down'). Very good; except that's not what the symptoms of bubonic plague are like, and the rhyme wasn't first recorded until almost 150 years after the Great Plague.

There's less argument about others; it's widely accepted, for example, that 'Hey Diddle Diddle' is an occulted version of some Elizabethan scandal, probably sexual – if only we knew who the cat and fiddle (not to mention the dish, the spoon and the little dog) were. 'Georgie Porgie' is said to refer the habits of the Prince of Wales[323], later George IV. 'Baa baa black sheep' remains completely impenetrable, although apparently originating in mediaeval times, when more or less everything was impenetrable to the twenty-first-century mindset.

But the meaning behind 'Pop goes the weasel', at least, seems not entirely lost. The 'weasel' was either a small tailor's iron or a

323 Or, if you believe one American commentator, is an early exposition of class and gender politics and the power-manifestations of sexual harassment.

mishearing of 'whistle and flute' – Cockney rhyming slang for 'suit'. The Eagle was a well-known music hall in London's City Road. And 'popping' something meant pawning it – deriving, probably, from the expression 'Popping out to see Uncle', Uncle being the local pawnbroker.

And so the story becomes clear: drinking and hanging around music halls sapped the money, so next day it was a case of popping the tools of the trade . . . which in turn meant you couldn't work, which meant no money, and so the vicious circle against which the song admonishes.

The modern equivalent would be the six-pack and the satellite telly. But that's less ruinous than the lure of the music halls, a hugger-mugger paradise for the working man whose fortunes in the period immediately before the Great War of 1914–18 were chronicled by J.B. Priestley in *Lost Empires*. The plot of which concerns Barney the Dwarf, who works for Ollanton, a mock-Indian magician working under the name of 'Gunga Din'. Barney, driven mad by the teasing of Nonnie Olmar, the company sex-interest, murders her. Ollanton and the hero, Harncastle, plot to get her corpse out of the country, and if that sounds fanciful and improbable, just read a copy of any supermarket celeb magazine and see what goes on in television . . .

. . . Which, coupled with changing public taste, led to the final decline and death of the music halls in the middle of the last century. The Eagle music hall, the itinerant performers criss-crossing the country between DIGS, meeting occasionally on Crewe Station to change trains in the rain, and the atmospheric, shabby-rich, tawdry escapism of the halls are all gone for ever now. But Uncle is still in business, and thriving more than ever; the new poor may demand more of life than rice-and-treacle pudding, but there is still a pawnbroker on the City Road. In three hundred years, will they be singing *Pop! goes the iPod?* And will our descendants know what it means?

260

Worlds, Lost

The contest between America and the USSR for supremacy in space seems to have produced nothing but the peripheral, the nasty or the naff: Teflon, spy satellites, orbiting bombs, freeze-dried ice cream, toothpaste tubes floating about the 'module' interior.

But it has also produced certainty. For the first time in our history, we finally *know* what our world looks like, and with that knowledge comes a near-infinity of lost cartographic worlds, constructed over the ages from curiosity, self-aggrandizement, speculation, greed and hope. What have we lost?

- The world of the Ionic philosophers, where Greece lay at the centre.
- The world of Sallust and other Christian cartographers, where Jerusalem was the *umbilicus terrae* (and so it persisted until around 1450, when the discoveries of Marco Polo and others forced the map-makers to rethink their world).
- Worlds where the past and present coexisted, Troy and Carthage depicted on the same page as Rome and Jerusalem, and the Labyrinth of the Minotaur and the Colossus of Rhodes were still there though they were long gone.
- Worlds subject to strange shifts and seizures, with Corinth the wrong shape (and seldom an isthmus), Cadiz in the middle of the Straits of Gibraltar, Palestine translated to central Africa.
- Worlds where places and events were conflated, Noah's Ark still on Ararat, GOD still raining destruction on Sodom and Gomorrah, the Tower of Babel and the Pharos at Alexandria still landmarks for seamen, and (space permitting) the Red Sea perpetually parted and Israel divided into its twelve tribes.

261

- Worlds where St Brendan's[324] 'Promised Land of the Saints' was clearly shown on maps until the mid-eighteenth century, variously located at Madeira, west of the Canaries, halfway to Japan and 100 miles off the coast of Ireland, before finally ending up in the West Indies.

- Worlds where the equally mobile and mythical Kingdom of PRESTER JOHN could drive cartographers to extremes of speculation in the general desire to prove the kingdom true[325], so that it would, over the centuries, move from the Far East to Abyssinia or, depending on the pleasure of the map-maker, to lower Scythia (Higden's *Polychronicon*), India (Marino Sanuto), over to Central Asia and back to Abyssinia again, as well as being separately mapped by the Dutchman Ortelius, complete with cartouche tracing the descent of Prester John from King David.

- Worlds like that of Behaim's Terrestrial Globe – the first constructed – of *c.* 1492, showing the Atlantic full of islands but no America.

- Worlds where mankind's enemies Gog & Magog[326] still flourish, penned behind great mountains by Alexander the Great, their rampart prison sometimes located

---

324 An Irish monk, *c.* 484–578, who set sail in search of paradise, which he assumed was somewhere in the Atlantic, thus becoming the first modern holidaymaker. His Paradise was eventually conceded to be a mirage, and thus he continued to be the first modern holidaymaker.

325 Everyone desperately *wanted* it to be true: Pope Innocent IV, for example, wanted Prester John to help 'convert' Genghis Khan, just as Henry the Navigator wanted the fabled wealth of the orient and a hand in defeating the Moors, not to mention the sea route to the Indies . . . so that, like other geographical fantasies, the false image guided and inspired real exploration.

326 And sharing their grim region with the Anie, Agit, Azenach, Fommeperi, Befari, Agrimandri, Casbei, Alanei and others besides.

beyond the Kingdom of Prester John, sometimes in Siberia[327].

- Worlds of the Western Nile which flowed through Africa, a natural canal across the continent.
- Worlds where Marco Polo's tall tales and Ptolemy's exaggeration of Europe and Asia drove explorers to hunt for the 'short voyage' to India and the Spice islands, and the notorious North-West Passage to the open water by the Kingdom of Anian.
- Worlds where myth and speculation could overrule observation, so that Christopher Columbus *knew* that he had discovered the short route to the Indies. (America? It was most certainly nothing of the sort . . . and he should know; had he not, damn it, been there *four times*?)
- Worlds where there was a great land at the southernmost part of the globe, running from Africa to India and landlocking the Indian Ocean: the land, marked, on Ortelius's 1589 map of the Pacific, as *Terra Australis, sive Magellanica, nondum detecta* – 'The Southern, or Magellanic, Land, as yet undiscovered' – and persisting as *nondum detecta* in the geographical imagination even after the discovery of Australia in 1605; the idea of a southern continent beyond Australia was only finally abandoned after Cook's second voyage of 1775. (But for once the imagination was right, and the great southern Terra Incognita was finally discovered and named Antarctica.)

---

327 Not to mention carved above the London Guildhall; Gog & Magog, in England, were the mythical survivors of a race of giants, obliterated by the founder of Britain, Brutus, who brought them in captivity as his palace porters.

Now we only have reality: the reality as seen from space. And yet, like the old cartographers, we still make mistakes. We think the Earth is big. We think we are important. The maps have not yet been fully redrawn . . .

Worlds, Lost, Tiny

When great worlds fall, we marvel and reach for our pens; when tiny worlds fall we are silenced. We live our lives under the shadows of lost love, when reconciliations fail or lie unsought, and each one is a small society, sometimes just of two, with its own language and history, its stories and memories that cannot survive on their own, in the dark. And worst of all, the jokes. Where do *they* go, when everything else has gone?

Zone, the Dead

You begin immortal. Later you realize you aren't theoretically immortal but there may have been an administrative cock-up. Later still you realize that there hasn't been an administrative cock-up. And for a while that's it. Then one night you wake at four in the morning, the suicide hour, and you *really* realize it. The distinguished thing. Hobbes's Voyage, that great leap into the dark, is *real*, and you are going to go on it, and it is simultaneously imaginable and wholly beyond comprehension. How can this thing happen? To *you*? **GOD** knows, if *anyone* deserves to be let off, it's you . . .

And you realize, too, that you don't know what to do, what's expected of you, how it will happen. You have heard stories of people turning their face to the wall; you have heard people willing themselves off the planet; but one day, when it's your turn . . . *what will you do?*

We've nowhere to turn now. Once we had **THE GODS**, in con-

264

stant negotiation with mankind about immortality; they resigned it to marry us, granted it to us in return for favours, were themselves transformed by each other, god 'A' turning god 'B' into a tree, a snake, a goat; transforming us in their turn, sometimes into stars, sometimes into other natural shapes or materials, so that what we would now describe in psychological terms, the ANCIENTS described in physical: they were petrified, cleft in two, turned to stone.

Then came GOD who kept it all to himself, made up his own mind, let nobody in on the secret; and, worse, Jesus, who performed the trick[328] but told nobody else how it was done. And now . . . we have little choice. Either we are done-for rationalists and at the end of the day it's lights out, or we are religious and equally in the dark, dependent on some celestial credit reference for our immortality and ignorant of the outcome until it's too late ('Your application has been declined at this time').

One may yearn for the ancient gods, who at least showed up from time to time, even if only as drunkards, thunderbolts or priapic swans.

But they aren't going to put in an appearance, and one wonders what the *hell* to do. Do you have to ask permission to die? Fill in a form? Does it just happen? Who will tell you how to pull the stunt off? Until one day your first friend, your first relation dies.

---

328 If he ever really existed, and if he *did* perform it; and of course, if it *was* a trick . . . But there was in those days a fine tradition of itinerant preachers doing magic to grab an audience, before proceeding to swipe them with the main message. The biggest trick of all was, of course, raising someone from the dead. How to top *that*? Why, by raising *oneself* from the dead. Difficult; but, were one cynical, one might recall the observation by the gonzo magicians Penn & Teller that the reason magicians get away with it is that the audience has *absolutely no conception* of the lengths to which a conjuror will go, or the money he will spend, to pull off an illusion.

At first it seems absurd, a foolish mistake, a wild improbability. Then another one dies, and another. A parent goes; an aunt, a colleague. Once you turn forty, it becomes a reality, and when the telephone rings with news of yet another bad diagnosis, you feel a stirring of sympathy but presently, like pornography, it loses more and more of its power to shock. It is (you say to yourself) rotten luck, but it is (you say to yourself) just one of those things. We all (you say to yourself) have to go some time, and anyway (you say to yourself) he's dead *and I'm not.*

But you don't say that out loud.

A friend and I were driving in his very fast car through France some years ago when a man coming the other way span out of control, all on his own with no provocation, crossed the central reservation and came hurtling towards us.

Time slowed down.

'Ah well,' said my companion, 'it's been a good life.'

Porsches are extremely good cars and in a series of manoeuvres which would have disintegrated a lesser vehicle, we evaded our fate and drove on while, in the rear-view mirror, the other driver sorted himself out and continued on his way, too. The gods had been too busy turning themselves into animals to turn us into meat.

I, as the driver, relaxed smugly in my seat, congratulating myself on my skills. My companion, however, looked rather puzzled and slightly cross.

'Actually,' he said, 'it hasn't.'

'Hasn't what?'

'Been a good life.'

But it was too late. Fate had twitched the curtain and shown us our destiny, and that destiny was obliteration. We were in the Dead Zone, and loss would be our portion.

A few years later, aged forty-nine, on the Stairmaster, climbing and climbing and heading nowhere, the very model of striving postmodern man, my friend had a sudden heart attack and was gone for good.

But such is the strange benignity of the Dead Zone that one's deepest fears are soothed. He knew what to do when the moment came; nor was life thereafter coloured by his loss, but by the knowledge that he had once been. He wrote the words at the beginning of this small meditation:

'The gifts he has . . . turn to dust in his hands as he realizes that everything he has is merely the shadow cast by what he has lost.'

But he was, for once, wrong. The gifts of life do not turn to dust, nor does loss cast a shadow. Loss sheds its light on what remains, and in that light all that we have and all that we have had glows more brightly still.

Further Reading,
If You Fancy It

Adams, Douglas, and Mark Carwardine. *Last Chance to See*. London: Heinemann, 1990.

Anderson, Bruce. 'The Decline and Fall of Footnotes.' *Stanford Magazine*, 1997.

Baden-Powell, Robert. *Scouting for Boys: A Handbook for Instruction in Good Citizenship*, 1908, edited with an introduction and notes by Elleke Boehmer. Oxford University Press, 2004.

Baker, Nicholson. *Double Fold: Libraries and the Assault on Paper*. Vintage, 2002.

Barber, Paul. *Vampires, Burial and Death: Folklore and Reality*. Yale University Press, 1988.

Barclay, Alexander. *The Shyp of Folys of the World*, 1509.

Battles, Matthew. *Library: An Unquiet History*. New York: Norton, 2003.

Beard, Mary. *The Parthenon*. London: Profile Books, 2002.

Berkow, Robert, Mark H. Beers, and Mark Burs, eds. *The Merck Manual of Diagnosis and Therapy: 17th Edition*. John Wiley & Sons, 5 March, 1999.

Biddulph, Steve, Karen Johns, and David Moore. *Stories of Manhood: Journeys into the Hidden Hearts of Men*. Finch, 2003.

Blainey, Geoffrey. *The Tyranny of Distance: How Distance Shaped Australia's History*. London: History Book Club, 1968.

Bly, Robert. *Iron John: Men and Masculinity*. London: Rider, 1990.

Bondeson, Jan. *The Great Pretenders*. New York: Norton, 2004.

Bowersock, G.W. 'The Art of the Footnote.' *The American Scholar*, winter 1983/4, 1983: 58.

Brigden, Susan. *New Worlds, Lost Worlds: The Rule of the Tudors, 1485–1603*. Penguin Books, 2002.

Burr, Chandler. *The Emperor of Scent: A Story of Perfume, Obsession and the Last Mystery of the Senses*. London: Heinemann, 2003.

Calvino, Italo. *Invisible Cities*. London: Secker & Warburg, 1974.

Campion, Edmund. *The Historie of Ireland*. Dublin: Society of Stationers, 1633. Quoted in Smith, Bruce, *Acoustic World*.

Cannadine, David. *In Churchill's Shadow: Confronting the Past in Modern Britain*. London: Allen Lane – Penguin, 2002.

Carr, Simon. *The Hop Quad Dolly*. London: Hutchinson, 1991.

Casson, Lionel. *Mysteries of the Past*. London: Mitchell Beazley, 1978.

Casson, Lionel. *Travel in the Ancient World*. Baltimore, MD; London: Johns Hopkins University Press, 1994.

Casson, Lionel. *Libraries in the Ancient World*. New Haven; London: Yale University Press, 2001.

Collins, John and Ross Glover, eds. *Collateral Language*. New York: New York University Press, 2002.

Comfort, N.A. *The Lost City of Dunwich*. Lavenham: Terence Dalton, 1994.

Connell, Evan S. *El Dorado & Other Pursuits*. London: Pimlico, 2002.

Cooper, Michael. *A More Beautiful City: Robert Hooke and the Rebuilding of London After the Great Fire*. London: Sutton, 2003.

Crane, Nicholas. *Mercator: the Man who Mapped a Planet*. London: Weidenfeld & Nicolson, 2002.

'Crystal homeopathy combines the principles of homeopathic medicine with the healing power of crystals.' *New Scientist* 177, 2003: 92.

Curl, James Stevens. *The Victorian Celebration of Death*. Stroud: Sutton, 2000.

'Current beliefs among the American public.' On website *Wolumne*. 4 April 2004. Available at <http://www.religioustolerance.org/aft_bibl2.htm>.

d'Israeli, Isaac. *Curiosities of Literature: Volume the Second*. London: J. Murray, 1743.

'Daily Life: August 12, 1835.' *The Times*. London, 29, 2003.

Davenport-Hines, Richard. *The Pursuit of Oblivion: A Global History of Narcotics, 1500–2000*. London: Weidenfeld & Nicolson, 2001.

'Dickens with a snarl.' *Observer*. London, 15, 24 August 2003.

Donne, John. 'A Nocturnall Upon St Lucies Day, being the Shortest Day', *Songs and Sonnets. c.* 1590–1601.

Donne, John. *LXXX Sermons preached by that learned and reverend divine Iohn Donne, Dr. in Divinity, late Deane of the Cathedrall Church of S. Pauls London.* (1630). London: Printed for Richard Royston, in Ivie-Lane, and Richard Marriot, 1640. (Edited by John Donne the younger, & prefaced by Izaak Walton's *Life of Donne*.)

Durant, Stuart. 'Ferdinand Dutert: Palais des Machines, Paris 1889.' In *Lost Masterpieces*. London: Phaidon Press, 1999.

Eco, Umberto. 'The Author and his Interpreters.' Italian Academy for Advanced Studies in America, 1996.

Ehrenreich, Barbara. *Global Woman: Nannies, Maids and Sex Workers in the New Economy*. London: Granta Books, 2003.

Ferry, Georgina. *A Computer Called LEO: Lyons Teashops and the World's First Office Computer*. London: Fourth Estate, 2003.

Flaubert. *Dictionnaire des Idées Reçues*. op. post.

Forrest, A. J. *A Dictionary of Eponymists*. Kettering: J.L. Carr, 1978.

Fox, Stephen. *The Ocean Railway: Isambard Kingdom Brunel, Samuel Cunard and the revolutionary world of the great Atlantic steamships*. London: HarperCollins, 2003.

Friedman, David M. *A Mind of its Own: A Cultural History of the Penis*. London: Robert Hale, 2003.

Fuller, Errol. *Extinct Birds*. Cornell University Press, 2001.

Gardner, Laurence. *Realm of the Ring Lords: The Ancient Legacy of the Ring and the Grail*. London: Element, HarperCollins, 2003.

Gleick, James. *Isaac Newton*. London: Fourth Estate, 2003.

Haig, Matt. *Brand Failures: The Truth About the 100 Biggest Branding Mistakes of all Time*. London: Kogan, 2003.

Hancock, Graham. *The Sign and the Seal: The Quest for the Lost Ark of the Covenant*. London: Heinemann, 1992.

Harris, Robert. *Pompeii*. London: Hutchinson, 2003.

Hayman, Ronald. *A Life of Jung*. New York: Norton, 2001.

Healy, John F. *Pliny the Elder on Science and Technology*. Oxford: Oxford University Press, 1999.

Henderson, John. *HORTVS: The Roman Book of Gardening*. London: Routledge, 2004.

Henry, John. *Knowledge Is Power: How Magic, the Government and an Apocalyptic Vision Inspired Francis Bacon to Create Modern Science*. Cambridge: Icon Books, 2003.

Hoffmann-Donner, Heinrich. *Der Struwwelpeter; oder lustige geschichten und drollige bilder für Kinder von 3-6 Jahren*. Frankfurt a. M.: Mütten & Loening, 1840.

Holland, Philemon. *The History of the World, Commonly Called the Natural History of C. Plinius Secundus, or Pliny*. London: Centaur Press, 1962.

Howell, Michael, and Peter Ford. *The Ghost Disease: And Twelve Other*

271

Stories of Detective Work in the Medical Field. Harmondsworth: Penguin, 1985.

Huxley, Aldous. *Brave New World Revisited*. London: Flamingo, 1983.

Jackson, Kevin. *Invisible Forms: Literary Curiosities*. London: Macmillan, 1999.

Jaynes, Julian. *The Origin of Consciousness in the Breakdown of the Bicameral Mind*. Boston, MA: Houghton Mifflin, 1976.

Kaplan, Robert, and Ellen Kaplan. *The Nothing That Is: A Natural History of Zero*. Oxford University Press, 2001.

Kivalszki, Anna. 'And the Pope will send us angels.' *The Michigan Daily*. Chicago, 15 September 1998.

Krakauer, Jon. *Under the Banner of Heaven*. London: Macmillan, 2003.

Lambrick, George *et al.* 'Lost treasure of Iraq.' *Guardian*. London, 15, 2003.

Lamont, Peter. *The Rise of the Indian Rope Trick*. Little, Brown, 2004.

Leech, John. 'A Court for King Cholera'. 25 September 1852.

Lost Masterpieces. London: Phaidon Press, 1999.

Lowenthal, David. *The Heritage Crusade and the Spoils of History*. London: Viking, 1996.

Maines, Rachel P. *The Technology of Orgasm: 'Hysteria,' the Vibrator, and Women's Sexual Satisfaction*. Baltimore: The Johns Hopkins University Press, 2001.

Mason, Michael. *The Making of Victorian Sexuality*. Oxford; New York: Oxford University Press, 1995.

McCrery, Nigel. *All the King's Men: One of the Greatest Mysteries of the First World War Finally Solved*. London: Pocket, 1999.

McKean, John. 'Crystal Palace: London 1851.' In *Lost Masterpieces*. London: Phaidon Press, 1999.

Medway, Gareth J. *Lure of the Sinister: The Unnatural History of Satanism*. New York University Press, 2001.

Menand, Louis. 'The End Matter: The Nightmare of Citation.' *New Yorker*. 6 October 2003.

Menzies, Gavin. *1421: The Year China Discovered the World*. Bantam, 2004. (Orig. pub. 2002)

Merck's Manual of the Materia Media, Together with a Summary of Therapeutic Indications and a Classification of Medicaments. (1899). Reprinted, New York: Wiley, 1999.

Merkur, Daniel. *The Mystery of Manna: the Psychedelic Sacrament of the Bible*, 2000.

Meyer, Hermann. *Karl Joseph Riepp der Orgelbauer von Ottobeuren*. Kassel: Baerenreiter, 1938.

Milton, Giles. *The Riddle and the Knight: In Search of Sir John Mandeville*. London: Allen & Busby, 1996.

Modern Boy's Book of Hobbies. London: Amalgamated Press, 1937.

Moggach, Deborah. 'Empire Building.' In *Smile and Other Stories*. London: Viking, 1987.

Mould, Philip. *The Trail of Lot 163*. London: Fourth Estate, 1997.

Moxon, Joseph. *Mechanick Exercises: or, the Doctrine of Handy-Works*. London: Joseph Moxon, 1693.

Moynihan, Brian. *If God Spare My Life: A Biography of William Tyndale*. London: Little, Brown, 2002.

Murray, Venetia. *High Society in the Regency Period 1788–1830*. London: Penguin, 1999.

Naughton, John. *A Brief History of the Future: the Origins of the Internet*. London: Phoenix, Orion, 2000.

Ogilvy, David. *Confessions of an Advertising Man*. (Revised edn.) London: Pan, 1987.

Parissien, Steven. 'McKim, Mead and White: Pennsylvania Station, New York 1905–10.' In *Lost Masterpieces*. London: Phaidon Press, 1999.

Paton, W.D.M. 'The Hexamethonium Man.' *Pharm. Rev.* 6, 59, 1954.

Phillips, J.R.S. *The Mediaeval Expansion of Europe*. Oxford University Press, 1988.

Pickart, Loren. 'The Lonely Crowd: Cleanliness Can Produce Loneliness.' On website *Skin Biology*. Available at: <<http://www.skinbiology.com/skin-pheromones.html#Skin%20Moisturizing,%20Healing%20and%20Mood%20Enhancing%20Body>>.

Pinker, Steven. *The Blank Slate: the Modern Denial of Human Nature*. London: Allen Lane, Penguin, 2002.

Pliny the Elder. *Natural History: A Selection*. London: Penguin, 1991.

Plumb, J.H. 'A Biography of Oliver Goldsmith (1728–1774).' On website *Volume*. Date. Available at <<http://www.ourcivilisation.com/smartboard/shop/goldsmth/about.htm>>.

Porter, Roy. *Blood and Guts: A Short History of Medicine*. London: Allen Lane, Penguin, 2002.

Pressley, Alison. *The Best of Times: Growing Up in Britain in the 1950s*. London: Michael O'Mara, 1999.

Prévinaire, P.J.B. *Abhandlung über die verschiedenen Arten des Scheintodes*. Leipzig: 1790.

Priestley, J.B. *Lost Empires: Being Richard Herncastle's Account of His Life on the Variety Stage from November 1913 to August 1914 together with a Prologue and Epilogue*. London: Granada, 1980.

Procter, Adelaide A. *The Poems of Adelaide Procter*. With an introduction by Charles Dickens. Boston: Houghton, Mifflin, 1858.

Puckle, Bertram. *Funeral Customs: Their Origin and Development*. Werner Laurie, 1926.

Rawlinson, Henry. *Empires of the Plain: Henry Rawlinson and the Lost Languages of Babylon*. London: HarperCollins, 2003.

Reich, Wilhelm. *The Function of the Orgasm*. New York: Farrar Straus Giroux, 1973.

Reif, Stefan C. 'The Genizah Framents: a Unique Archive?' In *Cambridge University Library: The Great Collections*. Cambridge University Press, 1998.

Renton, Peter. 'Has the Higgs boson been discovered?' *Nature* 428, 11 March 2004: 141–4.

Rhys, Ernest. *The Travels of Marco Polo*. London: Dent, 1908.

Robinson, Andrew. *Lost Languages: The Enigma of the World's Undeciphered Scripts*. London; New York: BCA/McGraw-Hill, 2002.

Rounding, Virginia. *Grandes horizontales*. London: Bloomsbury, 2003.

Schell, Jonathan. *The Fate of the Earth*. New York: Knopf, 1982.

Schlosser, Eric. *Fast Food Nation: What the All-American Meal is Doing to the World*. London: Allen Lane, Penguin, 2001.

Schwartz, Barry. *The Paradox of Choice: Why More is Less*. Ecco, 2004.

Schwartz, Barry. 'The Tyranny of Choice.' *Scientific American*, April 2004.

Smith, Bruce R. *The Acoustic World of Early Modern England*. University of Chicago Press, 1999.

Smith, Stephen. *Underground London: Travels Beneath the City Streets*. London: Little, Brown, 2004.

Spang, Rebecca L. *The Invention of the Restaurant: Paris and Modern Gastronomic Culture*. Cambridge, MA; London: Harvard University Press, 2000.

Stemman, Roy. *Atlantis and the Lost Lands*. London: Aldus, 1976.

The Booke of Common Prayer. London: Edward Whytchurche, 1549.

Toland, John. *The Great Dirigibles: Their Triumphs and Disasters*. New York: Dover, 1972.

Vermes, Geza. *The Authentic Gospel of Jesus*. London: Allen Lane, 2004.

Weinberg, Samantha. *Pointing from the Grave: A True Story of Murder and DNA*. London: Penguin, 2003.

Wells, H.G. 'The World Set Free.' In *The First Men in the Moon & The World Set Free*. London: The Literary Press, 1936.

Wolf, Gary. 'The curse of Xanadu.' *Wired*, 3 June 1995.

Wolmar, Christian. *Down the Tube: The Battle for London's Underground*. London: Aurum Press, 2003.

Wood, Gaby. *Living Dolls: A Magical History of the Quest for Mechanical Life*. London: Faber, 2003.

Wörsching, Josef. *Die Orgelbauer Karl Riepp*. Mainz, 1940.

Index

276

bed
    anti-lechery, of Prester John, 205
    three-in-a, not a sex romp, 47
    two-in-a, lurid scenes excised (*see*
        Noddy)
bedfellows, uneasy, psychoanalysis and
    Occam's Razor, 191n
bedrooms, cold, 66
Beer
    Keg, **57**
    airborne lifetime supply of, 153
    Elizabethan, unpleasantness of, 57
    impossibility of getting into safely, 58
    the man that waters the workers', 58n
belly, manly, an object of scorn, 211
beloved, consigning to the dustbin of, 61
Berkeley, Michael
    irrational thinking of, 213
    rational thinking of, 214
Berners-Lee, Sir Tim, denial of existence
    of Room 404, 17
Betjeman, John, 76–77
    origins of name, 252
Bierce, Ambrose, **59**
Big Ears, ambiguity of. *see* Noddy
Big Shopping God Stick, elusive meaning
    of, 115n
Billy, **61**
    recovered from terrible fate, 62
    Bunter, 82
birds, man-eating, 204
Bishops, warned against preaching, 198
Bisitun, the inscriptions of, 150
black and white, The Past really was, 164
Blair, Tony, not the maddest, 43n
Blake, William
    probably not a Muggletonian, 187
    mother probably a Muggletonian, 187
blankets
    electric, lethal, 66
    wolfskin, simple, 256
Bledlow, Old Man, 56
Blest, Isle of the, shifting locations of, 261
bliss, offered by vibrating chair, 114
Blower, the Double, **62**
Blyton, Enid, revisionism, 140–41
B. O., **45**
    sexy, 195
Bodmin, magical industry of, 248
Body
    Bending, 72
    parts, insertion of, 107
    Things of the, 208
Bogart, Humphrey, existence defined by
    his hat, 147, 172
Bogs, the V.D., 245

bolus, phlegmy, discharged, 232
Bomb, The
    most powerful ever (*see Tsar Bomba*)
    nightmare about, 253
bonbons, strawberry, 7
Bondi Beach, humiliation at, 258
Books
    the Terrible Flammability of, **63**
    burned by servants (*see* Carlyle,
        Thomas)
    diligent, profitable, 73
    eaten by dogs (*see* Newton, Isaac)
    lost, the graveyard of (*see* Cairo)
Borges, Jorge Luis, location of imaginary
    books reviewed by, 14–15
borrowers, dodgy, Sunday, 182
bosoms
    floury, vanished, 129
    jouncing, two-dimensional, 231
Boson, Higgs's, **64**
    Higgs fed up with, 65n
Botox, as obstacle to reading, 168n
Bottles, Water, Hot, **66**
    wrong material, 7
Bottom
    Baby's, 7, **67**
    Mozart's Little, **69**
    pipe, sodden, falls out, 176
Bowels
    necessity of Making Active, 72
    Ransackt, of the Ocean, 178
bowler hat, synonyms for, 147n
bowls, Hoover's scrotum-supporting, 151
Boy, Modern, tie-wearing, 131
Boyards Maïs, **70,** 195
    previously part-smoked, 196
Boys, Fry's Five, 6, **71**
Boys, Scouting for, **71**
brains
    of pheasants, 178
    the purpose of, 214
Breakfast
    Proper Cooked, **76**
    banishment following, 84
    proper, lethality of, 76
bricks, phenomenological, 32
Britain
    attitude to X-chromosomes, 107
    Prime Minister of, his little friends,
        172
Broad Street pump, 57
Brundin's Orchestra, 44
Brunel, Isambard Kingdom, obliterated
    for smoking, 96
Brut, the Great Smell of, **77**
Brylcreem, **78**

love and physics, 66
Crewe Station, 260
Cricklade, placed within five miles of,
	despite expensive education, 242
criticism, literary, Civil Service, 110n
Cronos, King of Atlantis, 44
crotch, Imperial, nibbled by "minnows,"
	122
Crowns, Three, **101,** 239
Croydon aerodrome, 50
cups, Melamine, lurid, 225
curtain, safety, reassuring, 202
Customer Relations, benefits of faking,
	200
customers, responsibility towards. *see*
	Passengers

D

Daaaaaaaaaaaaaaaaaaaa-NUH, **102**
Daily Mail
	desire to be editor of, 16
	making readers feel fat, 134n
	measured views on asylum-seekers, 86
	mistaken lynchings by readers of, 234n
	not a known cause of cancer, 82
	snobbery of its readers, 99
Damascus, the road to, closed by data
	and stealth, 23
damnatio memoriae, 8
	of Golly Town, 141
Damocles, the Walking-Stick of, 82
dance, incompetent, satirical, 200
danger, synthetic, safe, 136
Dansette Bermuda, 58
darkly, original glass for seeing through,
	177
date, confusion over, 186n
Dawson, The Very Rev. Roger, 90
de Morlay, Bernard, 26
dead
	the hallucinated voices of, 246
	they are, and we are not, 265
Dead,
	Land of the, postal scruples
		concerning, 162
	Methods of Disposal of, Fallen into
		Desuetude, **103** (*see also* coffin,
		Fogg's Patent)
Dearmer, Percy
	a glorious liturgical peacock, 197
	preoccupation with vestries, 198
	Songs of Praise, 198
death
	causes of, no longer fashionable, 121
	coming to terms with inevitability of
		(*see* Moore, Gyllian)

cure for, 62
entropy, 168
good, praying for, now uncommon, 29
lost causes of, 2
mistakenly regarded as unequivocal,
	63
packing for, 226
war against, 231
Debussy, Claude, musical inundation by,
	239n
Defoe, Daniel, on Destruction in the
	Womb of Time, 239
demeanour, perfectly serious but
	unwarranted, 19
Democracy, **104**
	expenditure on relative to fast food,
		17–18
	modern, unacceptable to Athenians, 105
dependency, easiest way to create, 234
depilation, Imperial, of concubines, 122
Deprave or Corrupt, Tendency to, **107**
	vulnerability dependent on social class,
		107
Descriptor Bloat, 245
desktop, pre-computer, 235
despair, not as bad as hope, 213n
Diabolus in Musica, probably not, 92
Dials, Analogue, Proper, **111**
Dick, Spotted, 35
die, seeking permission to, 264
dignity, architectural, paucity of models
	for, 95
Digs, **111,** 260
dildo
	chin, 152
	on a stick, 102
disappointment, phoney. *see* bank
	managers
disillusion, related to chocolate, 71
Disney, Honeyed Meretricious
	Sentimentality of, **112**
Disney, Walt, disagreeable character of,
	112
Doctor, the Non-, **114**
Doctors
	Proper, **116,** 201, 228
	faintly improper (*see* arse)
	harassed, gullible, 176
	impossibility of practising without
		Homburg, 147
	ships', easy diagnosis, 245n
Dodo, L'Estrange's, the Perishing of, **117**
Dog, The, **119**
Dog(s)
	the Ancients, dying like, 32
	bibliophage (*see* Newton, Isaac)

Dog(s) – *continued*
enforcing democracy, 104
generic, had it like everything else, 1
Mad, **120**
Mister Woofy-Woo, six months
without parole, 120
mythical, minatory, with teeth, 119
pink fluffy, urgent need for, 227
vomit, role in men's clothing, 123–24
your, death was its purpose, 119–20
Doll, Sir Richard, 69
Domitian, Emperor, Hair, Care of the,
Guide to, **121**
Donne, John, 23, 33, 183
and particle physicists, 65
Donnelly, Ignatius, chronicler of Atlantis,
42
dons, dead, 252
Donut nirvana, 130
dorsels, high, no room for, 198
dotard, valetudinarian, 77–78
doublets, old, 102
Douglas, the Pouch of, 21
Dove, Roja, Aladdin's Fridge of, 230
Dragons, Dungeons and, 123
drains, inexplicable attraction of, 85
dream
the American, number of acts in, 22
lifelong, Meccano, achievement of, 173
drug abuse, Victorian, legitimate, 239
Dundreary Weepers, disadvantageous
when sick, 117
dung, not speaking of, 188
Dungeons
& Dragons, **123**
latex in, 123
dunghill, Nature wants you for a, 7
Dunn & Co, **123**
testicle-protecting clothes, 124
Dunwich
the buried crown of, 101
overwhelmed by sea, 238
dwarf, imperial confidant, 121

E
ears, big, unmentionable, 141
Earth, the End of the, commemorated in
snuff, 126–27
éclair, second, 211
economy, role of proper banks in, 52
Eliot, T.S., role of poor air quality in the
poems of, 163
Elizabeth I, Queen, studiedly elegant
movements of, 137
Elizabeth II, Queen, interest in
contemporary opera, 214n

elves. homeopathic crystals mined by, 251
empires, fall of, 2
Endemol TV, absence of, a feature of
Arcadia, 188
endless loop. *see* loop, endless
entropy, temporarily cheated by eating, 2
Ephesus, 40
epidemiology, the birth of. *see* Snow, John
Epilogue, The, **124**
eponym
the author as, 191n
lost, various, 194
Erinna and Artemis, **40**
eschatology
Frank Zappa's contribution to, 99
need for negated by modern medicine,
30
euphuism, the sin of, concerning obesity,
210
Europe, the standardisation of, 195
everything, the boy who has, what to
give, 174
everywhere else, Paris now smells like,
195
Evil Mastermind, inability of West
Country man to be, 241
Exodus, cherubim of, detritus from, 33
experts, baffled, 94
exploration, driven by non-existent man,
205
eye, having someone's out with it, 158

F
face, vibrating, 115
facial hair, the musical influence of, 145
faith, the mystery of, obliterated, 98
fame
origins of word if not concept, 193n
Roman mistrust of, 28
fashion, the depredations of, 185
fashion and folly, the dismal progress of,
21, 36
fate, P.G. Wodehouse's observations on, 2
Father(s), **125**
elderly, outside prep schools, 125
gets home, wait until, 184
grooming, filial ambivalence about,
79
habits, rigidity of, and other fine
qualities, 125
heroic rescue by, 62
importance of holding pipe aloft, 131
irresistible opportunity to terrify sons,
113
feet, food tasting of, 227n
Ferguson, Euan, the poetry of, 24

282

ferry, real, with actual man, 85
fingers, wandering in the scented steam, 45
Finisterre, **126**
Fishing
fish not the point, 128
net, retractable, with secret paddle, 216
Rods, Built-Cane, **127**
Fitzgerald, F. Scott, quoted though unread, 22–22n
Fitzroy, Admiral, pioneering meteorologist, his barometers and *post mortem* radio career, 126–27
flamingos. *see* Phoenicopters
floors, bowling-alley, non-flammable varnish, 49
floppies, floppy, 7
Flour, **129**
ignorance of mistresses about, 129
mothers lightly coated in, 185
fluid, correction, 235
food
British, untempting nature of phrase, 225n
fads, difficulty of catering for, 39
fast, American spending on, 17–18
horrible, 227n
Scottish, imaginary, 208
Food Glamorizer, 216
fools
always one step ahead, 6
old, 6
Foreigner, Johnny, 89
fornication, origin of word (though not of practice), 45n
42, a coincidence, 192
Found, **129**
fountains, inadvertent, 202
404, the signifier of loss, **13**
Fox, Dr Peter, deployment of folio for shock, 11n
Frayn, Michael, *Clockwise*, 213n
Freeborn, Caron, 35n
French, tuition in, metaphorical, 18
Frenchman, the happy, 179
Fretwork, **130**
feverish rack-making in run-up to WW2, 131
Freud, Sigmund, nonsense about cigars, 89
fridge
Aladdin's (*see* Dove, Roja)
doing it in, 226
friendship, sublimated, ambiguous. *see* Noddy

frogs, lack of pluck of, 73
Fry, Stephen, speculation upon revenant potential of electromagnets, 69–70
Fry's Five Boys, 6, 71
Fug, **132**
Fuller, Errol, 118

G
Gadgets, **132**
gadgets, author's embarrassing collection of, 132–34
Garcia, Jerry, on rock and roll, what can be done about, 193
garden
overused as metaphor, 27, 185
when it looked better, 27
Gargantuas, fiery, imagined, 253
Gautier, Pierre (de Marseilles), fatal effects of financial prudence, 192
Gears
derailleur, skeletal, creepy, 136
Sturmey-Archer, 7, **134**
Genghis Khan, grandson of, 204
Genital Nervine Solution, Abercrombie's, 239
Gesualdo, Prince of Venoza, 93
ghost, turnip, 37–38
Giants, Volcano, 32
Gibbons, Orlando, 33
Gladstone, William, as supporter of Atlantis, 43
glands, 194n
Gloves, **136**
scented, burned at stake for, 137
glue, social, 208
goats, tallied in ancient writings, 10n, 150n
God, 7, 31, **138**
an ordinary fellow just like you or me, 98
anatomical proscription against sodomy, 107n
answers prayer of little boy, 16n
assumptions about attitude to hats, 148
dependency on fatherhood, 125
desecrator unpunished by, 192
desire to be like, as example of Unauthorised Request, 17
ecstatic contemplation of rewarded by caning, 83
the fly one of His creatures, 72
formal written disclaimer concerning, 34n
having a quiet word, 124
His particle, 65
His purposes, elegantly questioned, 35n

283

God – *continued*
  on His uppers, 53
  indifferent, 187
  kept it all to himself, 264
  love for His creation, undetectable, 257
  mouth, provided by, 186
  no alternative to believing in, 20
  not being allowed to talk about, 39
  pardoning not his true *métier*, 98
  person struck down by, known to Nanny Parkin, 66
  problems currently facing, 198
  satisfactory alternative to, 138
  seen as incompetent or horrible, 29
  similarity to a doctor, 116
  spirit of, moving upon the face of the waters, 64
  still raining destruction on Sodom and Gomorra, 261
  thanked for miniskirts, 221n
  tolerance for incest, 107n
  unmoved by prayer, 187
  what He did, 37
  will of, deducible from politicians, 97
  willing, 190
  the World ought to be considered as, 11n
Gods, The, 16, **139**, 182
  demise of, unconfirmed (Pan), 194
  fondness for metamorphosis, 264
  mean-spiritedness of (Gaia), 195
  pecs live on for ever, 258
  quirks and foibles of, 139
  too busy turning themselves into animals, 265
Gog and Magog
  brought to Britain as slaves, 263
  still flourishing, 261
Golden Age, 188
  nothing caused cancer in, 82
  personal, non-existent, songs yearning for (*see saudade*)
goldfields, the addictive cycle of, 60
Goldhill, Simon, 104
Golem, handwriting of, 156
Golly, Mister, **140**
goodness, 97
Google, 25
  role of in modern vice industry, 18
gorilla, silverback, 186
Gothick, bogus, 123
Grail, the Holy, **142**
The Grateful Dead, 193
  pivotal role of former member in defining cyberspace, 15

gravitas, the epitome of, 51
Greek, Ancient, **142**, 244
  as mark of a gentleman, 142
grey. *see* Dunn & Co
Grey-Turner, Elston, 185, 201, **229**
  realises he is a doctor, 116
  resemblance to Mr Pastry, 116
Greyfriars School, abuse of personhood, 235
Griffin and Spalding, unpleasant time had in, 197
Griffith-Jones, Mervyn, QC, opinions on obscenity and household management, 110
guarantee, as distinct from promise, 234
Guinness, strength, used to give you, 236
Guts, milky, of mullets, 178

H
haemorrhoids, bailiffs', 54
hair, men's
  consequences of running your hands through, 78
  lost guide to the care of, 121
Halliburton, Inc.
  failure of Solon to wait for permission from, 107
  importance of what it wants, 106
Hancock, Graham, 37–38
Handkerchief
  the Gentleman's, **143**
  not for the use of, 251
  reaching for on seeing book, 11n
  scented, vivid memories provoked by, 230
  used to bamboozle the lower orders, 143
The Handyman, celebrated turn of Mr Pastry, 200
happiness, equation for, failure of, 224
harbingers, turbulence and coincidence not, 191
Harding, Jehosophat Galitzine, 51
harmonium, played by revenants, 87n
Harmony
  Close, **144**
  overwrought metaphor concerning, 145n
harvest, failure of, reasons for, 32
hatchet, hotelier chasing wife with, 84
Hats, **145**
  Australian pub specialising in, 146
  author's, lost, 146
  bad (*see* Tiberius)
  Boyle's automatic self-raising, 150
  as cinematic device, 148

284

determining creditworthiness from, 72, 149
Evil Mastermind, 240
Parisian, 23
tipping, 90
Head
Vanishing, the Emperor's, **149**
chopped off, 103, 192
fell off, 61
reeling, 196
Hearne, Richard. *see* Mr Pastry
Hearst, William Randolph, 60
heat, lovely, absorbed by Mother, 177
Heisenberg, Werner, prostitution of Uncertainty Principle, 64
Heligoland, driven out by German Bight, 126–27
Hell
author bound for, reason why, 224n
a region of ice and silence, 1
Hellenophilia, Romantics' swooning, 142
heresy, Albigensian, harboured by beadles, 53
Hey Diddle Diddle, mystery of personnel in, 259
High Table, declined, 252
Hindus, strange, mystical, 210
history, great questions of, 47
Hobbes's Voyage, 264
hobbies, especially fretwork, 130
hobgoblin, gnarled and squatting. *see* Wad, Joan the
Hobson, Tobias, professional descendants of, 163
hod, coke, 177
hole, marketing opportunity for, 67n
Holland, Philemon, translation of Pliny the Elder, 11n
Holmes, Sherlock, 47
atmospheric conditions, 163
living conditions, 111
Holy of Holies, illegitimate penetration of, 192
home, waiting until your father gets, 184
homeopaths, as distinct from angel-believers, 250n
Homeopathy
Crystal, 251
potential role of elves in, 251
Homer
discredited by World War I, 142
role in discovery of Atlantis, 44
hoods, academic, fiddling with, condemned in footnote, 198n
Hoogstraaten, Nicholas van, purchase of immortality, 8

hope
devoured, 176
lost to pornography, 232
Horlicks, waterborne, 59
Horribilus, Cestius, 8
horror, peculiar, relentless, 238
horse
horsenessness disorder, suffering from, 207
the memory of, 91n
horsemen, headless, 184
soothing effects of, 113n
hospitals, the lost spirit of, 95
hot water bottles, 66
Human Genome Project, 2
human wishes, the fragility of, 6
humanity
the mark of, 97
the natural smell of, 46
our sense of, an affront to, 207
the wonderful diversity of, 211
Hunter, William, 21
Hunter-Dunn, Miss Joan, 252
hyde, -Nauga, 39, 201
hydraulic power, 2
hydrophobia, omnipresence among Foreigners, 120

I
I Ching, how it actually works, 191n
idiots, the contemptibility of, 106
ignorance, posing as knowledge, 256
Imeson, Kenneth, 83
immortality
a characteristic of the young, 6
credit reference for, 264
impotency, 2
Inclined, That Way, 212
Incomprehension, Absolute, **150**
incontinence, sexual, of Vicar's husband, 197
infantilism, the triumph of, 172–73, 245
Innamincka (Australia), pub hat department, 146
intimacy, healthy English avoidance of, 89
Inventions, **151**
crazed or otherwise, 152–5
iPod, Pop Goes the, 260
Iron Curtain, railway manifestations of, 164

J
Jacobus of Liège, on musical diabolism, 93
Jantzens, **155,** 257

285

Minerva, the Shield of, **178**
Minoxidil, Emperor Domitian born too soon for, 123
mission statements, decoding, 163n
Mister, **179**
  unfortunate connotations of, 179
mistresses, as means of smoothing relationships with fellow-men, 179
Mitchell, Joni, expensive quote from lyrics of, 212
mob, the common, its role in founding democracy, 107
Moby-Dick, modern version celebrating tofu, 176
Modern, Pride in Being, **179**
  the most Victorian of values, 180
Modernism, the exemplifying material of, 49
Moleskine, **180**
Mollies. *see* buggeronies
Money, **181**
  not in cyberspace, 15n
  the only model for human behaviour, 199
Monkey Town, built upon ashes, 141
Monmouthshire, obliteration of, 54
Monsieur, smoothing things over with, 179
Monteverdi, Claudio, the foxy cunning of, 93
Moon
  clifftop madness by light of, 84
  the locus of love, 182
  sound-bite, fluffed, 184n
  World War II Bomber Found on, **182,** 255n
Moore, Gyllian, 2
moquette, uncut, 39
Morrison, Van, 183
mortal remains, as souvenirs, 104
Mothers, **184**
  bad legs of, 90
  fear of offspring putting someone's eye out, 158
  good, as cause of coronary heart disease, 35n, 76
  heat-absorbing, 177
  lightly coated in flour, spiritually, 185
  men who live with, 212
  signified solely by roasting smell, 131
  William Blake's possibly a Muggletonian, 187
Mouchoir de Monsieur, grim warning to husbands, 144
mountaineering, paleographical, 150
mouse potatoes, 130

Moustaches
  Walrus, **185,** 228
  linked with polygamy, 66
  waxed, tendencies revealed by, 72
Mozart, the little bottom of, 69
Mr Pastry, 185, 228
  resemblance to Elston Grey-Turner, 116
Muggletonian, The Last, **186**
Mull of Kintyre, pornography, 109
Mullets, Milky Guts of. *see* Phoenicopters
Mumbles Railway, closure, lachrymose effects of, 50
Muscovite, pale, eventually singed, 177
music, popular
  rubbish, 33n
  rude words in, 24
mutilés de guerre, reserved seats for, 50
mystery, lunar, gone, 184

N
na gCopaleen, Myles, 48n
The Name of the Rose, possibly a mistranscription, 26
Nanny Parkin
  omniscience and disapproval, *passim*
  knew little boy who petted dog and died in spasms, 120
  knew man struck down by God, 66
  garden shears, present from, 158
  sharp knife, present from, 158
  another sharp knife, present from, 158
  possible ambivalence of, revealed by choice of presents, 158
Nature, **188**
  abhorrence of vacuum, 67
  general nastiness of, 188
navvies, Latvian, 86
les neiges d'antan, "ou sont...?", the answer to, 15
Nessun Dorma, ghostly harmonium version, 87n
Nettlinhame, Doreen. *see* Wad, Joan the
New Delhi, unavailability of agents in, 87
Newton, Isaac, book eaten by his dog, 2
Nineveh, still here, though gone, 150
Noah's Ark, still on Ararat, 261
Noakes, Mr Philip, of Matfield near Tunbridge Wells, the last Muggletonian, 187
Noddy, 7, **189**
  poor workplace discipline of, 141
Normality, **190**
nose, numbing the inside of, an epiphanic moment, 115n

R

Rabbit, Rampant, as measure of female secrecy, 114n

racks, multiple, fretwork, essential in 1930s home, 131

radiators, randomly coming into existence, 224

Radio, Car, Removable, **212**

rafters, hanging from to sleep. *see* Schoolmasters

raincoats, dirty, men in, 18

Random Lovecraft Generator, The, 182n

Ravel, Maurice
consequences of boating trip, 227
lost manuscript, 81

Rawlinson, Henry, paleographical mountaineering, 150

razzle, sad, Saudis on a, 86

rear, regular daily, vital importance of, 72

Received Pronunciation, clenched suavity of, 242

reconciliations, lost, 247

Red Sea, perpetually parted, 261

redhead, naked, wriggling, 256

Refresca Café/Bar, actually neither, 199

Relativism, the Age of, 34

religion
difference between it and science, 38n
its position on loss, 2

Rendlesham, the buried crown of, 101

reprobates, the obligation to curse, 187

Rhinoceros
the Nasal Membrane of the, **214**
inability to understand modern drama, 215

Rilke, Rainer Maria, on transformation of love, 170–71

risk assessment, formal, lack of, consequences to tent. *see* Noddy

Roanoke, the Lost Tribe of, 69

Robertsons Jams, political correctness of, 141

Robot, Magic, yearning for, 225

rock, flesh-eating, 103

rocking-chair, self-ventilating, 151

rodent offences, 130

Rolfe, John, saved Colony of Virginia with tobacco, 69

Romans, young, their wishy-washiness and lack of go, 74

Romantics
as causes of natural phenomena, 188
swooning, 176

Ronalds, Fanny, yoking of sex and death, 92

Ronco, **216**

Roses, Ring a Ring of, nothing to do with plague, 259

rubber
head, tendency of to perish, 61
multicoloured, seaside toys, 84

rules, Draconian, in casinos, 87

Rumsfeld, Donald, intelligible remark by, 64n

Ryan, Paddy (pen-name of Dr R.E.W. Fisher), 62

S

Saatchi, Charles, 5

saddened, Microsoft feeling, 178

sadism, predatory and imaginative, 122

"Sailing By," the comfortable melancholy of, 126

salesmen
snake-oil, 82
the unknown agenda of, 225

sandals, Clarks, 84

Sandwich
Ham, the Railway, 199, **217**
tomato, soggy, 84, 135

Sanhedrin, alternative opinion on Jesus, 9n

Satie, Eric, what was behind his piano, 81

satirists, their absurdity compared to politicians, 20

saudade, paradox of, 189

sausage, flying, pun on, 169

savannah, the ancestral, 138

Sayers, Dorothy L., on chastity and the Life of the Mind, presently renounced, 244

Scale, Lost, alleged rediscovery of, 94

Schell, Jonathan, 254

Schliemann, Heinrich, genuine discovery of Troy, 44

Schliemann, Paul, fake discovery of Atlantis, 44

Schocking de Schiaparelli, firmly-stoppered, 131

Schoolmasters, **217**
favoured weaponry of, 82–84
not hauled off to pokey, 234

Schwartz, Barry, on the paradox of choice, 226

science
difference between it and religion, 38n
uncertainty of, mistake about, 64

Scotland
inhabitants' dedication to venery, 208n
mythical, 208

Scouting for Boys, **71**

the Gravelly, 205
organist lost at, 192
receding or overwhelming, 238–39
Sea, Carpathian, 178
sea areas, British, illusory permanence of, 126–27
sea-foam, Dutch, solid, 176
seal, as accoutrement of Evil Mastermind, 240
seaside, English, measureless delights of, 84
secrets, lost, all the same, 38
senses, purposes of, 214
Septum, the Nasal, **217**
sermons, keeping order at, no longer necessary, 53
serotonin, quite possibly, 176
17th century, speech, misrepresented, 98
Seventies, The, **218**
sex
bed-wrestling as synonym for, 122
in the fridge, 226
incomprehensibility of abjuring, 48
playing the organ taking precedence over, 128n
romp, improbability of, 20n
type of B.O. conducive to, 195
war against oblivion, 231
Welsh?, 76n
what not to say after, 100
shame, vanishing, led from the top, 209
Shape
manly, stylish, of Cigarillo, 236
the One True, 211
Shaw, George Bernard, mones abowt speling, 241n
ship, the camel of the sea, 42n
Shoes, Just, **223**
shop, bookie's, the smell of, 196
Shop, Left in the, **226**
shopkeepers, British, disobliging, 227
Shops, The, **227**
Shulamite, her role in the envy of youth, 23
Sibelius, not just a composer, 214
Sign, Elston Grey-Turner's, 228, **229**
signs, threatening, 233
Sillage, 227, **229**
rosy, 26
Simpson, Homer, donut intake of, counted by academics, 20
666, supplanted by Y-chromosome, 125n
skully-dhù, imaginary, 208
slipper, tobacco in the, 47
smell
of beef, symbolic of motherhood, 131

of blood and rubble, 195
of bookie's shop, 196
of Brut, the allegedly great, 77–78
of the English seaside, 84
of French vicar's garden, 230
of hot Bakelite, 50
natural, of humanity, role in family breakdown, 46
proper, of schoolmasters, 217
unique
of maggots, 127
of Paris, 50
Smith, Mister John Aloysius Podicarp, non-existent, 179
smoke, medical, misguided, 63
Smoker's Companion, positioned on favourite armchair, 40
snake oil, 192, 240
snakes, 120-foot, 205
SnoCreme, banana, 84–85
Snow, John, 57
Snuff, **231**
meteorological, 127
soap, Lifebuoy, shame-inducing, 46
sofas, the true obscenity in pornography, 109n
software
essential, mostly inessential, 133
Microsoft, this book written without any, 178n
Soho, Atlantis never located in, 43
Song of Solomon, echoes of Noah's Flood in, 256
songs, pop, purpose of existence, 212
Space Race, pointless spin-offs from, 261
Span, Spick and, **231**
Spangles, 7
spanking machine, for initiation rites, 152n
Spanner
Club, for Meccano Men, 175
Trial, for men differently inclined but still handy, 175
speech, modern, attempts to address the unfathomable in, 98
sperm oil
the author's illegal enjoyment of, 68
warm, fragrant, 176
Spitting, No, **232**
spleen, damp on the, 250
spot, tiny, life dwindling to a, 124
squeaks, pip, 81
St Brendan, the first modern holidaymaker, 261
St Thomas, trip to India, improbable tales of, 203